COOKING
FOR FRIENDS

RAYMOND BLANC

COOKING FOR FRIENDS

HEADLINE

First published in Great Britain in 1991
by HEADLINE BOOK PUBLISHING PLC

First published in paperback in 1994
by HEADLINE BOOK PUBLISHING

Some of the recipes in this book originally
appeared in a different form in the *Observer*.

10 9 8

ISBN 0–7472–7892–X

Typeset by Medcalf Type Ltd, Bicester, Oxon
Designed by John Hawkins
Edited by Susan Fleming
Illustrations by Vana Haggerty

Colour reproduction by Hilo Offset Ltd,
Telford Way, Colchester, Essex, CO4 4QP

Printed and bound in the UK by
Butler Tanner & Dennis Ltd

HEADLINE BOOK PUBLISHING
A division of Hodder Headline PLC
338 Euston Road
London NW1 3BH

To various
ancestors – grandmother and mother –
who made me a good cook

Note

I have suggested an appropriate season for each of the recipes, although many of them can be enjoyed throughout the year. Tinted panels denote the seasons: green for spring, yellow for summer, brown for autumn and blue for winter.

Acknowledgements

Warm thanks and appreciation to Susan Fleming my editor who kept on smiling no matter what, and of course to the Headline editorial team of Alan Brooke and Celia Kent.

My heartfelt gratitude to my loyal testers who ate their way through all the recipes and difficulties – Patricia McKenzie, Annie Colbeck, Pauline Budd, Ginette Gould, Julie Kavanagh, Loraine Fergusson, Cecile Harris and Sue Jones.

Many thanks to my secretary Marita Dover and my assistant Elena Giacomelli, as well as the Le Manoir team led by Clive Fretwell and Nicolas Jambert, *Chef Pâtissier*. Thanks are due also to Bruno Asselin, our young *sommelier*, who helped me to select the wines.

I have the greatest admiration for the photographer Michael Boys, whose brilliance speaks for itself in the food photographs, so thanks are due to him and his assistant Virginia Dehanes.

Many thanks to M. Philippe Dadé, who owns a bakery in London, and helped me write the material on bread; Patrick Rance and his son, Hugh, who helped me with the cheese information; and to Felicity Bryan, my agent and friend.

A lot of appreciation to Peter Lewis and Villeroy and Boch for providing most of the beautiful tableware; and to Miele, who provided the kitchen at my own home, where many of the pictures were taken.

Contents

Introduction

When I was asked to write my first book on the *cuisine* of Le Manoir, I had already considered writing this one to follow; to balance and contrast the sophistication and relative difficulties associated with the Manoir book, and write one on the beauty of simple home cooking; to show another angle where cooking, eating and enjoying oneself did not necessarily involve elaborate or expensive dishes.

This dual perception is very much part of my own background, characteristic of both earlier and later developments in my craft. My childhood was very strongly associated with simple and delicious home cooking, and that ingenuity, mostly inspired by poverty, must have had a powerful influence on my approach to food.

The fact that I am self-taught is also relevant, and means that I have a strong empathy with anyone who approaches cooking with some trepidation. I have had to learn through my own mistakes, flops, trials and tribulations, all the while nurturing an inexhaustible curiosity about *why* and *how* the mistakes occurred, and how best to avoid and correct them. It has been an exciting journey from simplicity to subtlety and sophistication, and back to simplicity again – a rather natural and magical cycle which I believe can inspire anyone.

Another factor, of course, is to show that while the food at Le Manoir has a particular profile, my cooking and eating at home are entirely different, and it would be a mistake to compare them. My wife, although she loves the food of Le Manoir, would refuse to eat it all the time. We both have simple, wholesome food at home and far from being the intimidating monster of our kitchen, I rather like enjoying the rare luxury of putting my feet up once in a while and enjoying an uncomplicated earthy meal which we share with good wine and lively conversation.

This book has not been written for chefs but for cooks at home. Nor are the dishes in this book influenced by trends: I am not a follower of the current fashion and the coming back to grandmother's *cuisine*. My aim instead is to reflect traditional skills. Hence I have reproduced the great classics of family *cuisine* that I used to enjoy at home. My culinary curiosity has also led to lots of new dishes and ideas influenced by modern *cuisine*; these too can be done with ease in your home. All of these recipes highlight the fact that tradition is not static or frozen, but moves along with our different needs and lifestyles. The dishes that you will find in this book are the ones that my family and friends come to share with me at home.

I hope the book and the recipes will give inspiration and confidence to anyone who wants to experiment with the alternatives to pre-packed, ready-made, convenience foods, without sacrificing too much time. It is a definite statement to return to quality and to the essential ingredients of good eating. I hope that I have shown that we can prepare delicious meals with excellent ingredients without the necessity of either expert skills or exotic foodstuffs. And of course the joy and fun of reverting to one's own imagination is something I hope will be contagious.

All the recipes in this book have been tested to ensure that they work. Tester Julie Kavanagh made the following comments in her report:

> If *Recipes from Le Manoir Aux Quat' Saisons* challenges even the real professionals, this new collection is a welcome handbook for amateur foodies with professional lives. For me, sampling the recipes was much more than an ephemeral pleasure: they taught me how to cook. There are two to single out as examples – *filets de lièvre rôtis au lard* and *queue de lotte à la moutarde et estragon*. The depth of flavour of the sauces would woo a constellation of stars from the most dyspeptic Michelin inspector, and yet they each took less than half an hour to concoct. More to the point, I've since adapted the principles to other recipes with great success.

However, some of the testers came unstuck with the more difficult recipes; this report from Loraine and Colin Fergusson describes their problem with a *millefeuille* of potatoes that didn't make the grade and does not appear in the book:

> For over an hour we tried different approaches. First the very hot dry pan – [the potatoes] still uncooked in four minutes and rather singed at the edge. Then the slow cook in the butter-brushed pan – again they broke up. Then the very hot pan – fish and chip shop smoke filled the kitchen and we produced a sad,

soggy raffia mat. Then Colin tried the egg ring method, holding the mixture flat inside with the end of a rolling pin – it stuck to the rolling pin. At this rate the *millefeuilles* were taking an hour over the estimated time. 'Perhaps,' we mused, looking at our pile of soggy raffia mats, 'our potatoes were wrong.'

When it came to serving the dish hysteria seized us. Our little soggy mats hung limply around the chicken livers, their burnt bits sticking out sideways and giving the appearance of tiny bonfires. As I placed the shallots on top Colin suggested a small Guy Fawkes would be more appropriate.

Food for Thought

The idea that food is simply fuel to get us through the duties and functions of daily existence is a hideous and unacceptable thought. Similarly, if one looked on a car as a four-wheeled object only designed to take us from A to B, a bed only for sleeping and wine only for getting drunk, life would indeed be dull and boring. For the same reason I shall argue that hot dogs (a label clearly indicative of a rabid beast about to seduce a female partner) and burgers, the proudly proclaimed 'fast food', are an affront to good taste, digestion and family itself. How dispiriting it is that a plasticised, ready-made convenience food is preferred to a natural choice fuelled by one's imagination or craving. One also has to query the advantage of 'fast'. What is the hurry? You can cut your finger just as easily on an electric tin opener as you can on a knife peeling a delicate vegetable which still has life, texture and taste. Where is the convenience of battery (or rather battered) chickens and thin, sickly, anaemic eggs? When it comes to eating these nightmarish metamorphoses of a bygone era when animals lived, ate, and reproduced in open, unrestricted and, dare I say it, natural surroundings, I feel that 'speed' masks 'greed' in our attitude to present-day convenience food.

What we achieve through the madness of mass production, processing and packaging takes a terrible toll on quality, the balance of nature and our over-abused planet; not to mention its equally nasty side-effects on our criteria of what is acceptable to our palates and bodies. It breeds an apathy, both towards ourselves and to our environment, which is very dangerous. I shall not go into the details of this argument, for luckily it too is becoming a cliché. I say 'luckily' because out of sheer necessity and panic we are now waking up to the sad fact that over-industrialisation and over-use of technology without an insight into their consequences have tipped the balance of our entire planet to the point where we all have to take action urgently.

Another sad effect is the slow extinction of craft skills. There is less and less choice for the consumer now, but it is he who has helped bring about the death of excellence, by accepting mediocre products, many of which have been bred to look, rather than taste, good. Tomatoes will continue to be red, shapely and good looking, but where are the tomatoes of my childhood – fleshy, plump, bursting with the robust flavours of summer. . . . Where are those real farm chickens which used to be fed on corn and maize, and wandered about with lots of space and a happy sex life! A chicken labelled free-range in Britain should imply that happiness and freedom, but how wrong can you be? Its flesh is often like cotton wool with an unremarkable taste, and it has such a weak bone structure that you could almost eat the whole carcass without noticing. Eating foods such as these does not demand any effort, chewing hardly plays a part in eating any more, and I can foresee the day when man's morphology will be transformed; our jaw muscles will atrophy and our whole facial structure will be altered.

Nature has established certain rules, but man has forcibly bent them, and there will come a time when that interference damages the fragile order. Should we be reduced to the role of mere witnesses and spectators? Of course not. At the moment we are actively participating and perpetrating, and as a consumer group we have immense power. We can demand that quality, craft and excellence are not lost to the mediocrity of mass production.

However, agriculture, sadly, has slowly become agrochemistry. In order to revert to the former, farmers will have to substantially cut down on the use of petrol-based fertilisers, etc. It would be naïve to believe that *all* food could be produced organically – there would be great shortages on the shelves – but we, the consumers, must demand that there is a choice. Food stores already exist – Marks and Spencer, for instance – who have understood this and who have anticipated the demand; they are presently establishing a new order and have introduced a dual market, so that the consumer has a choice between the very best, available with a small premium, and better-quality mass-produced food.

In 1992 Europe will become an open market, a reality which must be quite scary for the farming community. If unprepared, the British market could be flooded with all sorts of goods from our European 'partners'. Why should we have to import, when most of these foods can be grown in Britain, and at the same cost or less?

Food brings the family together

For years, British farmers have traditionally grown barley, corn, wheat, etc., some of which we do need, but most of which is dumped at cut prices. Every industry has a need to adapt and change in order to compete, and British farmers too will have to undergo these changes. They will have to become adventurous and diversify, a move which will be beneficial to both the industry and to the British consumer.

Service

There is a curious phenomenon, particularly British, that makes a great number of small shopkeepers feel they are being victimised. They feel that they cannot compete with the supermarkets, and feel that they are being squeezed out of existence. I understand and appreciate that they are unable to compete in the sense of choice of goods, but I am unwilling to accept that they cannot compete as far as standards are concerned. In any enterprise, small or large, there is one factor that is unbeatable – the human factor. Being of service, giving a personalised service with full knowledge of what they sell, and giving lots of goodwill – this is what will keep small shops in business. Not only will they survive, but they will also thrive, of that I am convinced.

If only butchers could proudly rediscover their craft, would hang their meat properly, bone it out, trim the fat, make their shops attractive, and display the meat enticingly. If they would only cater for special needs and orders, listen attentively and offer advice with a smile – even learn certain basic cooking principles and how they are applied to the meat they sell. If they did, small butchers would thrive in this country.

This also applies to greengrocers. Imagine going into a shop, wanting to make a purée of potatoes for your family. You would ask for potatoes, but how astonished you would be if the greengrocer asked, 'Excuse me, what dish are you making?' Of course, if you didn't know any better, you might not understand the point of the question. But he would then explain to you that potatoes have a personality and an identity, and that some varieties would be far too starchy to make into a purée, but would be perfect for frying or making sauté potatoes. How delighted you would be! As with butchers, if he sold only the freshest vegetables and fruit, tried to market some lesser-known varieties, enticing the customer to cook them by offering a small accompanying recipe, for instance, I know for a fact that that particular greengrocer would have this particular customer (and many others) for life.

Fishmongers should not escape either. How many times, when you have been approaching a fish shop or stall, have strong 'fish' smells emanated from it? And then, as you come closer, you can actually see the flabby, dead-eyed creatures. How many times too, have you dared to ask to have the fish boned, scaled and filleted? Often one is met with indifference or, worse, blatant rudeness.

Service does not mean servitude. It is something to be done with pride. Every business has to have an ideal and to be able to offer competitive alternatives if it is to survive. The empathy I once had for small shopkeepers has partly vanished as I have experienced this sort of attitude. If a shopkeeper/butcher/fishmonger, etc. is interested in or passionate about his produce, he will never lose customers, because he can communicate that enthusiasm he has for his product to them.

The customer is partly responsible for this lack of service, as many of us rarely complain. It is important to realise how much power we have as customers; only by exercising this power can we alter and improve standards of service. We have got to become much more critical and demanding. We must be equally appreciative when we get what we want. I know many small shops who try to help and who give a service with pride, and those people deserve their success.

The Pleasures of Preparing, Sharing and Giving

Not very long ago, I saw a brilliant marketing trick. On a packet it said 'make-it-yourself'. This amounted to no more than cracking an egg into a ready-prepared mixture, then shoving it in the microwave. I realise now why that selling point was so clever; it suggested a primeval, semi-instinctive involvement with the food, that nowadays only echoes in fragments of our imaginations – an illusion of a lost creativity.

What we lose in the convenience of speed are many essentials of our general existence – the joy, the feeling of achievement, the appreciation, the adventure, the curiosity, the trying. Business as well as family communication revolves around the table and around meals. Good food is a present to be shared and enjoyed – it is a catalyst for discussions, friendships and love. Presenting one's friends or family with a TV dinner or a quick take-away is simply not the same as cooking for them yourself. Something is missing. The 'mmm, this is so good' always is the response to a personal offering, not to a packet.

In my family, the creative nature of my mother's cooking was fuelled by sheer poverty – where any leftovers had to be utilised, where things were never to be wasted. I have learned to have a great deal of respect for her cooking, for she produced different dishes time after time.

There is something very elemental and satisfying about our relationship with food. I know I may be preaching to the converted, because presumably people keen on cooking buy cookery books, but so often we imagine that, unless it is some special occasion or an especially elaborate dish, it is hardly worth attempting. Not so. Just by throwing a few roughly chopped carrots, a leek, some celery and a few herbs into water you will get the most delicious soup. This is much more satisfying than buying a packet or opening a tin. Instead of buying an over-sweet chocolate mousse full of preservatives, emulsifiers and additives, in five minutes you can turn out the most delicious confection that both grown-ups and children will love.

Cooking is also an offering, and it is a gesture of care and love to bring one's own creation, however humble or simple, to the table. Of course, nurturing and mothering are intimately connected with cooking. The impulse to provide is one keenly felt across tables the world over. Sharing food is so rich in symbolism, of our deepest human needs, that it is hardly surprising all our festivities and celebrations take place around tables, be they birthdays, anniversaries, engagements or . . . funerals. No one would have a take-away for a wedding or anniversary party, unless they were keen on an early divorce! Nor would that many people wish to have an important business deal discussed over tinned soup and a pizza.

Nowadays, I feel that an increasing number of families do not meet, do not share or communicate, and do not eat together. The pace and stress of life are proving destructive, and this is unlikely to yield a caring, thoughtful, kind society in the future. But families *can* be brought together again by the seemingly insignificant means of cooking at home. From the excitement of choosing the ingredients, to the preparing and the assembling of the dish, the entire process from beginning to end is full of rewards. These are crowned by the sharing and enjoying of both the food and the company it has brought together.

CHAPTER ONE

Ingredients, Basic Recipes and Techniques

Choosing and Buying Ingredients

For the best results, you need the best ingredients, and the following brief details should help.

Butter

At last more and more British consumers are switching from salted to unsalted butter for cooking. Unsalted butter is definitely better as it holds fewer impurities, less whey and, of course, no salt. It can be heated to a higher temperature without burning, and its flavour will not interfere with the taste of the dish. British farmers are at last producing it.

Cheese

Cheese plays an important part in a dinner party; whether you choose to serve it before or after the dessert being a matter of taste and tradition. My opinion is bound to be influenced by my early French education, and even after many attempts I still cannot enjoy cheese after the dessert. I find the transition from savoury to sweet and back to savoury again totally confusing and conflicting.

Until recently (about five years ago), apart from a few classic varieties, British cheese-making concerned itself with colour more than taste. Today, however, we are witnessing a revival in cheese-making, with almost every county boasting its own particular style. We are now spoilt for choice.

The enthusiasm and professionalism of one single man, Major Patrick Rance, author of *The Great British Cheese Book* and *The French Cheese Book*, has helped to promote the interest in cheese-making in Great Britain, and helped a number of new craftsmen to create new businesses and revive their traditional skills. The demand is so great that it cannot be fully satisfied. The small and successful cheese-maker cannot easily expand as the Milk Marketing Board cannot increase the milk quotas set by the EC regulations.

Because of the unsatisfactory classification and labelling, what qualifies as a farmhouse cheese can be as different as a burger from an Aberdeen Angus fillet. The customer is led to believe that a farmhouse cheese is an artisan product; unfortunately these cheeses are often made at factory scale with pasteurised milk and bear little resemblance to the real thing. For example, amongst the many farmhouse Cheddars, only two are made from unpasteurised milk. This very loose labelling leaves the situation wide open for malpractice.

Equally, supermarkets are dictating what is to be produced. They protect themselves by insisting on pasteurisation and often sell cheeses which are not properly matured, and keep them at too low a temperature.

How to select cheese Because of the confusion over farmhouse labelling, this is very difficult. Look will tell you a lot about the condition of the cheese, and where possible ask to taste the cheese (although this might prove unpopular!). The best place to buy cheese is naturally in a specialist shop or a delicatessen.

How to keep cheese The best place is, of course, the cellar but very few people have cellars these days. The next best place would be the garage, but neither is this very convenient. Cheese does not benefit from being stored in a very cold place for too long, but I would advise you to keep your cheese in the lowest part of the refrigerator, wrapped up well in a cloth or aluminium foil.

Serving cheese It is always better to offer a small selection of cheeses − perhaps only two that are mature and at their best − rather than a vast array of cheeses which have not reached their prime. Cheese should be served at room temperature. Remove from the refrigerator 1 hour before serving.

Chocolate

In the United Kingdom chocolate was once a highly prized commodity, partly due, perhaps, to its secretly addictive and exciting properties. This respect was lost as commerce took over from the artisan. Now with the consumer desire for pure unadulterated product, real chocolate is returning. As with cheese and wine, chocolate draws its character from the soil and the plant, and offers the discerning consumer a chance to develop a taste appreciation.

The cocoa tree grows in the tropics around the Caribbean, Pacific and Indian Oceans, having been discovered for society by Christopher Columbus in 1502. The unique flavour of chocolate and its exciting properties soon

Always use the very best ingredients

became very popular. Like many raw materials it has been refined and contaminated dramatically since and indeed its true flavour and excellence are only now being rediscovered.

To make truly great chocolate the perfectionist starts with only the best raw materials selected on the estates. The pods are harvested twice a year. The beans within are fermented then dried by the farmer who performs the 'cocoa dance' to pass air through the carpet of beans laid under the tropical sun.

Arriving at the manufacturer, the beans are roasted – a skilled task as with coffee – then ground – in a great chocolate very fine indeed, to 17 microns! Finally comes the mysterious 'conching' process – the mixing of the solids and fats extracted from the ground beans. In great chocolate this goes on and on for up to 5 days without interruption.

Cooking chocolate is often far too sweet and will be detrimental to the quality of the dessert you are preparing. Sugar is now considered public enemy number one, and the health factor has certainly helped us to rediscover the unadulterated taste of real chocolate! Le Meunier is good, and Valrhona is quite arguably the best chocolate available, the latter now becoming more readily available to the consumer in the UK.

When choosing chocolate for a dessert, choose an extra bitter one which should contain no less than 60 per cent cocoa.

Coffee

The French have never excelled in the art of making tea, but one thing is certain – they know their coffee beans! However witty and persuasive the instant coffee ads are, this is not real coffee, it's only a convenient substitute. I would never dream of offering it at the end of a beautiful meal; it would spoil all my efforts and certainly would be in bad taste. To enjoy real coffee you need a very small investment, a *cafetière*, and good coffee beans (whole or freshly ground). I would recommend pure Arabica as it has a wholesome and gentle flavour and taste. Only then will you enjoy and rediscover the real taste of coffee plus the fun of making it (and not cheating on your guests by making silly noises as some of the ads suggest!).

Cream

Unless stated otherwise in the recipe, the cream to be used should be whipping cream.

Eggs

All the eggs used in the recipes, unless otherwise stated, should be size 3. Only buy free-range eggs if possible, and the fresher the better.

Gelatine

Use gelatine leaves which weigh 2g (about $\frac{1}{16}$ oz) each. You could use the same equivalent in powdered form, but obviously the leaves are more accurate as it is always difficult to weigh such small amounts. Gelatine leaves can be found in most delicatessens and specialist food stores.

For vegetarian use, a form of gelatine is made from seaweed compounds, and can be found in health-food shops.

Herbs

The scents of herbs are often stronger than the taste itself, sometimes pungent and spicy, almost overpowering; sometimes fragile, fresh and dainty. Since time immemorial, herbs have been used medicinally, both for good and evil; those with a knowledge and understanding of their power were greatly revered or feared. While I am no expert in herbal medicine, herbs have always fascinated me. They can make or break a dish, round off the character or ruin the whole creation, or give life to an otherwise uninteresting roast.

I am very privileged to have a small herb garden at home and can grow most herbs. Actually you do not need much space, and with just a few square feet you would be amazed at what you can produce – plus the satisfaction and fun associated with it.

Most of the herbs used should be fresh as the drying often alters the flavour. Stronger or tougher varieties such as rosemary, thyme, sage, marjoram and bay can be dried successfully, but be very careful using them because of their strength. More tender herbs such as basil, chives, tarragon, chervil and mint should be used fresh.

Do not shy away from experimenting with these challenging little plants. Try different combinations; the clever and imaginative use of herbs can give new, exciting character to a well-tried dish. My visit to Joël Rebuchon's famed establishment in Paris illustrates this well: out of the whole excellent meal one dish was outstanding –

Some of the wonderful cheeses you can buy now

none other than the side salad, which was an innovative and delicious mixture of herbs and salad leaves which surprised my palate, almost disconcertingly simple, yet highly sophisticated. Although there was a generous grating of truffle adding its earthy scent, the originality came mostly from the unusual alliance of herbs.

Oils

Groundnut oil is a general purpose, non-scented oil which can be used as much for vinaigrettes as it can for frying. Grapeseed too is a non-scented oil, and it is best used in mayonnaise as it does not congeal when left in a cool place. Sunflower is an equally good non-scented oil – the advantage of the non-scented being that there is no taste to the oil that can interfere with that of the food being cooked.

The best olive oils are undoubtedly from Italy. In Great Britain, the labelling on olive oil bottles is very imprecise and 'loose'; never be tempted by such advertising as 'pure' olive oil, as this does not mean very much, is misleading, and often is the result of a second pressing. The olive oil to look for is *extra virgin* olive oil; this comes from the first, cold, pressing of the fruit, and is unrefined. Using olive oil is extremely healthy, as it is unsaturated, and of course its flavour is heavenly in salads, marinating and frying.

Obviously there are lots of other oils such as sesame (good in dishes with an oriental touch), and the nut oils, walnut and hazelnut. In a dressing, these should be mixed with a non-scented oil as they can overpower.

Vegetable oil should be used mostly for deep-frying rather than in dressings and mayonnaise, etc., as it can reach a very high temperature without smoking.

Puff Pastry

Puff pastry is the most difficult of all pastries to make, so I would propose in this book that you buy it ready-made. Try to find one that has been made with butter.

Rice

I personally use mostly basmati rice and North American wild rice, both of which are unrefined and untreated. Tilda have got a good variety and quality of rice which you should be able to find in most stores.

Spices

Spices play an essential role in the kitchen and, if appropriate, it is always better to buy them whole rather than powdered. If possible, keep a small coffee grinder to prepare them. They should be kept at room temperature.

Caraway seeds These will keep very well if stored in sealed jars and are used for flavouring bread and cheeses; they can also be used quite successfully in various sauces.

Cinnamon This is a spice native to Asia, thought to be one of the oldest spices, and it is very well known in Britain. It is best if bought whole – it is the bark of a small tree – and it should be kept in sealed jars as it is very strong. Use sparingly.

Cumin Cumin seeds are very similar to caraway seeds (they belong to the same botanical family), but cumin is less attractive in flavour. It is mostly used in Indian *cuisine*.

Nutmeg and mace Nutmeg is a shelled seed of an eastern tree. You should buy it whole, and grate it fresh as needed. Mace is the thin membrane that separated the nutmeg seed from the surrounding fruit. You will only find this in powdered form.

Paprika Being married to a Hungarian has made me well acquainted with this spice, the national spice of her country! It is the product of a special type of capsicum pepper, and is available in several degrees of pungency. Use hot paprika as it is the best.

Pepper Peppercorns are the fruit of a tropical vine, native to Asia. The fruit is picked when it is green and then dried (for black peppercorns) or brined (for green peppercorns). For white peppercorns, the fruit is allowed to mature on the tree then it is soaked in water, its red skin removed, and the seed is then dried. It is less pungent than black pepper and, unless stated otherwise, this is what I use in my recipes.

Saffron The spice consists of the pistils of a crocus flower which are dried. They are painstakingly collected and harvested by hand, so it is easily understood why saffron strands are so costly.

Saffron powder is less expensive and extremely convenient to use. It is sold in 1g sachets and can be kept for a long time. Beware of using it in hot fat as it will burn.

Star anise This is the star-shaped fruit of a tree of the magnolia family, and contains some very strong oils. It can be used in many Provençal dishes.

Vanilla Whenever possible, use the real thing, the pod, which comes from a South American vine. Before you buy, make sure that the pod is moist; pods that have dried out will have lost much of their flavour. Buy up to six at a time, and store them in sugar in an airtight container; this will give you vanilla sugar.

For the best results, split the pod lengthways, scrape out the inside and add these scrapings to the liquid. Chop and add the pod. This may not be economical, but it makes the most delicious custard.

For a lighter flavour, infuse a whole pod in the milk for a custard, say, then wash and dry it and store it in caster sugar for further use. This way, a vanilla pod can be used at least two or three times. Split the pod when using it for the last time.

Never use vanilla flavouring. You may, however, be able to find a good quality vanilla essence or extract. Check carefully before buying as most are the products of chemical flavouring.

Vinegars

Twenty years ago, malt vinegar was used as a deadly weapon in just about every dish. The image of the waiter coughing over the red cabbage soaked in malt vinegar is not too distant! Malt vinegar should be used only for pickling.

Red and white wine vinegars are the most commonly used for sauces and dressings. Always buy the best quality.

Xérès vinegar is made from sherry wine and can, of course, be used in dressings. It is also very good in sauces where Madeira or port are used.

Aceto balsamico, or balsamic vinegar, originates from Italy and it is made from grapes which are picked very late so they have a very high concentration of sugar; these are then crushed, cooked to stop the fermentation and left to mature in oak and other wood casks for a minimum of 10 years up to 50 years. Of course, the older the better. This vinegar has a balance of sweetness and acidity which is very pleasant and unusual. Its colour is dark, mostly due to the ageing process.

Raspberry, passion fruit and kiwi vinegars are by-products of *nouvelle cuisine*, and were invented mostly for their novelty value – and used for the same reason. If you use these highly flavoured vinegars, add only one part to five parts of white wine vinegar.

Wine
Wine used to be the monopoly of European countries such as France, Germany and Italy, but all this has now changed! Quality wines are now available from many countries such as Australia, New Zealand, North America, South Africa, etc. All this is very beneficial for the customer as it provides healthy competition both in price and quality, and must have helped enormously in the revival of interest in wine drinking. No longer is wine drinking for the privileged few.

Regional wines are now made with even more care, and it is worth looking for them on the shelves. Equally, wines from eastern bloc countries such as Romania, Hungary and Bulgaria are particularly worth looking for as their prices are very low, and you can find some exceedingly good wines for a few pounds per bottle.

In this book I have tried to guide you mostly towards regional wines rather than the expensive and well-known labels. The pocket book written by Hugh Johnson will guide you in choosing your wines and expand your knowledge of wine. His *World Atlas of Wine* will also prove invaluable.

Measurement Conversions
It is not practical to give exact equivalents when converting from metric to Imperial measurements. To avoid complications, the conversions have been rounded up or down to the nearest ounce or fluid ounce. Please remember that you must use either metric or Imperial measurements, but not a mixture of both.

Please note that all spoon measurements are level spoonfuls unless otherwise stated.

Oven Temperatures
It is important that the oven is preheated to the required temperature for at least 20 minutes before cooking the dish.

Pastries, Sponges and Crêpes

The recipes in this section will be used as the basis of many flans, both savoury and sweet, and of many desserts.

Savoury Shortcrust Pastry

This quantity of pastry will make one large tart (28cm × 3cm diameter/11 × 1¼in), with a little pastry left over.

Preparation time: 10 minutes, plus at least 6 hours' resting in the refrigerator.

Planning ahead: Make sure to prepare the pastry at least 6 hours in advance so that it can firm up and lose its elasticity. The pastry can also be prepared 24 hours in advance and refrigerated; it is suitable for freezing as well (it will keep for up to 4 weeks).

250g (9oz) plain, medium strength flour, sifted
1 egg yolk
70ml (about 2½fl oz) water
1 coffeespoon caster sugar
1 coffeespoon salt
65g (2½oz) unsalted butter, diced

Place the flour in a large bowl. Separately, in another bowl, mix together the egg yolk, water, sugar and salt. Reserve.

With your fingertips, rub the diced butter into the flour until it becomes sandy in texture. Make a well in the middle and pour in the egg-water mixture. Mix until the dough is holding together well.

Lightly flour your work surface and place the dough on it. Knead with the palms of your hands until it is totally blended, then form into a round shape. Wrap in cling film and refrigerate for at least 6 hours prior to using.

CHEF'S NOTES
According to which flour you are using, the amount of water may vary slightly. It is advisable to use a little *less* than stated, and add some more if the pastry seems dry.

Sweet Shortcrust Pastry

This quantity of pastry will make two medium tarts (23cm × 2.5cm diameter/9 × 1in approximately).

Preparation time: 10 minutes, plus at least 6 hours' chilling.

Planning ahead: The pastry must be prepared at least 6 hours in advance to allow it to rest. It can also be prepared 48 hours in advance, wrapped in cling film and refrigerated.

75g (3oz) icing sugar
2 egg yolks
120g (4½oz) unsalted butter, creamed
½ coffeespoon baking powder
a pinch of salt
250g (9oz) plain flour, sifted
2 tablespoons water

In a large bowl, mix together the icing sugar, egg yolks, creamed butter, baking powder and the pinch of salt.

Add the flour to the butter mixture and rub together using your fingertips, until it becomes sandy in texture. Add the water, then mix and press together.

Lightly flour your work surface and place the dough on it. Knead with the palms of your hands until it is well blended, then knead vigorously for a few more seconds. Wrap in cling film, and refrigerate for at least 6 hours.

CHEF'S NOTES
The resting time for the pastry is important as it will ensure that the pastry can relax and lose its elasticity. It will then be easier to roll.

Pâte Sablée Fine

Sweet Shortbread Pastry

Preparation time: 10 minutes, plus at least 2 hours' resting in the refrigerator.

Planning ahead: This pastry must be prepared in advance and refrigerated.

250g (9oz) medium-strength flour
a pinch of baking powder (optional)
2 egg yolks
2 tablespoons whipping cream
85g (3¼oz) icing sugar, sifted
a pinch of salt
a dash of vanilla essence (optional)
175g (6oz) unsalted butter, diced,
at room temperature

This pastry is unashamedly rich, delicate, melting and crumbly. This quantity of dough will make one 28cm (11in) diameter tart, or sixty 4cm (1½in) tartlets.

Thoroughly sift and mix together the flour and baking powder (if using).
   In a large mixing bowl, beat together the egg yolks, whipping cream, icing sugar, salt and vanilla essence (if using), then mix in the softened butter until well blended. Slowly sift in the flour, incorporating it with your fingertips until you obtain a crumbly, sandy dough. Do not overmix.
   Place the dough on a lightly floured work surface and work it quickly with the palms of your hands, shaping it into a ball. Wrap in cling film and chill in the fridge for at least 2 hours before using.

CHEF'S NOTES
This pastry is particularly delicate, so handle it with care and do not overmix at any stage. Remove the pastry from the fridge 30 minutes before you wish to use it, which makes it easier to roll.

Sponge Biscuit

Preparation and cooking time: 20 minutes

Special equipment:
1 pastry tray, 30 × 40 cm (12 × 16in).

Freezing: The sponge can be wrapped in cling film and kept in the freezer for 1 month.

2 egg whites
60g (2¼oz) caster sugar
2 egg yolks
60g (2¼oz) plain flour, sieved
10g (¼oz) unsalted butter, melted

This multi-purpose light sponge is used as a base for many desserts – see the Truffière de Chocolat on page 255, for instance – and cakes.

Preheat the oven to 350°F (180°C) Gas 4.
   Beat the egg whites until they reach soft peaks, then add the sugar gradually, continuously beating. When all the sugar is beaten in, whisk in the egg yolks. Finally fold the flour in delicately, followed by the melted butter.
   Line a pastry tray with silicone paper, pour the mixture over and spread out on the tray to 1cm (½in) thickness. Cook in the preheated oven for 10 minutes. Remove and leave to cool before using.

CHEF'S NOTES
When adding the flour to the egg whites, the best way is to place the flour in a sieve and sprinkle it at the same time as gradually folding it into the mixture (this will prevent lumps forming). A little help from a friend would be very useful.

Sheets of silicone paper are very practical as they do not stick to the sponge. Alternatively, use good greaseproof paper, or butter and flour the pastry tray.

Variations
Naturally, the biscuit mixture can be baked in a pastry ring or cake mould. Depending on the size of these, the cooking time will vary. To check, test with a needle which should come out dry if the sponge is cooked.

Grated orange and lemon zest can be added to the basic mixture, or any other flavours such as ginger or vanilla essence.

Chocolate Sponge Biscuit
Follow the ingredients and method exactly, but use only 50g (2oz) flour mixed with 10g (¼oz) unsweetened cocoa powder.

Crêpes (pour desserts)

Sweet pancakes

Makes 12–14 pancakes

Preparation and cooking time: about 30 minutes

Resting time: 30 minutes

Special equipment:
1 pancake frying pan 5mm (¼in) deep.

Planning ahead: The pancakes can be cooked a few hours in advance.

60g (2¼oz) unsalted butter
2 eggs
30g (1¼oz) caster sugar
a pinch of salt
100g (4oz) plain white flour, sifted
350ml (12fl oz) milk
finely grated zest of 1 orange
butter for greasing

Making the batter
Heat the butter in a frying pan until it foams and has a delicate nutty colour. Pour into a mixing bowl, and add the eggs, sugar, salt and flour. Mix thoroughly with the whisk, adding the milk little by little. Whisk until the mixture is completely smooth. Strain through a conical sieve into a bowl, and finally add the orange zest.

Leave the mixture to rest for 30 minutes at room temperature.

Cooking the pancakes
Lightly butter the pancake frying pan. Heat until it is very hot, pour in a small ladleful of batter and rotate so that it covers the whole frying pan surface. Cook for 30–40 seconds, then turn over with a spatula and cook the other side for another 30 seconds. Reserve on a tray. Proceed with the remaining batter as above.

CHEF'S NOTES
It is advisable to use a special pancake pan of this depth, and preferably made from cast iron. Never wash it after you have cooked the pancakes. Grind salt on to the surface of the pan, wipe it dry with a cloth, and rub in a tiny drop of oil to create a film. Put aside until required.

If you do not have a pancake pan, use a non-stick frying pan.

It is important that the batter is allowed to rest so the mixture will lose its elasticity.

When cooking the pancakes, the temperature of the butter is very important. If it is not high enough, the pancakes will be leathery. If it is *too* high, holes will form in the middle . . . Practice makes perfect!

Do not stack pancakes on top of each other as they will stick together. Lay them flat on a tray overlapping each other by half.

Variations
To make savoury pancakes, simply omit the sugar and orange zest, and add two more pinches of salt.

Soufflé-making

I still remember my despair when I first attempted soufflés. Time and again they failed – such is the price of learning by yourself. Books were of little help; they merely described a succession of apparently simple operations, none of which helped me to understand where I was going wrong.

I hope that my explanation will help you to achieve a perfect soufflé every time.

Sweet Soufflés

THE TRADITIONAL METHOD
There are many ways to make soufflés, but with this basic recipe, you can make almost any variety (e.g. Soufflé au Chocolat, or Soufflé aux Fruits de la Passion, see pages 258 and 214).

EQUIPMENT
Mixing bowl for beating the egg white Use scrupulously clean china or stainless steel. Copper bowls (traditionally used to obtain the best bulk) are now thought to release tiny particles of dangerous copper.
Whisk (for beating the whites by hand) Use a large supple balloon whisk to make beating easier and give more bulk. Alternatively, use an electric mixer with a whisk.
Supple spatula Use for folding the soufflé mixture into the pastry cream.
Soufflé dishes These should be made of ovenproof china – the finer the better, for heat conduction. I prefer individual dishes to one large one, as they give you more control over the cooking. The heat permeates the soufflé mixture better and faster, leaving the soufflé just cooked outside and barely cooked inside. The presentation is better, too.
Oven Always check the accuracy of the oven thermostat with a thermometer. Cook soufflés towards the bottom of the oven: if cooked higher up, strong heat is reflected off the top of the oven on to the top of the soufflés, which impairs the rise and may cause the tops to burn.

Soufflé au Grand Marnier

Grand Marnier soufflé

For four people

Preparation and cooking time: 55 minutes

Special equipment:
4 soufflé dishes, 9cm (3½in) diameter, 6cm (2¼in) high.

FOR THE SOUFFLÉ:
200ml (7fl oz) warm Pastry Cream (see page 47)
2 egg yolks

2 tablespoons Grand Marnier
8 egg whites
40g (1½oz) caster sugar
1 teaspoon lemon juice

FOR THE SOUFFLÉ DISHES:
1 teaspoon unsalted butter, at room temperature
2 tablespoons caster sugar, to line the soufflé dishes

Preheat the oven to 375°F (190°C) Gas 5.

Preparing the moulds
Using your hands, evenly butter the inside of the soufflé dishes, then put 2 tablespoons sugar in the first bowl and rotate until competely coated. Tip the excess into the next bowl and repeat.

This isolates the soufflé mixture from the dish, enabling the soufflé to rise without hindrance. Badly buttered bowls will produce an uneven rise or prevent it completely. Butter fixes the sugar in place and gives a delicious crust.

Preparing the soufflé base

Put the warm pastry cream into a mixing bowl, add the egg yolks and Grand Marnier and whisk well together. Keep warm.

The pastry cream is the soufflé base and holds the flavour. Check the degree of moistness: if it is too wet, the egg whites will not be able to absorb and lift it. The cream should still be warm when incorporated into the egg whites: this helps to prevent lumps and gives better lifting power.

The egg yolks are added for richness, not binding power; in some soufflés (e.g. raspberry, passion fruit and blackcurrant) they are not needed at all.

Many flavouring liqueurs can be substituted for the Grand Marnier. Fruit *coulis* can also be used; some (e.g. raspberry, blackcurrant and apricot) must be reduced beforehand to concentrate the flavour and keep the base firm. Strongly textured and flavoured *coulis*, such as lime, lemon and passion fruit, do not need reducing.

Adding the egg whites

Beat the egg whites at medium speed to soft peaks, then add the sugar and lemon juice. Increase the speed and beat for a few more seconds until just firm but not too stiff. This will give the soufflé a wonderful melting texture. During the whisking, the egg white will expand to create millions of tiny air bubbles which will expand during baking and cause the soufflé to rise. If the whites are beaten too stiffly the mixture will be too close-textured.

One-week-old eggs are best: very fresh egg whites have a high water content and are prone to graining. The mixing bowl must be scrupulously clean, as any trace of fat or yolk will severely reduce the bulk obtained by beating.

Whisk one-quarter of the beaten egg white into the warm pastry cream mixture for 2–3 seconds, until smooth. This brisk, brief whisking lightens the base mixture and eases the incorporation of the remaining egg white.

Using a spatula, delicately fold in the remaining egg whites with large circular movements until just incorporated. Do not overmix, or you will break down the air bubbles in the egg white and impair the rise.

Filling the soufflé dishes

Fill the soufflé dishes right to the top and smooth the surface with a spatula. Push the mixture about 1cm (½in) away from the edge of the bowls with your thumb; this prevents the soufflé from catching on the lip of the dish as it rises.

Cooking and serving the soufflés

Space the dishes well apart in the lower part of the preheated oven, allowing the heat to circulate freely, and bake for 12–13 minutes. After about 5 minutes, the soufflés will begin to rise. Check that they are rising evenly; if not, free the edges with a knife.

Dust the tops with a thin layer of icing sugar once or twice; it will melt and produce a delicious caramelised glaze. Remove the cooked soufflés and serve.

CHEF'S NOTES

Soufflés are not as fragile as you may think. You *can* open the oven door for a few seconds without them disintegrating. Do not remove them as soon as they have risen, however, as the centres must also be cooked. If they are removed too soon, they will indeed collapse. Overcooking produces the same result, as the air bubbles will eventually burst open.

An ideal soufflé should have a melting texture, with a barely cooked and soft, creamy centre. It will stand for at least 2 or 3 minutes without deflating.

A soufflé should have enough flavour of its own, and should not need a sauce poured into the centre. This is unsightly and immediately destroys the texture. I often serve a sorbet or slices of the same fruit used in the soufflé.

Savoury Soufflés

These are basically made in the same way as sweet soufflés.

Line the buttered dishes with fine breadcrumbs and add an extra squeeze of lemon to the egg whites instead of sugar during beating to improve the flavour and prevent graining.

Mousse-making

Many people rightly regard mousses as the ultimate culinary achievement – a feat worthy of respect and admiration. The basic method is actually quite simple but a really melting tasty fish or meat mousse requires a great deal of care at every stage.

Puréeing the main ingredient A food processor is necessary for this as the fibres and tissues must be puréed properly or the mousse would turn out grainy. Rub the mixture between your fingers; it should be perfectly smooth. When processing, stop the motor at least twice and use a supple spatula to stir in any mixture trapped under the blade.

Adding salt and pepper Salt and pepper added at this stage will be evenly distributed. The salt causes the proteins in fish and meat to swell: this firms up the consistency of the mousse mixture and helps the subsequent incorporation of cream.

Adding eggs or egg yolks Both yolks and whites provide the binding element (although meat and fish often contain enough natural proteins to bind the mixture on their own). I prefer to use egg yolks to enrich the mousse rather than whites, which need to be counterbalanced by more cream and thus dilute the mousse's essential flavour.

Chilling the mixture The friction of the food processor blade causes the mousse mixture to heat up as it is puréed. It is then essential to chill it for about 30 minutes per 150g (5oz) of basic ingredient. If cream were to be added to a tepid mixture, the liquids, fats and solids might separate.

Incorporating the cream Chilled whipping cream gives the lightest results. Use a food processor (the easier method) or incorporate it by hand (for the lightest result).

Using a food processor With the motor running, add the cream to the chilled mixture in a steady trickle. Make sure it is absorbed steadily: if you add too much at once, you may whip the cream and the mixture will separate. If it is absorbed too slowly, the mixture will warm up and separate. Halfway through mixing, scrape out any mixture trapped under the blade, then continue: it takes about 2 minutes to incorporate 600ml (1 pint) cream.

Sieving the mousse This removes all the small fibres and nerves from the mixture.

Use a fine mesh circular sieve and a plastic scraper (you can make your own from a plastic ice cream carton), or a fine conical sieve and a ladle. Force through only a small amount of mixture at a time.

If you do this last, there is hardly any waste: the mixture is light and creamy and passes easily through the sieve. Traditionally, the mixture is sieved before adding the cream, but I find this wastes time and effort, not to mention good basic ingredients and expensive sieves which collapse under the pressure!

To improve the lightness of the mousse, work the mixture with a wooden spoon to incorporate as much air as possible.

Testing the mousse Cooking is an inexact science: the quantity of cream needed depends on the type and freshness of the meat, fish and eggs used for the mousse. Start by adding only four-fifths of the cream and reserve the rest until you have tested the mousse.

To test, quarter fill a small buttered ramekin with the mousse mixture. Cook in a *bain-marie* with water at just below simmering point. Taste to check seasoning and texture: the mousse should have a melting texture but still hold its shape. Add the remaining cream to the main mixture and correct the seasoning if necessary.

Cooking the mousses Great care must be taken when cooking mousses as their structure is so delicate.

Preparing the moulds Butter the insides lightly, the fine film of butter makes unmoulding the mousses easier.

The bain-marie Use a deep roasting pan lined with greaseproof paper to protect the mousse from the heat from beneath.

Pour in enough hot water to come at least three-quarters of the way up the sides of the moulds: this ensures that the temperature of the mousses is constant throughout.

Cover the *bain-marie* with pierced foil or buttered paper, which allows the steam to hover above the mousses before escaping and keeps the surface moist. If the foil or paper is sealed too tightly, the heat builds up and the mousses rise like tiny soufflés, then collapse miserably, especially when a high proportion of egg white is used.

Temperature I prefer to cook my mousses at a relatively low temperature (325°F/160°C/Gas 3). This produces a delicate, trembling mousse, just bound together. A higher oven temperature will produce an overcooked and less delicate mousse. Most oven thermostats are inaccurate: check with an oven thermometer until you get to know the behaviour of your oven.

Timings may vary according to the thickness of the moulds, quantities being made, etc., so always check whether the mousses are ready. The surface should be slightly convex and the centre should feel firm when pressed with your finger.

Serving the mousses Hold the ramekin and shake it sideways; this should free the mousse. If not, slide a knife down to the bottom of the mould and, pressing the blade firmly against the side, make one continuous circle around the edge. Hold a plate firmly over the mould and invert.

Vegetable Mousses

Vegetable mousses do not need as much care and attention since they contain no binding proteins and the cream can simply be poured in. Most often the vegetables are puréed and chilled, then the cream, eggs and salt are all added at once and the mixture is forced through a sieve.

Cooking Vegetable mousses retain a lot of liquid. To reduce the risk of sticking, line the bottom of the moulds with buttered greaseproof paper, then pour in the mixture and cook gently.

Pasta-making

I really believe a pasta machine is an essential piece of equipment everyone should have in their kitchen. The pasta dough is very easy to make and a pasta machine makes the whole job child's play! It will give you a sense of achievement and all the family can join in to provide you with a great many delightful, simple, healthy recipes.

A pasta machine is not expensive to buy, and can be found in most large department stores.

Rediscover the joy of making rather than buying something ready made!

Pasta for Ravioli or Fresh Noodles

Makes 30 raviolis (with some extra dough which can be made into noodles).

Preparation time: 15 minutes

Resting time: 1 hour

Special equipment:
A pasta machine.

250g (9oz) plain flour
4 egg yolks
1 whole egg
1 level teaspoon salt
1 tablespoon olive oil
2 tablespoons water

Making with a food processor

Put all the ingredients in the given order into the food processor and mix for about 30 seconds until just blended. Knead the dough until perfectly smooth, wrap in cling film and leave to rest in the fridge for 1 hour before using.

Making by hand

You will need strength!

Place the flour in a mixing bowl and make a small well in the middle. Put in the egg yolks, whole egg, salt, olive oil and water and mix with your fingertips, gradually drawing the flour into the centre. Work the dough until fairly homogeneous, adding another tablespoon of water if necessary. Place the dough on a lightly floured surface and knead it thoroughly until perfectly smooth. Wrap in cling film and leave to rest in the fridge for 1 hour.

Rolling by hand
This is no easy matter and you cannot really produce as fine a result by hand as you can by using a pasta machine.

Cut the rested dough into four or five pieces. Place on a lightly floured surface, flatten, then roll out as thinly as possible. Roll the pasta sheets on to themselves and cut into strips, wide or narrow, for ravioli or noodles, tagliatelli, etc.

Rolling in a machine
Fix the machine to the side of a table. Cut the dough into four and flatten slightly with a rolling pin. Roll the dough using the thickest setting, then fold each sheet on itself and repeat, thinning it each time on a finer setting until the pasta is as thin as possible. Place in the machine and cut to the desired width (as above).

Drying the pasta
If you are not going to use the pasta immediately, drape it loosely on a tray or a stick to dry. Store it in a glass storage jar in your kitchen for future use. This will not only be useful but will look decorative.

Cooking
Bring to a fast boil 2 litres (3½ pints) water with 2 level tablespoons salt, and cook the fresh pasta for about 2 minutes (3 minutes if dried), depending on thickness, stirring occasionally to prevent sticking. (It is not necessary to add oil, as this simple floats to the surface and does not help.) Taste after 1 minute; the pasta should be *al dente*.

Drain under cold running water to remove excess starch.

To finish the noodles, heat 30g (1¼oz) butter with 2 tablespoons of water. Add the pasta and cook for 1 minute, stirring from time to time. Add a pinch of salt and freshly ground black pepper to taste and the noodles are ready to serve with any number of additional ingredients. Try shredded basil leaves, cooked tomatoes, minced meat, *julienne* strips of ham, cream, etc.

CHEF'S NOTES
When rolling out the dough, use no flour, or as little as possible; if too much is absorbed, the pasta will become glutinous and slimy when cooked.

After boiling the pasta, refresh it with cold water to rinse out the starch and prevent the noodles from sticking together.

Garnishes and Miscellaneous

A few basic recipes which will be useful in a variety of ways throughout the book.

Chapelure Provençale

Breadcrumbs scented with olive oil, garlic and herbs

Makes about 120g (4½oz)

Preparation and cooking time: 10 minutes

100g (4oz) dried bread, without crusts
2 garlic cloves, peeled
3 tablespoons olive oil
leaves from 1 large sprig of thyme
salt and freshly ground pepper
15g (½oz) parsley, finely chopped

These breadcrumbs are delicious sprinkled at the last moment on to something like a fricassee of mushrooms or roasted fish (see pages 90 and 137).

Grind the bread to crumbs in a food processor and turn out into a small bowl.
   Crush the garlic, chop finely and mix with the olive oil.
   Strain the oil through a fine sieve into the breadcrumbs and mix to obtain a fine, sandy texture. Season, then mix in the thyme and parsley.
   Store in a covered container in the refrigerator for 1 week or for up to 3 weeks in the freezer.

CHEF'S NOTES

The bread must be completely dry before you grind it, or the moisture combined with the olive oil will make the mixture lumpy.

Pat the parsley dry only once, before chopping. It is common practice to press parsley in a tea towel once chopped, but this will weaken its vigorous taste, and leave you with tasteless pieces of green fibre.

Vary the herbs and add more to suit your taste or the dish it accompanies; rosemary, basil, tarragon and chervil are good additions.

Lardons

Lardons are strips cut from belly of pork where the layers of lean and fat meat are juxtaposed, giving them their succulent, melting mellowness. They can be cut from cured and smoked belly, or from unsmoked 'green' belly. Use them to garnish salads and meat dishes.

Remove the rind and bone out any cartilage, then cut into slices about 5mm (¼in) thick, 5mm (¼in) wide, and 3cm (1¼in) long. (The size can vary to suit the dish.)
   Blanch the lardons in unsalted boiling water for 2–3 minutes, then refresh and drain. (Smoked lardons need cooking a little longer, due to the high salt content.)

Croûtons

2 slices bread
(about 150g/5oz), diced

30g (1¼oz) unsalted butter

Croûtons can either be sliced from a small *baguette* or diced from slices of a sliced loaf of bread.

Preheat the oven to 425°F (220°C) Gas 7.
   Melt the butter, add the diced bread, and toss to cover the dice with butter. Roast in the preheated oven for about 5–8 minutes until they are golden. Drain on absorbent paper and reheat gently when needed.

Variations
Olive oil croûtons can be cooked in exactly the same way as above, by simply replacing the butter with olive oil.
   Of course, the croûtons can be flavoured with garlic. Simply add 1 teaspoon of finely puréed garlic, after cooking, then mix.

Zestes Confits

Candied citrus zests

For six to eight people

Preparation and cooking time: 20 minutes

Planning ahead: The syrup must be made in advance.

4 oranges, or 6 limes or lemons, or 3 grapefruit
at least 1 litre (1¾ pints) boiling water
200ml (7fl oz) Stock Syrup (see page 46)
juice of ½ lemon

Use as a decoration to add colour, taste and texture to many desserts.
   Cut long strips of zest from the fruit, using a potato peeler. Cut these into fine *julienne* strips.
   Blanch for 8–10 minutes in the gently boiling water, then put in a colander and refresh under cold running water.
   Place the *julienne* strips in a small saucepan with the syrup acidulated with the lemon juice. Bring to the boil and simmer for 3 minutes.
   Draw off the heat and taste to check the texture is right. Transfer to a small bowl and leave to cool. Seal with cling film. The zests will keep for up to 2 weeks in this covered container.

CHEF'S NOTES
The blanching is done to remove excessive bitterness from the zest. It is important to blanch the zests in at least 1 litre (1¾ pints) water to disperse the bitterness, which would be recycled into the zests in a smaller quantity of water.

Lemon juice is added to the syrup to counter-balance its sweetness.

The cooking time will vary slightly depending on the thickness of the *julienne* strips. Check by tasting after 3 minutes' simmering. If undercooked, the zests will be unpleasantly bitter and hard; if overcooked, they will be mushy and too sweet.

Variations
Lemon, lime, orange and grapefuit zests can all be used.

Bouquet Garni

several parsley stalks   *½ bay leaf*
1 sprig of thyme   *a leek leaf or 2 small celery stalks*

A *bouquet garni* is traditionally made with a few stems of parsley, bay leaf and thyme. These herbs are wrapped in a leek leaf or two small stalks of celery, then tied.

The *bouquet garni* is there to enhance flavour, and some additional herbs could be added to create a different flavour. Unless stated, however, use this traditional recipe.

Place the parsley, thyme and bay leaf inside the leek leaf or celery stalks, and tie together with string. Use as required.

Clarified Butter

Clarified butter is necessary in many recipes. With the milk solids removed, the fat will be able to reach a higher temperature.

You must use only the very best quality unsalted butter. Melt 225g (8oz) butter gently in a heavy saucepan. Allow to foam for a minute or two, but not to burn. Remove from the heat and leave to settle for 20 seconds. Pour through a strainer lined with muslin into a bowl. The butter will be clear, the milk solids left in the muslin.

Purée de Coings

Quince purée

For four people

Preparation and cooking time: 25–30 minutes

500ml (18fl oz) cold water
juice of ½ lemon
100g (4oz) caster sugar, plus a pinch (optional)
40g (1½oz) unsalted butter

1kg (2¼lb) very ripe quinces
2 litres (3½ pints) water, acidulated with
2 tablespoons vinegar

A wonderful accompaniment for any game. Use the peel to make the liqueur on page 295.

Preparing the quinces
Peel, core and quarter the quinces and cut them roughly into 2.5cm (1in) squares, dropping them into a bowl with the acidulated water as you go.

Cooking and puréeing the quinces
In a large saucepan, bring the cold water to the boil with the lemon juice and 100g (4oz) sugar.

Drain the quinces, put them in the boiling water, cover and simmer for about 15 minutes until soft. Remove with a slotted spoon (the chilled cooking liquid makes a most pleasant drink), drain in a colander, then purée for about 3 minutes until completely smooth.

Finishing and serving
Pour the purée into a medium saucepan and if too liquid, stir over medium heat until it reaches a good consistency. Stir in the butter, taste and add a tiny pinch of caster sugar if necessary.

CHEF'S NOTES

This recipe calls for very ripe quinces; they should be a deep yellow colour and have a strong scent. Less ripe quinces will need a longer cooking time and that extra pinch of sugar at the end.

Variations

A tiny slice of root ginger can be added during simmering.

For an even smoother texture, force through a fine sieve after puréeing.

Ecorces de Pamplemousse Confites

Candied pink grapefruit peel

Makes 50 pieces

Preparation and cooking time: 40 minutes

Marinating time: 2 hours

1 pink grapefruit
2 litres (3½ pints) water

FOR THE SYRUP:
juice of 1 grapefruit
100g (4oz) caster sugar

FOR THE COATING:
50g (2oz) granulated sugar

Slice off the rind and part of the pith of the grapefruit to a thickness of 5mm (¼in). Cut the peel into sticks 5cm x 5mm (2 x ¼in) thick, then place in the cold water. Bring to the boil then simmer for 20 minutes. Drain.

Bring the grapefruit juice and caster sugar to the boil to dissolve the sugar, then add the grapefruit sticks and simmer for about 10 minutes. Leave the grapefruit sticks to cool down in the syrup for 2 hours.

Drain the grapefruit sticks then leave to dry on a cooling rack for about 30 minutes. Roll them in the granulated sugar until they are completely coated.

CHEF'S NOTES

The grapefruit sticks can be kept for up to 2–3 days in a sealed container.

Variations

Grapefruit can be replaced by oranges or lemons.

Equipment

As a general rule, it is better to invest in good equipment. What seems expensive to start with might prove a very good investment in the long term, including the pleasure it will give you. To get such equipment, you need to go to a specialist shop.

Whisk

A good whisk should be supple and made of stainless steel.

The simple task of whipping cream could turn into a very taxing experience if you use one of those rigid-lined wire whisks, which may also discolour and change the taste of the cream.

Knives

There are a lot of cheap-looking knives with plastic handles, made of poor quality steel. Do not be tempted, but always buy the best.

You will need a few knives such as vegetable, chopping, cook's, boning and butcher knives.

Ladles
Try to find ladles which are made in one piece, from stainless steel.

Sieve
A good fine conical sieve may be expensive, but will prove useful in so many ways. A round flat sieve is good for mousse-making.

Mouli-légumes
A good old traditional *mouli-légumes* or vegetable mill is essential. Again find the best quality.

Casseroles and Pots
For braising, nothing is better than a good, old-fashioned cast-iron pan, with a lid. A good stock-pot is vital if you want to make stocks (and the best sauces), and it is also useful for sterilising jams, etc. (see page 304).

Pans
Non-stick pans of all kinds, and roasting trays are very handy. One of their main advantages is that you need to use little fat. The trays are also very useful as *bain-maries*.

Dishes
A number of my recipes require lidded terrine dishes: these come in various sizes. Ramekins and egg dishes are useful too.

Baking
For this you will need good baking or pastry sheets or trays that will not buckle in the oven. Pastry cutters and rings are useful, as are fluted flan tins with removable bases. There are a number of more specialised tins and moulds which are specified in individual recipes.

Mixer
An electric mixer with a few attachments such as a liquidiser, whisk, dough hook, etc. will perform many duties for you.

Food Processor
This is just as useful as the mixer for chopping, mixing, blending, etc.

Pasta Machine
A hand pasta machine will turn pasta-making into fun, and the cost of it is not too high.

Sorbetière
These machines are expensive, but they are so easy to handle and will help you to create so many easy sweets and sorbets instantly. Forget about those ice creams full of preservatives and additives. It would make a really special Christmas present.

Oven
Whatever oven you may have, you need to know how the heat is distributed, as this will have an enormous influence on the final result.

CHAPTER TWO

Stocks and Sauces

Stocks

General rules for all stocks

Vegetables Dice or chop them finely so that they release their flavour more quickly.

Wine Any wine used must be boiled to remove the alcohol, then reduced to remove some of its acidity.

Water You must use *cold* water so that when the stock is brought back to the boil the heat will solidify all the impurities. These are carried to the surface during simmering and can be skimmed off.

The stock must be simmered, not cooked at full boil, or the impurities would be recycled and turn the stock cloudy again.

Seasoning None is added to basic stock recipes since the meats already contain some, and a stock is often reduced and used to enrich a sauce. Add salt then if necessary.

Fond Blanc de Volaille

Light clear chicken stock

Makes 1 litre (1¾ pints)

Preparation time: 20 minutes

Cooking time: 1 hour

2kg (4½lb) chicken wings or *chopped carcasses,*
or *turkey legs,* or *a plump boiling fowl*
15g (½oz) unsalted butter or *chicken fat*
1 small onion, peeled and finely chopped

white of 1 small leek, *finely chopped*
1 small celery stalk, *finely chopped*
100g (4oz) button mushrooms, *washed and finely sliced*
1 garlic clove, *peeled and crushed*
10 white peppercorns, *crushed*
200ml (7fl oz) dry white wine *(optional)*
1 litre (1¾ pints) cold water
1 bouquet garni *(see page 30)*

This subtle stock is used to enrich and enhance the flavours of many dishes, or to prepare soups.

In a large saucepan, sweat the chicken wings in the butter for 5 minutes without colouring. Add the chopped vegetables, garlic and crushed peppercorns, and sweat for a further 5 minutes. Pour in the wine, if using, and boil to reduce by one-third.

Cover with the cold water, bring back to the boil and skim. Throw in the *bouquet garni* and simmer for 1 hour, skimming from time to time. Strain through a fine sieve and leave to cool.

Store in a covered container in the fridge for 3 or 4 days, or for up to 2 months in the freezer.

CHEF'S NOTES
Do not add salt at this stage – salt will be added when you use the stock for the dish.

Jus Brun de Volaille

Brown chicken stock

Makes 450ml (15fl oz)

Preparation and cooking time: 1 hour, 10 minutes

Planning ahead: The stock can be made in advance and refrigerated for 1 week, or frozen for 3 weeks.

1.5kg (3¼lb) chicken wings or carcasses, chopped finely
100ml (3½fl oz) non-scented oil (see page 17)
1 medium onion, peeled and finely chopped
1 garlic clove, peeled and crushed
100g (4oz) mushrooms, wiped and chopped
1 tablespoon tomato purée
6 black peppercorns, crushed
½ bay leaf
1 sprig of thyme
approx. 900ml (1½pints) water
10g (¼ oz) arrowroot or cornflour,
diluted in 50ml (2fl oz) water

Very often, the home cook wishes he could reproduce the sauces that are made in professional kitchens. Usually the stocks for these are very time-consuming, complicated and out of reach of the home cook. This recipe has many merits: it is cheap, the yield is good and the stock is well flavoured with a good colour . . . and will not take up hours of your time. Of course this recipe is not as easy as dissolving a stock cube in water, but the results are not comparable and are well worth the effort. It is the simplest way I know to add that touch of magic to your sauces!

Once the stock has been made, it can be stored in small containers in the freezer to use as and when required.

Preheat the oven to 450°F (230°C) Gas 8.

In a large roasting pan, heat the oil until smoking, then over the strongest heat, brown the chicken wings or carcasses for 8–10 minutes, stirring occasionally with a wooden spoon. Add the chopped onion, garlic and mushrooms and cook for another 5 minutes until lightly coloured.

Cook in the preheated oven for 20 minutes until the chicken wings and vegetables turn a rich brown. Spoon out the excess fat and discard. Add the tomato purée, peppercorns, bay leaf and thyme and stir.

Deglaze the pan with 200ml (7fl oz) of the water, scraping up all the caramelised bits from the bottom of the pan.

Transfer the bones and liquid to a saucepan, cover with the remaining water (about 700ml/23fl oz) and bring to the boil. Skim, then simmer for 20–30 minutes. Strain off the juices and skim off any fat.

Whisk the diluted arrowroot or cornflour and water into the stock, and bring to the boil to lightly bind the stock. Cool, then refrigerate or freeze.

CHEF'S NOTES

I prefer to keep this stock neutral tasting so that it will not interfere with the flavour of the sauce to which it is added, but if you want more depth to the taste, add a glass of white wine or dry Madeira before deglazing the bones with water.

Chop the chicken bones into small pieces, about 5cm (2in) square. The smaller the chicken pieces are, the less cooking time will be needed, thus producing a clearer, stronger flavour and also a better colour.

The degree of the browning of the bones will determine the taste and quality of the stock. If it does not have sufficient colour, add a teaspoon of soy sauce.

Variations
The chicken carcasses can be replaced by game or veal trimmings.

Fumet de Poissons

Fish stock

Makes 400ml (14fl oz)

Preparation and cooking time: 40 minutes

Planning ahead: Order the fish bones from your fishmonger well in advance. Ask him to chop the bones into small pieces, about 5cm (2in), so that they will impart their flavour to the stock more readily.

*400g (14oz) fish bones
(sole, lemon sole, turbot or plaice)
50g (2oz) shallots, peeled and finely chopped
25g (1oz) unsalted butter
250g (9oz) button mushrooms, washed,
patted dry and sliced
200ml (7fl oz) white wine
500ml (18fl oz) water
1 bouquet garni (see page 30)
freshly ground pepper*

This stock can be used for a variety of fish dishes, and adapts to make a wonderful sauce for fish (see page 42). It can be stored to use as required, but try to make it from the bones of the fish you are using in the recipe. This will give the finished dish a unified flavour.

In a large saucepan, sweat the shallots in the butter for 2–3 minutes without colouring. Add the sliced mushrooms and the chopped fish bones, and sweat for a further 5 minutes. Add the white wine, bring to the boil, then boil to reduce by approximately one-third.

Cover the fish bones with the cold water and bring to the boil. Skim, add the *bouquet garni* and pepper, and simmer for 20 minutes.

Strain through a fine sieve into a bowl, cool down, cover with cling film and refrigerate.

CHEF'S NOTES
Sole bones are highly recommended for this fish stock.

There is no salt in this recipe as one often needs to reduce the fish stock; salt can be added at that stage.

The reduction of the wine is very important. If it is not reduced enough, the stock will be very acidic and 'heady'. If the wine is reduced *too* much, the stock will be bland, with no depth whatsoever. The reduction of the wine, therefore, is approximate and may vary according to which wine you are using.

Nage de Légumes, Herbes et Condiments

A clear, scented stock made from vegetables, herbs and spices

Makes 500ml (18fl oz)

Preparation and cooking time: 30 minutes

Infusing time: 5–6 hours

*½ onion, peeled and finely chopped
white of 1 small leek, finely chopped
1 carrot, peeled and finely chopped
¼ celery stalk, finely chopped
peelings of 1 fennel bulb,
finely chopped, or some fennel seeds*

*2 garlic cloves, peeled and finely chopped
4 pink peppercorns
1 star anise
8 white peppercorns, crushed
zests of 1 lemon and 1 orange
1 sprig of thyme
500ml (18fl oz) cold water
a small bunch each of tarragon and chervil, chopped
1 teaspoon chopped coriander leaves
(or 6–8 coriander seeds)
100ml (3½fl oz) dry white wine*

This involves a lot of chopping, but once that is done, the recipe is very simple. The stock is mostly used for accompanying or poaching fish.

Put all the vegetables, spices, zests, and thyme into a large saucepan and pour in the cold water. Bring to the boil and skim, then simmer for about 10 minutes.

Add the chopped tarragon, chervil and coriander, pour in the wine, and simmer for a further 2–3 minutes. The gentle acidity of the wine will 'lift' the stock.

Take the pan off the heat and leave uncovered for 5–6 hours so that the flavours infuse. Strain the stock through a fine conical sieve, pressing with a ladle, into a storage container. Seal.

Keep in a covered container for 2 or 3 days in the fridge, or several weeks in the freezer.

Variation
This stock can be used as the basis for a sauce for steamed fish. Reduce the quantity of stock by half, to 250ml (9fl oz). Add 2 tablespoons whipping cream, then whisk in 40g (1½oz) cold diced unsalted butter. Season with salt and pepper, and add lemon juice and your favourite herbs or spices.

Fumet de Légumes
Vegetable stock

Makes about 600ml (1 pint)

Preparation and cooking time: 20 minutes

1 onion, peeled and finely chopped
1 large courgette, trimmed and finely sliced
1 small leek, washed, trimmed and finely chopped

½ fennel bulb, finely sliced (optional)
1 garlic clove, peeled and finely chopped
12 black peppercorns, crushed
600ml (1 pint) cold water
2 sprigs of tarragon, chopped
a tiny bunch of chervil, chopped

This light vegetable stock is the base for many of my sauces. It has a wonderfully concentrated aroma of the garden, and is very simple to make: prepare a large quantity and keep it in the fridge (1 week) or freezer (1 month).

In a medium saucepan, place all the vegetables and the peppercorns. Cover with the cold water, bring to the boil and simmer for 15 minutes.

Add the chopped herbs, and simmer for a further 5 minutes.

Using the back of a ladle, force the liquid through a fine conical sieve into a small bowl (or a plastic container for freezing).

CHEF'S NOTES
Vary the herbs according to the dish you are cooking; add them at the last moment to preserve their fragrance and colour.

Do not exceed 15 minutes in cooking time in order to preserve the freshness of flavour.

Add salt only when using in a recipe.

Clarification

For clarifying 1 litre (1¾ pints)

Special equipment:
A piece of muslin.

1 litre (1¾ pints) stock
3 egg whites

100g (4oz) raw fish, or lean meat, very finely chopped
herbs (according to taste and recipe) for flavouring
½ leek, washed and finely chopped
¼ celery stalk, finely chopped
1 tomato, finely chopped
1 carrot, peeled and finely chopped

This is sometimes necessary to produce the clearest possible stock for a consommé or jelly. Finely chopped raw meat, fish or vegetables (depending on the main ingredient in the recipe) are mixed with egg white, vegetables, herbs and spices, and added to the stock.

Place the stock in an appropriately sized saucepan.

Place the egg whites in a bowl, and lightly break them with two or three movements of the whisk. Add the chopped meat or fish, herbs and vegetables, and mix thoroughly.

Whisk all these clarifying elements into the stock, and bring to the boil, stirring continuously. Simmer for 30 minutes. Use a ladle to make a hole in the crust which forms on the surface, at the point where the bubbling is strongest.

Take the pan off the heat and leave to rest for a few minutes.

Pour the clear stock through a fine sieve lined with damp muslin. Leave to cool, cover and refrigerate: keep in the fridge for 5 days, freeze for 1 month.

CHEF'S NOTES
The addition of meat or fish compensates for the loss of flavour caused by clarifying.

While the stock is simmering, the proteins in the meat or fish and egg white will coagulate and trap all the impurities present in the stock. The gentle simmering carries the solidified impurities to the surface, forming a light crust, and leaving a completely clear stock.

The hole in the crust prevents a build-up of heat and the stock will not boil over.

Savoury Sauces

Never allow a sauce to overpower the dish it accompanies. A sauce is an ally, not an oppressor: let it be the catalyst which brings out all the essential qualities the dish has to offer.

General advice on sauce making

Mirepoix Diced vegetables form part of the build-up of flavours. The sizes of the dice vary according to the cooking time of the sauce.

Browning the meats, vegetables or bones This most important stage adds colour and flavour to a brown sauce. If the ingredients are not sufficiently browned, the sauce will be too light in taste and colour, but if they are too brown, the sauce may be too strong or bitter (although the colour will be good). Practice makes perfect! Make sure that the fat is hot before browning the meats.

Vinegar This must be reduced completely. It should give the sauce a gentle acidity; if insufficiently reduced, the sauce will be too acid and difficult to correct.

Wine Use a decent quality wine for a wine sauce. A good wine will lend its characteristics to the sauce – so will a bad one.

Unless otherwise stated in the recipe, always reduce wine by boiling to remove first the alcohol, then some of the acidity. Sweet wines do not need reducing, since they contain little or no acidity: boil only briefly to remove the alcohol but keep the flavour intact.

Red wine sauces Always use a full-bodied wine with plenty of flavour and a deep colour, like a Rhône or good table wine.

White wine sauces Use a dry white wine unless otherwise stated and reduce as above.

Port Ruby port has a more pronounced flavour and colour than tawny.

Madeira Use a dry Madeira, as a medium or sweet wine will often spoil the sauce.

Herbs Some are robust enough to withstand long simmering (e.g. thyme, rosemary, bay leaf) and can be added at the outset. More delicate herbs quickly spoil, so add them at the end, a little at a time, tasting frequently so that they do not overpower the sauce.

Spices Add sparingly at the beginning and adjust towards the end.

To correct a sauce Sauces should be seasoned sparingly, first with salt, then pepper and finally with spices. It is more difficult to correct an over-seasoned sauce than one which is under seasoned.

Too sharp Add a dash of cream, whisk in a tiny quantity of butter or add a pinch of sugar, a touch of redcurrant jelly or honey.

Lacking acidity Enliven with a tiny drop of vinegar, wine or a dash of orange or lemon juice.

Beurre Blanc

Butter sauce

For four people

Preparation and cooking time: 15 minutes

50g (2oz) shallots, peeled and finely chopped
2 tablespoons white wine vinegar

3 tablespoons dry white wine
2 tablespoons cold water
200g (7oz) unsalted butter, chilled and diced
salt and freshly ground white pepper
lemon juice

This classic sauce is almost legendary, but it still shines alongside the lighter modern sauces despite its richness. It makes a simple and delicious accompaniment to poached or grilled fish. It is also very easy to do.

In a small heavy-bottomed saucepan, combine the chopped shallots, vinegar and wine, and boil until you have about 1 tablespoon of syrupy liquid left.

Add the cold water (this extra liquid will help the emulsion) then, over a gentle heat, whisk in the cold diced butter, a little at a time, until completely amalgamated.

The finished sauce will be creamy and homogeneous, and a delicate lemon yellow. Season with a tiny amount of salt and pepper and enliven with a squeeze of lemon. Keep warm.

CHEF'S NOTES
Shallots have a tough fibrous second layer of skin. Remove this as well as the peel, but leave the finely chopped shallots in the sauce for a pleasant, rustic flavour and texture.

The success of the sauce depends greatly on the quality of the butter. Use the very best unsalted butter you can find. The butter must be *cold*. If too soft, it will melt too quickly and not emulsify. Ideally, the temperature of the sauce should be 150°F (60°C) when incorporating the butter. Test with your finger from time to time – the heat should be bearable. If the sauce is too cold, the butter will cream and separate. Try to maintain an even temperature.

If the liquid is not sufficiently reduced, the sauce will be too sharp. (If this is the case, add a little more butter or 2 tablespoons whipping cream at the end.)

Beurre blanc is an emulsified sauce. The emulsion is made possible by the water in the butter, which helps the binding, then by fast whisking and finally the application of heat which stabilises the emulsion. Constant whisking is extremely important to produce a smooth emulsion, especially at the beginning.

As there are no emulsifiers to stabilise the sauce completely, it will remain rather delicate, and should be kept for no more than 1 hour in a warm *bain-marie* at 122–150°F (50–60°C). Whisk from time to time to maintain the emulsion. If the sauce *does* separate, in a clean saucepan bring to the boil 2 tablespoons whipping cream, then slowly whisk in the separated sauce.

Variations

This 'mother' sauce can produce many offspring: add *julienne* strips of ginger, blanched for 15 minutes; lemon or orange zests blanched for 3–4 minutes; or scent the sauce with shredded coriander, tarragon or other herbs.

Beurre Noisette

'Hazelnut' butter

Beurre noisette is butter which has been heated to a sufficiently high temperature for the solids contained in the butterfat to start cooking. This turns the butter a rich golden colour and gives it a distinct taste of hazelnuts.

Be warned, though; the stage beyond *beurre noisette* is *beurre noir*, which is black, rather nasty and pretty indigestible.

Sauce Mayonnaise

Serves four people

Preparation time: 10 minutes

2 egg yolks
1 teaspoon Dijon mustard

salt and freshly ground white pepper
250ml (8fl oz) best quality non-scented oil
1 teaspoon white wine vinegar
2 teaspoons lemon juice

Mayonnaise is an emulsified sauce which once more illustrates the magical power of egg yolks. Smooth and delicious, this classic sauce is very simple to make.

In a large mixing bowl whisk together the egg yolks, mustard, 2 pinches of salt and 3 turns of pepper.

Start adding the oil in a steady trickle, whisking energetically until the oil is absorbed and the mixture turns pale yellow and thickens (usually after adding 150ml/5fl oz of the oil).

Loosen the consistency with the wine vinegar and lemon juice, then whisk in the remaining oil. Taste and correct the seasoning if necessary.

Store in a covered container for 2–3 days in the lower part of the fridge.

CHEF'S NOTES

All ingredients used must be at room temperature – especially the oil. If too cold, it will be difficult to incorporate.

If you are not going to use the mayonnaise immediately, make it with grapeseed oil, which prevents it from separating in the fridge.

At first the incorporation of the oil must be done gradually, and with constant vigorous whisking. The emulsion is created at this stage and the emulsifying agents within the egg yolk cannot cope with too much oil at a time. This is the most important stage of mayonnaise making. Once the sauce is emulsified, it will be stable. The rest of the oil can be added in greater quantities and with less vigorous whisking. If the mayonnaise separates, put 1 teaspoon Dijon mustard (which contains an emulsifier) in another bowl and gradually incorporate the separated mayonnaise, whisking vigorously.

Variations
Mayonnaise is a 'mother' sauce from which others can be made – by adding tomato *coulis* (see page 122), paprika, curry powder or saffron, etc.

To make a light *rouille*, replace the non-scented oil with olive oil and add a pinch each of saffron and cayenne pepper, and 2 garlic cloves, peeled, crushed and puréed.

Sabayon Base for Savoury Sauces

For four to six people

Preparation time: 5 minutes

Cooking time: 10 minutes

3 very fresh egg yolks
4 tablespoons cold water

A *sabayon* is the lightest base used for binding sauces and creams, and is the foundation of many sauces in this book (see the next recipe and page 268). It is a simple process really, although it all sounds rather complicated. Only practice will give you confidence, however, so have a go now!

Emulsifying the egg
Combine the egg yolks and water, whisking continuously. This is easier in an electric mixer (2½ minutes at speed 3, to be precise!), but can be done in a bowl. (An electric hand whisk is a good investment.)

The mixture will expand to four or five times its original volume and become light and foamy, but it needs heat to stabilise it.

Stabilising the egg
The foam is composed of millions of little air bubbles wrapped in a film of egg yolk. While the yolk remains uncooked, the air will escape through its fragile walls, so you must now partially cook the protein wall (the yolk) to strengthen it. Do not use *direct* heat for this process, but a bowl and a *bain-marie*.

Set the mixing bowl in a hot *bain-marie* (with the water at about 175°F/80°C) so that the heat permeates the *sabayon* very gradually. Continue whisking vigorously for about 5 minutes at a constant temperature.

The mixture will now be firmer and have the consistency of lightly whipped cream.

Keeping the *sabayon*
Keep warm in a *bain-marie*. If you are not using the *sabayon* immediately, cool it over ice, still whisking to minimise the loss of lightness. Since it is now fairly stable, the *sabayon* will keep for an hour or so before being used in your sauce.

CHEF'S NOTES
You may be tempted to remove the *sabayon* from the heat as soon as it begins to thicken, but this may be too soon and the mixture will quickly deflate and separate. If, however, you allow the temperature to rise above 175°F (80°C), the *sabayon* will be ruined and you will end up with scrambled egg: the first warning sign is the appearance of flecks of darker yellow solid yolk. Test the temperature by dipping your finger into the *sabayon*; the heat should be bearable.

Lemon Sabayon

A light hollandaise

For four people

Preparation and cooking time: 20 minutes

Planning ahead: The sauce can be prepared 30 minutes before use and kept in a warm *bain-marie* (at about 122°F/50°F) covered with buttered greaseproof paper to prevent a skin forming.

3 egg yolks
4 tablespoons water
50g (2oz) clarified butter (see page 30), warmed
a pinch of salt
a pinch of cayenne pepper
juice of ¼ lemon

Traditional hollandaise sauce is made with 250g (9oz) butter per three egg yolks, which is a real killer. This sauce uses only 50g (2oz) butter and will still serve four people. Delicious – and no feelings of guilt!

The sauce can be served with poached fish, or lightly cooked vegetables such as broccoli, asparagus or spring greens.

Preparing the *sabayon* base

With the ingredients at room temperature, place the egg yolks in a *sabayon* bowl, add the water, and whisk vigorously until you obtain a beautifully light, bulky foam about four or five times its original volume. (Use an electric mixer with a whisk, which will make the beating much easier.)

Place the bowl over a *bain-marie* (no hotter than 175°F/80°C) and continue whisking until the egg yolk is coagulated by the heat and the foam becomes stable.

Incorporating the clarified butter

Pour the warmed clarified butter into the *sabayon* in a steady trickle, whisking constantly. Taste, season with a tiny pinch of salt then a pinch of cayenne pepper, and finally add most of the lemon juice. Taste again and add the remaining lemon juice if necessary.

Use immediately, or keep for no longer than 30 minutes (see Planning Ahead).

CHEF'S NOTES

The clarified butter should not be hot, just warm. If too hot, it will raise the temperature of the *sabayon* too much and may cook the egg yolk.

Variations

You can use this lemon *sabayon* as the basis for many sauces. For a *sauce mousseline*, for instance, add 100ml (3½fl oz) whipped whipping cream. Any herb such as tarragon or basil could also be added. Equally, if you're feeling rich, 50ml (2fl oz) truffle juice would be a delight, or a few drops of truffle essence . . .

Sauce Vin Blanc

White wine sauce for fish

Makes 400ml (14fl oz)

For eight people

Preparation and cooking time: 35 minutes

300ml (10fl oz) dry white wine
50g (2 oz) shallots, peeled and chopped

25g (1oz) unsalted butter
400g (14oz) fish bones, chopped into 5cm (2in) pieces
500ml (18fl oz) whipping cream
200g (7oz) button mushrooms,
washed, patted dry and finely sliced
salt and freshly ground pepper
lemon juice

A great classic sauce which is still enjoyed in spite of its richness.

Boil the white wine to reduce it to 200ml (7fl oz). Reserve.

In a large saucepan, sweat the shallots in the butter for 2–3 minutes without colouring. Add the fish bones and sweat for a further 5 minutes. Add the reduced white wine, cream and mushrooms. Bring to the boil for 30 seconds, then gently simmer for 25 minutes.

Pass through a sieve pressing the bones and mushrooms with a ladle to extract as much liquid as possible. Reduce until the sauce is the right consistency, then taste and season with salt and pepper.

Enliven the sauce with a dash of lemon juice. Cool down and reserve.

CHEF'S NOTES
As for the Fish Stock recipe on page 36.

Variations
This sauce can produce a lot of offspring. For a saffron sauce, add a pinch of saffron powder or strands when sweating the shallots. For a ginger sauce, add 20g (¾oz) finely chopped ginger when you add the cream. Various herbs such as tarragon, chives or basil can also be added: do this at the end of cooking before the sauce is served.

Vinaigrettes

Much of the success of a salad lies in the harmony of its dressing, which should be neither too oily nor too thin, neither too overpowering nor too bland. The following popular vinaigrettes show how many different flavours you can use.

Always add the vinaigrette to the salad at the last moment; the acid in the vinegar quickly attacks the colour and texture of the more fragile leaves.

The ingredients for a vinaigrette should always be at room temperature. The quantities given here are generally for immediate use, but larger quantities can be made and stored in sealed bottles or jars at room temperature. Shake well before use.

All the vinaigrettes are quick and easy to make; they will serve four to six people.

Vinaigrette à l'Huile de Noisette

Hazelnut oil vinaigrette

½ tablespoon hazelnut oil (see page 17)
3 tablespoons non-scented oil (see page 17)
1 tablespoon white wine vinegar

a large pinch of salt
4 turns freshly ground white pepper

The most scented of all the vinaigrettes.

Mix all the ingredients together.

CHEF'S NOTES
Do not be tempted to increase the quantity of hazelnut oil; the vinaigrette will then be too highly scented and will overpower the salad.

Variation
For a walnut oil vinaigrette, use walnut instead of hazelnut oil.

Vinaigrette à l'Huile d'Olive

Olive oil vinaigrette

4 tablespoons extra virgin oil (see page 17)
1 tablespoon non-scented oil (see page 17)
1 tablespoon white wine vinegar

a large pinch of salt
4 turns freshly ground white pepper

. . . With all the evocative scents and flavours of sunny Provence.

Simply mix all the ingredients together.

Vinaigrette à l'Huile d'Arachide

A non-scented vinaigrette

4 tablespoons non-scented oil (see page 17)
1 tablespoon white wine vinegar

a large pinch of salt
8 turns freshly ground white pepper

If you do not enjoy scented oil, this vinaigrette is ideal, and will not interfere with the flavours of the salad or other ingredients used.

Mix all the ingredients together.

Variation
A few freshly chopped leaves of tarragon or chervil and a finely chopped shallot will give this vinaigrette a little more depth.

Vinaigrette au Coulis de Tomates

Tomato vinaigrette

200g (7oz) ripe tomatoes
a large pinch of salt
a large pinch of caster sugar
a dash of white wine vinegar

2 tablespoons extra virgin olive oil (see page 17)
freshly ground white pepper
basil or coriander leaves, finely shredded (optional)

The success of a tomato *coulis* depends on the ripeness of the tomatoes. Use fat, fleshy Marmande, olive-shaped Roma or sweet cherry tomatoes.

Halve the tomatoes and remove the seeds with a teaspoon. Chop the flesh roughly and purée finely, then force through a fine conical sieve into a mixing bowl, using a ladle. Season with salt and sugar, add the vinegar then whisk in the olive oil until well emulsified. Finally, season with four turns of pepper and add the herbs, if using.

Vinaigrette à la Moutarde

Mustard vinaigrette

Makes about 300ml (10fl oz)

Planning ahead: The dressing can be prepared 4–5 hours in advance of use.

1 tablespoon Dijon mustard
3 tablespoons groundnut or grapeseed oil
50ml (2fl oz) soured cream
1 tablespoon white wine vinegar
2 tablespoons water
salt and freshly ground pepper

This is a delicious accompaniment to the Terrine de Poireaux on page 66, but also is good with any salad.

Place the mustard in a large bowl and slowly whisk in the oil followed by the soured cream.
  Add the vinegar and water to loosen the texture, then season with salt and pepper.

CHEF'S NOTES
White truffle oil is available in most delicatessens and if you can find it, replace the groundnut oil with 1 tablespoon white truffle oil. This would make the sauce extra special!

Sweet Sauces

Apart from the basic sweet sauces here, there are several others throughout the dessert chapter, principally the *coulis* (see pages 222 and 237). These are cooked or uncooked juice and pulp from puréed and sieved fruits.

Sauce au Chocolat

Chocolate sauce

For six to eight servings

Preparation time: 10 minutes

Planning ahead: You can make this sauce a few hours in advance and keep it covered in a *bain-marie* or in the fridge. Reheat over a gentle heat, stirring constantly.

100g (4oz) best dark dessert chocolate
150ml (5fl oz) water
20g (¾oz) unsalted butter

Break the chocolate into small pieces and melt it in a small bowl over a saucepan of gently simmering water, stirring occasionally. Add the water, bring to the boil, stirring constantly and finally whisk in the butter.
  The sauce can be served tepid or cold (in which case, loosen it with a little more water).

CHEF'S NOTES
Choose the best quality chocolate; it will determine the quality of the sauce. If you cannot find unsweetened chocolate, add 1 tablespoon cocoa powder when melting the chocolate.

Stock Syrup

100g (4oz) caster sugar   *100ml (3½fl oz) water*

This is used in many recipes such as sorbets, sweet tarts and puddings, etc.

Place the water in a saucepan, then add the sugar. Bring to the boil, skim off any impurities, then simmer until the sugar has dissolved. Reserve.

Crème Anglaise

Vanilla custard or cream

Makes 500ml (18fl oz)

Preparation and cooking time: 10 minutes

5 egg yolks
75g (3oz) caster sugar
500ml (18fl oz) milk
1 vanilla pod, split lengthways and scraped

Seldom in the course of culinary history have the French borrowed recipes from Britain, but *crème anglaise*, or 'English cream', is an exception, although it bears little resemblance to the original English recipe! It is used as a base for ice cream, mousses and sauces, and as an accompaniment to many sweets.

In a large mixing bowl, cream together the egg yolks and sugar until a pale straw colour.
    Combine the milk and vanilla pod in a heavy-bottomed saucepan, bring to the boil and simmer for about 5 minutes. Draw off the heat.
    Pour the milk on to the egg and sugar mixture, whisking continuously, then return the mixture to the saucepan over medium heat. Stir to bind the custard until it thickens and coats the back of a wooden spoon.
    Strain immediately into a bowl through a sieve. Stir for a few minutes, then keep in the fridge.

CHEF'S NOTES
For more information on vanilla pods, see page 18.

Although this recipe is very simple, there are still a few difficulties. If the egg yolks are subjected to too strong a heat, the custard will curdle. The partial cooking of the yolk binds and thickens the custard. Stir constantly to distribute the heat and watch carefully – there is a precise moment when the custard will be ready.

Even when strained, the custard can still curdle, so continue stirring for 1 or 2 minutes until tepid.

A longer, but foolproof (well, almost!), method is to use a *bain-marie*. Stand the saucepan in water heated to 194°F (90°C), and follow the recipe.

Variations
Lemon cream: Add 6 strips of lemon zest to the milk during simmering, and proceed as above.
Orange cream: Add 8 strips of orange zest during simmering, and a dash of Grand Marnier when cool.
Chocolate cream: Add 25g (1oz) good chocolate, broken into small pieces, during simmering.
Coffee cream: Dissolve 20g (¾oz) Nescafé in 50ml (2fl oz) boiling water. Cool and mix in. Or add ½ cup of very strong espresso coffee, or 50ml (2fl oz) coffee essence (see opposite).

Crème Pâtissière

Pastry cream

Makes 600ml (1 pint)

Preparation and cooking time: 20 minutes

Planning ahead: The cream can be made up to 4 days in advance and kept covered in the fridge.

500ml (18fl oz) milk
1 vanilla pod, split lengthways
6 egg yolks
100g (4oz) caster sugar
25g (1oz) plain flour
20g (¾oz) cornflour
1 teaspoon caster sugar for dusting

Pastry cream has many uses – as a lining for fruit tartlets, as a filling for cakes and éclairs, as a base for sweet soufflés (see page 24), etc.

In a large heavy-bottomed saucepan, bring the milk to the boil. Add the split vanilla pod and infuse at just below simmering point for about 5 minutes. Draw off the heat and remove the vanilla.

Cream together the egg yolks and sugar, then whisk in the flour and cornflour.

Pour 100ml (3½fl oz) of the hot milk into the egg, sugar and flour mixture, and whisk until well blended. Bring back to the boil, whisking until smooth. Add the remaining milk and boil for 1 minute, whisking continuously.

To store, transfer to a bowl or container, and sprinkle the surface with caster sugar to prevent a skin from forming. Cool, seal with cling film and refrigerate.

CHEF'S NOTES
The split vanilla pod can be re-used (see page 18). If you want a stronger flavour, scrape the inside and chop the vanilla pod.

The constant whisking is very important to remove any small lumps.

Essence de Café

Coffee essence

Makes 100ml (3½fl oz)

Preparation time: 15 minutes

2 level tablespoons instant coffee powder
175ml (6fl oz) hot water
100g (4oz) caster sugar
50ml (2fl oz) espresso coffee (optional)

This essence is very useful for flavouring cream and sauces for desserts. It makes enough to flavour 1 litre (1¾ pints) *Crème Anglaise*.

Dissolve the coffee powder in the hot water.

Place the sugar in a sugar pan and cook to a dark, bitter caramel. Tilt the pan away from you and add the dissolved coffee and espresso, if using. Simmer, swirling the pan from time to time, until the caramel is diluted. Leave to cool, pour into a jar, cover and keep at room temperature.

CHEF'S NOTES
It is extremely important to make a *dark* caramel, or the sauce will be far too sweet.

CHAPTER THREE

Hors d'Oeuvres

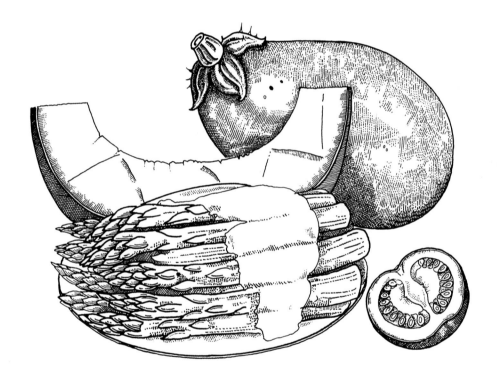

Cold Hors d'Oeuvres

These have the great advantage that, in most cases, they can be prepared in advance. This helps enormously in the good organisation and flow of the meal, and of course puts much less pressure on the host, allowing him or her plenty of time to enjoy the guests' company and equally to ensure that the presentation is excellent. All this in the good cause of making your guests feel loved and spoiled.

One often mistakenly believes that cold hors d'oeuvres are just for warm days; in fact one can prepare them all year round. Most of the following recipes are extremely light and appetising, and make a perfect introduction to a meal. Some of them belong to tradition, some are part of my mother's repertoire, and most are new ideas which will fit very well into a busy lifestyle.

For eight to ten people

Preparation time: 50 minutes

Cooking time: 30 minutes

Special equipment:
1 pastry ring, 25cm (10in) wide and 3cm (1¼in) high.

Planning ahead: This dish can be prepared a day in advance. The Tomato *Coulis* can also be prepared in advance.

FOR THE MOUSSE:
½ onion, peeled and chopped
50ml (2fl oz) olive oil
2 medium ripe tomatoes,
seeded and finely chopped
5 red peppers,
seeded and finely chopped
salt and freshly ground pepper
4 gelatine leaves
(soaked in cold water to soften)
100ml (3½fl oz) white wine vinegar
1 teaspoon raspberry vinegar
cayenne pepper
400ml (14fl oz) whipping cream

FOR THE JELLY AND *JULIENNE*
OF PEPPERS (optional):
100ml (3½fl oz) reserved
vegetable juices
1 gelatine leaf
(soaked in cold water to soften)
1 red pepper, skinned and seeded

FOR THE SAUCE:
300ml (10fl oz) raw Tomato
Coulis (see page 122)

Bavarois de Poivrons Rouges

Mousse of red peppers

A cold starter for a spring dinner party. The texture of this mousse is so delicate, so melting, and the taste so sharp and lively, that the dish is well worth all the effort.

Preparing the mousse
In a large pan, sweat the onion in olive oil for 5 minutes. Add the tomatoes and red peppers. Season with salt and pepper and cook on a medium heat for about 8 minutes, covered with a lid.

Spoon out 100ml (3½fl oz) of juices that the peppers and tomatoes have released. Strain into a bowl, reserving for the jelly. Cook the vegetables for a further 20 minutes without the lid. All the moisture will have evaporated. Add the gelatine leaves and stir until dissolved. Cool down the pulp a little, then purée and force through a sieve or mouli-légumes.

Separately mix the two vinegars in a casserole and boil to reduce by two-thirds in volume. Add to the purée. Taste, then add salt and cayenne pepper. Cool down completely at room temperature.

Whip the cream in a bowl until firm and fold delicately into the purée. Taste and adjust seasoning.

Place the pastry ring over a flat serving dish and pour in the mousse. Smooth the top with a palette knife and refrigerate for a minimum of 4 hours to allow to set.

Preparing the jelly and *julienne* of peppers (optional)
Bring the reserved juice to the boil and dissolve the single leaf of gelatine in it. Allow to cool down.

Cut the pepper halves into strips. Divide each strip in half horizontally, and cut into very fine *julienne* strips of about 3mm (⅛in) thick. Season with salt and pepper, and reserve.

Finishing the dish
Scatter the *julienne* strips of pepper over the mousse and spoon the nearly set jelly out on to the top. Refrigerate.

Bavarois de Poivrons Rouges

Serving

Loosen the mousse from the ring with the blade of a warm knife, and lift the ring off. Place raw Tomato *Coulis* in a sauce boat and serve to your guests.

CHEF'S NOTES

Place onion, tomatoes and peppers in the largest saucepan you have, so moisture can evaporate more quickly.

It is important to remove most of the moisture when drying off the mixture of tomato and pepper. The quantity of purée you should be left with is about 175–200ml (6–7fl oz).

When folding in the cream, do it very delicately with a spatula. You would lose the lightness if you over-mix the mousse. The purée must be at room temperature.

⇒ WINE ⇐

A Gewürztraminer from Alsace. The fruity flavour of the grapes and the fine spice overtones (*Gewürz* means spice in German) will make this wine a delightful experience for the palate. Or try Domaine de la Bernarde, a rosé.

Salade aux Légumes Croustillants et Herbes du Jardin

A selection of salad leaves and deep-fried vegetable ribbons scented with garden herbs

Salads are now exciting. In the past we knew what to expect: limp leaves of lettuce with a rather acidic dressing. Now the varieties of salad leaves available are incredible – the peppery taste of rocket, the textured and lemony flavour of purslane, the rich sweetness of *mâche*, the bitterness of radicchio . . . And the vinaigrettes are just as exciting: walnut, lemon, meat juices, herb dressing, and the many textures you can add to the recipe such as langoustines, little fillets of ham, duck, monkfish. This dish makes a brilliant starter to any dinner party.

For the salad
Prepare, wash and dry all the salad leaves, then mix with the chopped herbs. Set aside.

Preparing and deep-frying the vegetables
Cut the turnips into the very finest slices, about 1mm ($\frac{1}{16}$ in) thick. Do the same with the carrots and unpeeled courgettes. Cut the aubergine into fine *julienne* strips of 1mm ($\frac{1}{16}$ in) thick and 6cm (2½in) long. Cut the leek leaves to the same length. Pat all the vegetables dry very carefully, and keep them all separate.

Place the vegetable oil over a medium heat and wait until the temperature has reached 300°F (150°C). Deep-fry the vegetables separately until they acquire a golden colour and have a crispy texture.

Drain on kitchen paper, again separately, and season lightly with salt and pepper. Reserve on a tray lined with fresh kitchen paper.

Finishing the dish
Combine all the liquid ingredients for the vinaigrette in a large bowl, and season with salt and pepper. Add the chopped shallot, then mix in the salad leaves and herbs. Toss, taste and correct seasoning.

Serving
Arrange the salad attractively on four plates in mounds. Scatter the deep-fried vegetables around each mound, placing the fine leek *julienne* strips on top. Serve to your guests.

CHEF'S NOTES
The choice of herbs can be varied according to what is available. The rocket leaves, though, are very important to the salad because of their earthy, peppery taste.

Other deep-fried vegetables could also be used, such as potatoes. Parsley, coriander, celery and basil leaves can also be deep-fried: they will add a touch of colour and flavour.

For four people

Preparation time: 20 minutes

Cooking time: 6–8 minutes

4 handfuls of different salad leaves (oakleaf, chicory, lettuce, radicchio and frisée, if possible)
20 rocket leaves
12 peppermint leaves, finely chopped
1 tablespoon chopped fresh coriander
2 tablespoons chopped fresh dill
6 small basil leaves, finely chopped
2 tarragon leaves, finely chopped (optional)
salt and freshly ground pepper

FOR THE DEEP-FRIED VEGETABLES:
2 small turnips, peeled
100g (4oz) carrots, peeled
2 small courgettes
100g (4oz) aubergine, peeled
4 outer leaves of leek
1 litre (1¾ pints) vegetable oil or best deep-frying oil

FOR THE VINAIGRETTE:
2 tablespoons Xérès (sherry) or balsamic vinegar
6 tablespoons olive oil
2 tablespoons water
1 shallot, peeled and finely chopped

⇒ *WINE* ⇐

Due to the presence of the vinaigrette in the salad, no serious wine should be drunk – but try a table wine, *rosé* or red.

If you have difficulty in obtaining Xérès or balsamic vinegar, use white wine vinegar.

Make sure that the vegetables for the deep-frying are completely dry, otherwise the oil will spit.

Variation
If you want a more substantial salad, add fine slices of roasted monkfish fillet or scallops, lightly roasted lamb tenderloin or fillet scented with rosemary, or fine duck ham slices.

Filets de Harengs au Vin Blanc

*Fillets of herring marinated in white wine,
spices and finely sliced vegetables*

Serve this spring *hors d'oeuvre* for every day or at a dinner party. It can be accompanied by a side salad or a new potato salad.

Marinating the fish
Mix all the marinade ingredients together. Put the fish in an appropriate dish, and pour in the marinade, ensuring that the fish is well covered. Cover with cling film and marinate for a minimum of 16 hours in the fridge.

Serving
Arrange the fish fillets, spices, vegetables and herbs attractively on a serving dish. Serve to your guests.

CHEF'S NOTES
If small herrings prove difficult to obtain, use two large herrings and increase marinating time to 28 hours minimum.

Variations
This dish is also delicious made with small mackerel or sardines.

A very good accompaniment would be a potato salad, served separately. Boil 450g (1lb) new potatoes until barely tender, then skin and slice them. Mix with 2 finely chopped shallots (or 1 small onion), 4 tablespoons olive oil, 2 tablespoons white wine, 1 tablespoon white wine vinegar, salt and freshly ground pepper. Sprinkle with freshly chopped parsley.

For four people

Marinating time: 16–28 hours

Planning ahead: Ask your fishmonger to fillet the herrings for you, and to remove the bones running along the middle of the fillet. The dish must be prepared at least 16 hours in advance and then kept in the marinade.

4 small herring fillets

FOR THE MARINADE:
100ml (3½fl oz) water
150ml (5fl oz) dry white wine
50ml (2fl oz) distilled malt vinegar
1 teaspoon Pernod or Ricard
juice of ¼ lemon
1 star anise
1 bay leaf
1 sprig of thyme
2 pieces of orange peel,
1cm (½in) wide and 2cm (¾in) long
4 lemon slices
1 celery stalk, washed,
peeled and finely chopped
1 large carrot, peeled and
finely sliced (about 2mm/⅛in thick)
1 small onion, peeled and finely sliced
5 basil leaves
10g (¼oz) parsley leaves
1 teaspoon caster sugar
2 level teaspoons salt
1 level teaspoon freshly ground pepper

⇒ WINE ⇐

Whenever you have vinegar in a dish, it is not really advisable to drink any great wine. For this dish, I would propose a delicate crisp wine such as Muscadet de Sèvre et Maine.

Salade d'Agneau Parfumée au Romarin

Lamb salad scented with rosemary

For four people

Preparation time: 15 minutes

Marinating time: 24 hours

Cooking time: 20 minutes

Planning ahead: The vegetables can be prepared in advance. Order pork back fat from the butcher and have him cut it into four very thin rectangles of about 18cm (7in) × 8cm (3¼in).

*4 small lamb tenderloins,
about 300–400g (11–15oz) total weight
4 large squares of thinly cut back fat
(to wrap around the lamb)
3 tablespoons olive oil
3 sprigs of rosemary
salt and freshly ground pepper*

FOR THE VEGETABLES:
*1 small aubergine,
200g (7oz) in weight
2 small courgettes,
100g (4oz) in weight
150g (5oz) French beans,
topped and tailed
2 tomatoes
100ml (3½fl oz) olive oil*

FOR THE VINAIGRETTE:
*1 tablespoon cooking juices
from the lamb
1 tablespoon white wine vinegar
3 tablespoons olive oil*

Marinating the lamb (24 hours in advance)
Lay the back fat on the table and place the lamb tenderloins in the middle. Sprinkle with 2 tablespoons of the olive oil and the rosemary leaves, and wrap up in the back fat. Tie with string and marinate in a cool place for 24 hours.

Preparing and cooking the vegetables
Cut the aubergine and courgettes into 1cm (½in) dice.

Pan-fry the aubergine dice in the hot olive oil for 1 minute, then remove and allow to cool. Season with salt and pepper and reserve.

Blanch the courgette dice for 2 minutes in plenty of boiling salted water, then refresh in cold water. Drain and reserve.

Blanch the beans for 3 minutes in plenty of boiling salted water, then refresh in cold water. Drain and reserve.

Blanch the stemmed tomatoes in plenty of boiling salted water for 3 seconds. Peel off the skin, cut in half, seed them and cut into dice. Reserve.

Mix all the vegetables together in a dish.

Preheat the oven to 450°F (230°C) Gas 8.

Cooking the lamb
Sear the lamb all over in the remaining tablespoon of olive oil in a pan, then roast in the preheated oven for 7 minutes. Remove, cover with aluminium foil and rest for 10 minutes in a warm place.

Preparing the vinaigrette
Pour into a bowl any juices that the lamb has released during the resting period. Add the vinegar and oil and some salt and freshly ground pepper. Taste and reserve.

Serving
Unwrap the lamb fillet, discarding the fat, and remove and discard the rosemary. Season the lamb with salt and pepper, and cut into fine 5mm (¼in) slices.

Add the vinaigrette to the vegetables, stir lightly, then taste and season with salt and pepper. Arrange them on each plate and divide the little slices of lamb around. Give two or three turns of freshly ground pepper, then serve to your guests.

CHEF'S NOTES
If you cannot find tenderloins, you can use fillets of lamb. Obviously this is more expensive and the cooking time will be a little longer (8 minutes).

The lamb is wrapped in the back fat to protect it during cooking and to concentrate the flavour of the rosemary, but the fat can be omitted.

54

Salade d'Agneau Parfumée au Romarin

Instead, you can simply marinate the lamb with the rosemary in a dish covered in cling film, then pan-fry and roast as per the recipe.

Do not whisk the vinaigrette, simply mix ingredients and stir.

Variations
Of course all sorts of summer vegetables can be used to add colour and taste to this dish.

 *WINE*

A light Pinot Noir such as a Givry will suit the dish well.

Marinade de Légumes à l'Italienne

An interpretation of a traditional Italian dish made with marinated vegetables

For four people

Preparation time: 1 hour

Marinating time: 6 hours minimum

Planning ahead: This dish may be prepared 1 day in advance.

1 medium firm, ripe aubergine
salt and freshly ground pepper
150ml (5fl oz) olive oil
2 red peppers
1 small onion
2 medium courgettes
1 litre (1¾ pints) water
4 ripe tomatoes

FOR THE MARINADE:
150ml (5fl oz) olive oil
3 tablespoons balsamic vinegar
50ml (2fl oz) water
2–3 fine slivers of peeled garlic
12 basil leaves
2 sprigs of thyme

Preheat the oven to 400°F (200°C) Gas 6.

Preparing and cooking the vegetables
Cut the stem off the aubergine and discard it. Slice the aubergine into 1cm (½in) slices, and sprinkle with 1 level teaspoon salt. Leave for about 30 minutes, then rinse and pat dry.

In a large pan heat 6 tablespoons of the olive oil, and sear the aubergine slices on both sides, colouring them slightly. Roast in the oven for 8 minutes, 4 minutes on each side. Remove them from the oven, drain on absorbent paper, and reserve.

Increase the temperature of the oven to 450°F (230°C) Gas 8.

Make a few slits lengthways down each of the peppers, brush with 1 tablespoon of the olive oil, and place on a roasting tray lined with aluminium foil. Roast in the hot oven for 20 minutes, until the skin has blistered. Remove from the oven, peel, cut them in half and remove the stem and seeds. Slice each half in two. Reserve.

Peel the onion and cut it into four 5mm (¼in) large rings. Pan-fry in the remaining olive oil on a medium heat, covered. Turn them after 5 minutes with a fish slice so as not to disturb the rings and cook for a further 5–6 minutes, colouring them lightly. Season with salt and pepper.

Slice the courgettes into 5mm (¼in) thick slices at a slight angle. Bring the water plus 1 tablespoon salt to the boil, and boil the courgettes for a maximum of 1 minute. Drain, reserving the cooking water. Refresh the courgettes under cold running water to keep their colour. Pat dry and reserve.

Remove the stalks from the tomatoes and plunge them for 3–5 seconds into the boiling water reserved from cooking the courgettes. Lift out of the water, cool under cold water, then drain and skin. Slice flesh into quarters, and remove the seeds. Reserve.

Marinating the vegetables
Mix the marinade olive oil with the balsamic vinegar and water, and season with salt and pepper. Lay the slices of aubergine, peppers, onions, courgettes and tomatoes in a single layer in a large dish. Sprinkle the vinaigrette over them, then add the garlic, basil and thyme, and a few turns of freshly ground pepper. Cover with cling film and leave to marinate for a minimum of 6 hours.

Serving
Either serve to your guests from the marinating dish, or alternatively arrange on individual plates.

Marinade de Légumes à l'Italienne

CHEF'S NOTES

If the aubergine is over-ripe, it will be hollow and full of seeds. During the marinating time the slices will also lose their colour. Always choose aubergines that are heavy and firm and which do not sound hollow when tapped.

The olive oil used should be the very best quality, first-pressing (virgin) oil (see page 17).

The salting of the aubergine is done for two reasons: it removes some of the excessive bitterness, and also draws out some of the water.

Variations

Anchovies, black olives in olive oil, marinated sardines, fennel, pan-fried little fillets of red mullet, courgette flowers, artichoke hearts, or slivers of Parmesan cheese could be added as well.

A tomato vinaigrette could be served separately (see page 44).

Deep-fried tarragon or basil (see page 137) could also be added to give that festive look.

⇒ WINE ⇐

The food and wines from Italy are now very popular. Why not discover a little Chardonnay from Italy with this wholesome dish – Il Marsocco.

Terrine de Betteraves et Suprêmes de Pigeon Sauvage

Terrine of beetroot and breasts of wild pigeon

For eight to ten people

Marinating time: 12 hours

Preparation and cooking time: 2 hours

Setting time: 12 hours

Special equipment:
1 terrine, 24cm (9½in) long, 10cm (4in) wide and 10cm (4in) deep;
a wooden board that will fit the top of the terrine;
a 1kg (2¼lb) weight.

Planning ahead: The terrine can be prepared 2 days in advance.

8 breasts of wild pigeons
1 tablespoon groundnut oil
salt and freshly ground pepper

FOR THE MARINADE:
1 tablespoon olive oil
2 tablespoons red wine
2 juniper berries, crushed
freshly ground pepper
1 bay leaf

FOR THE TERRINE:
1kg (2¼lb) beetroots
1 tablespoon caster sugar
12 black peppercorns, crushed
2 tablespoons white wine vinegar
5 gelatine leaves
(soaked in cold water to soften)

FOR THE GARNISH SALAD
AND DRESSING:
2 handfuls of various salad leaves
(lettuce, radicchio, rocket, etc.)
3 tablespoons olive oil
½ tablespoon walnut oil
1 tablespoon white wine vinegar

Marinating the pigeon breasts

Mix the marinade ingredients together. Place the pigeon breasts flesh side down on a small tray, then pour over the marinade, cover with cling film, and leave to marinate for 12 hours.

Cooking the beetroot

Wash the beetroot and place them in a saucepan. Add 1 teaspoon salt, the sugar, peppercorns and vinegar, then cover with water and simmer for 50 minutes (according to size). Check to see if they are cooked with the tip of a knife blade. Leave to cool in the liquid (which you retain).

Peel the beetroot and chop them into dice about 1cm (½in) wide. Taste and season with salt and pepper.

Preparing the gelatine

Place 300ml (10fl oz) of the strained beetroot cooking liquid in a saucepan and bring to the boil. Add the softened gelatine leaves, turn off the heat, and stir. Put aside to cool. Strain, taste and correct seasoning.

Preheat the oven to 450°F (230°C) Gas 8. Place the terrine dish in the freezer for at least 20 minutes.

Cooking the pigeon breasts

Remove the pigeon breasts from the marinade, and pat dry. Pan-fry them in the hot oil, searing the meat for 30 seconds on each side. Season with salt and pepper.

Place the breasts on their skin side on a baking tray, and roast in the preheated oven for 3 minutes. Discard the oil, cool, then remove skin from the breasts. Season with salt and pepper.

Building the terrine

Remove the terrine from the freezer. Place a 3mm (⅛in) thick beetroot jelly film on the bottom of the terrine, which will set immediately. Place half of the beetroot dice in the terrine, then arrange the pigeon breasts in a line on top. Cover with the remaining beetroot dice.

Pour the remaining beetroot jelly into the terrine. Cover the terrine with cling film, place the wooden board on top, then arrange the weight on top to press it down. Refrigerate for a minimum of 12 hours.

Serving

Remove the weight, wooden board and cling film. Dip the terrine in hot water, then run the blade of a knife that has been dipped in hot water along the inside. Turn the terrine upside down on to a flat working surface. Using an electric knife (if possible), cut slices and arrange on a cold plate.

Combine the salad dressing ingredients, seasoning with salt and pepper. Add the salad leaves, toss and arrange dressed leaves attractively around each terrine slice. Serve to your guests.

Terrine de Betteraves et Suprêmes de Pigeon Sauvage

CHEF'S NOTES

The pigeon legs and carcasses, etc., can be kept to be used for a sauce.

Do not be tempted to cook the pigeon breasts for longer as they would be tough and inedible.

Carving the terrine is a delicate operation. An electric knife would be ideal. If this is not possible, use a very sharp, serrated edge knife.

 WINE

A fruity wine from the Loire Valley such as Chinon or Bourgueil will do very well. As would a red Alsace, Pinot Noir.

Assiette de Crudités Maman Blanc

A display of summer vegetables and salads

This is one of my favourite starters. My father would grow these vegetables and my mother would place them on the table on Sunday; the simplest, purest transition from the earth to the table.

Preparing and cooking the ingredients

Beetroot Cook in plenty of lightly salted water for 25–30 minutes according to size. Leave to cool in the water, then drain in a colander. Skin.

Potato Chop into 1cm (½in) dice, and cook in lightly salted water for 5–6 minutes. Refresh and drain, then reserve.

French Beans Blanch the French beans in plenty of boiling salted water for 3–4 minutes according to size, then refresh and reserve.

Cucumber With the seeds still in, slice the peeled cucumber finely and scatter with ½ teaspoon salt. Stir, then marinate for half an hour before rinsing under cold water, and draining.

Celeriac Grate, and mix in a third of the lemon juice.

Carrots Grate.

Tomatoes Slice finely.

Shallots Chop finely.

Eggs Boil gently in simmering water for 10 minutes. Refresh then shell and quarter them.

Adding the dressings to the vegetables

Beetroot Mix in 2 tablespoons of vinaigrette and a quarter of the chopped shallots. Season with salt and pepper and reserve.

Potato Mix in 2 tablespoons mayonnaise, one-third of the remaining shallot, and a quarter of the chopped parsley. Season with salt and pepper and reserve.

French beans Add the remaining shallot and 2 tablespoons vinaigrette. Season with salt and pepper and reserve.

Cucumber Add 1 tablespoon of vinaigrette then taste and correct seasoning with salt and pepper. Reserve.

Celeriac Add 2 tablespoons mayonnaise and half of the remaining lemon juice. Season with salt and pepper and reserve.

Carrots Mix in 2 tablespoons of vinaigrette and the remaining lemon juice. Season with salt and pepper and reserve.

For four to six people

Preparation and cooking time: 1¼ hours

Special equipment:
1 oval dish, 35cm (14in) in diameter.

Planning ahead: The dish can be prepared 4–5 hours in advance of the meal.

4 medium raw beetroot,
washed and trimmed
salt and freshly ground pepper
1 large potato, peeled
150g (5oz) French beans,
topped and tailed
½ cucumber, peeled
300g (11oz) celeriac, peeled
juice of ¾ lemon
2 large carrots, peeled
4 tomatoes, Roma if possible, washed
4 shallots, peeled
4 eggs

FOR THE DRESSINGS AND GARNISH:
about 150ml (5fl oz) non-scented vinaigrette
(see page 44)
200ml (7fl oz) Sauce Mayonnaise
(see page 40)
15g (½oz) parsley leaves,
washed, patted dry and chopped
1 whole lettuce,
washed and prepared (see page 195)

Assiette de Crudités Maman Blanc

Serving

Arrange the lettuce leaves around the dish. Place a mound of carrots in the middle and surround with the French beans. Surround these with the cucumber. Arrange the potato, celeriac, tomatoes, beetroot and eggs on the lettuce leaves, and then sprinkle everything with the remaining parsley.

Serve the remaining mayonnaise separately.

CHEF'S NOTES

Surprisingly enough, raw beetroot cannot often be found – they're usually cooked! So long as the beetroot has not been *over*cooked, or in too much vinegar, it will suffice.

Cucumber contains certain enzymes which often have the unpleasant effect of causing indigestion. The marinating of the cucumber in salt for half an hour will draw out all these nasty enzymes.

Grate the celeriac thickly enough so that the shreds will have a good texture. Grate the carrots slightly thinner than the celeriac if possible.

Variations

Obviously this dish should trigger your imagination. There is a wealth of ingredients which you could use whether to replace or to add to the dish – artichokes, bean salad, finely shredded cabbage, etc. Each part of this dish is a dish on its own!

WINE

A light *rosé* would be the perfect complement to this dish. No 'serious' wine should be drunk with a dish containing vinaigrette.

Salade de Foies de Canards Confits

Duck livers gently cooked in duck fat

This dish is well worth battling with your butcher in order to get the livers of these noble birds.

Preparing the duck livers
Choose very fresh livers which are a delicate pink colour, not red or bruised. It is very important to remove all traces from the liver of green from the gall bladder; this would spoil the dish, giving it a bitter taste.

Preparing the duck skin
Roll up the duck skin, wrap in cling film, then twist and secure both ends. Place in the freezer for a minimum of 1 hour, so it becomes hard and easy to slice.
  Preheat the grill.
  When frozen, remove the cling film, and slice the duck skin very finely. Place on a rack under the hot grill for 7 or 8 minutes until very crisp and golden. Drain on absorbent paper, season and reserve.

Cooking the garnish shallots
Sear the shallots in the duck fat for 4–6 minutes until brown, then add the vinegar, thyme, bay leaf and some salt and pepper. Cover the pan and cook very gently for 15–20 minutes. Remove the shallots with a slotted spoon, and reserve in a warm place.

Cooking the duck livers
Place the duck fat in a casserole and warm to 160°F (70°C), just under simmering point. Add the cleaned livers, and leave to poach gently for 5–6 minutes. Turn off the heat, and leave in the fat to keep warm.

Finishing the dish and serving
Place the vinaigrette into a mixing bowl, add the prepared salad leaves and toss. Season with salt and pepper. Arrange dressed salad leaves around each plate, and scatter with the duck skins.
  Remove the duck livers from the fat with a slotted spoon, and pat dry with absorbent paper. Place in the middle of each plate. Arrange the shallots around, and serve to your guests.

CHEF'S NOTES
If the livers are slightly red, soak them overnight in the refrigerator in 50/50 lightly salted milk and water.

Reserve the fat which runs off when you roast a duck, and refrigerate until required (see *Millefeuille de Confit de Canard* on page 88). You can also buy ready-prepared duck or goose fat in delicatessens.

When cooking the livers, the fat must be under simmering point for the heat to penetrate slowly; if the fat boils, the livers will be overcooked, grey and dry.

For four people

Preparation time: 20 minutes

Cooking time: 20 minutes

Planning ahead: The salads can be prepared in advance. The livers can be poached in the duck fat 1 or 2 hours in advance, and kept in the duck fat. The garnish may be prepared 1 or 2 hours in advance. Mix vinaigrette and salads at the last moment.
  Order duck livers well in advance. If unobtainable, use chicken livers.

150g (5oz) fresh duck livers
30g (1¼oz) duck skin (optional)
salt and freshly ground pepper
300ml (10fl oz) duck fat

FOR THE GARNISH SHALLOTS:
24 shallots, peeled
2 tablespoons duck fat
1 tablespoon white wine vinegar
1 sprig of thyme
½ bay leaf

FOR THE SALAD:
4 handfuls mixed salad leaves
(frisée, radicchio, salad bowl, etc),
prepared (see page 195)
4 tablespoons Walnut Oil Vinaigrette
(see page 43)

WINE

A Jurançon *sec* from the south-west, where the dish comes from, will perfectly complement it.

Pavé de Saumon aux Pointes d'Asperges

Fillet of salmon with spring asparagus, dressed in balsamic vinaigrette

Preparing the vinaigrette
Mix all the ingredients except for the chives together, then season with salt and pepper.

Preparing and cooking the asparagus
Trim and wash the spears. Cut off the bitter ends and discard. You will now have spears of about 10cm (4in) long. Cut off tips about 4cm (1½in) long. Cut the middle stalk bits into fine *julienne* strips of about 3mm (⅛in) square, and 4–5cm (1½–2in) long. Reserve.

Bring the water and 1 tablespoon salt to the boil. Cook the asparagus tips for about 3–4 minutes according to size, then add the *julienne* strips and cook for a further 30 seconds. Refresh in cold water, drain and reserve.

Cooking the salmon fillets
In a non-stick pan, melt the butter over a medium heat until it becomes a delicate blond colour. Pan-fry the fillets of salmon for 1 minute on each side. Season with salt and pepper and squeeze a dash of lemon juice over each fillet. Keep warm.

Serving
Add the asparagus tips and *julienne* strips to the vinaigrette in a small pan and warm up gently without boiling. Add the chopped chives just before serving.

Place a fillet of salmon in the middle of each warm plate. Arrange asparagus spears and *julienne* strips around the fish, and spoon all the vinaigrette over and around. Serve to your guests.

CHEF'S NOTES
Very good farmed salmon is available, if wild is too expensive. However, quality is variable so choose carefully and avoid those orange-looking fillets.

If salmon is overcooked, it has a dry unpleasant texture. A minute on each side is enough to leave it just medium and moist.

This dish is served warm, not hot.

Variations
Salmon trout fillets can be used instead. Diced tomatoes or chopped chervil could be added to the vinaigrette.

For four people

Preparation and cooking time: 25 minutes

Planning ahead: The vinaigrette can be prepared in advance; the asparagus can also be blanched and refreshed in advance.

4 × 100g (4oz) wild salmon fillets
salt and freshly ground pepper
20g (¾oz) unsalted butter
juice of ¼ lemon

FOR THE ASPARAGUS
JULIENNE STRIPS:
24 small asparagus spears
500ml (18fl oz) water

FOR THE VINAIGRETTE:
6 tablespoons olive oil
2 tablespoons balsamic
or Xérès vinegar (see page 18)
2 tablespoons water
1 tablespoon chopped chives

 WINE

Due to the dressing, do not choose too serious a wine. A young white Chardonnay will match the richness of the salmon very well.

Terrine d'Aubergines Pressées au Coulis de Tomates

Aubergine terrine served with a tomato vinaigrette

For eight people

Marinating time: a minimum of 6 hours

Preparation and cooking time: 45 minutes

Maturing time: 12 hours

Special equipment:
1 terrine mould, 8 × 24 × 9cm (3¼ × 9½ × 3½in);
1 rectangular wooden board, to fit the inside of the terrine, 7.5 × 23 × 8cm (3 × 9 × 3¼in);
a 4kg (9lb) weight.

Planning ahead: The terrine can be made 2 days in advance. The tomato vinaigrette can be made in advance also.

6 medium aubergines,
about 1.9kg (4¼lb) total weight
200ml (7fl oz) olive oil
salt and freshly ground pepper
12 basil leaves (optional)
1 quantity Tomato Vinaigrette (see page 44)

FOR THE MARINADE:
100ml (3½fl oz) olive oil
50ml (2fl oz) water
50ml (2fl oz) balsamic vinegar
1 teaspoon salt
1 teaspoon sugar
1 teaspoon freshly ground white pepper

TO WRAP THE TERRINE:
18 large spinach leaves

Preheat the oven to 425°F (220°C) Gas 7.

Cooking and marinating the aubergines
Cut off the ends of the aubergines and slice them in half widthways, to make 12 'barrels'.

Heat the olive oil in a roasting tray on top of the stove, add the aubergines and sear them for 2 minutes on each side until they are golden. Season with salt and pepper. Roast them in the preheated oven for 20 minutes on each cut side, covered loosely with aluminium foil. Place the aubergine slices in a deep tray and leave to cool down.

Mix all the ingredients of the marinade and pour over the aubergine slices. Cover with cling film and refrigerate for a minimum of 6 hours, turning them at least twice during this period.

Cooking the spinach leaves
Cook the spinach leaves in plenty of boiling salted water for about 40 seconds. Refresh in cold water, drain and pat dry gently with a tea cloth. Open up the leaves.

Building the terrine
Place the terrine on a tray and line it with a double sheet of cling film, making sure that you have about 15cm (6in) overlap on each side. Then line the mould with the spinach leaves, leaving an overlap on each side again. Place six aubergines slices upright along the bottom of the terrine, pressing them well together; season with salt and freshly ground pepper and scatter with the basil leaves (if using). Top with the remaining six aubergine slices (these should come 2cm/¾in above the rim of the terrine).

Wrap with the overlapping spinach leaves and cling film, place the wooden board over and place the 4kg (9lb) weight on top. Refrigerate for at least 12 hours.

Serving
Remove the weight and board, and turn the terrine gently out on to a cutting board. With a serrated knife or electric knife, cut into 2cm (¾in) thick slices. Place one in the middle of each plate, remove the cling film and spoon the tomato vinaigrette (see page 44) around. Serve to your guests.

CHEF'S NOTES
Choose young, firm aubergines. The large ones are often hollow and seedy and will also oxidise (discolour).

There is no binding ingredient in the terrine. It only holds together because of the weight which has been put on it, so the slicing must

⇒ *WINE* ⇐

A rosé from Provence such as Domaine de la Bernarde will suit the dish perfectly.

be done delicately. To help the slicing, it is best to leave the terrine wrapped in cling film and peel it off the individual slices; an electric knife would also help.

Variations
Artichoke hearts or French beans could be added to the terrine.

Terrine de Légumes d'Eté à la Grecque

Terrine of summer vegetables soused in a spicy white wine and olive oil marinade

Making the marinade
In a saucepan, combine all the ingredients of the marinade together and bring gently to the boil. Simmer for 5 minutes.

Cooking the vegetables
Add the onions, carrots and celery sticks to the marinade and simmer for 5 minutes, then add the peppers and simmer for 2 minutes; add the mushrooms and cauliflower florets and simmer for a further 2 minutes. Finally, add the courgette sticks and cook for 1 minute.

Strain the cooking liquid into a small saucepan, and spoon out any fat. Add the softened gelatine leaves, stir, cool down, then add the coriander leaves, lemon juice and sugar.

Pack all the vegetables into a terrine dish and cover with the cooking juices. Cover with cling film and refrigerate for a minimum of 5–6 hours.

Serving
Place the bottom of the terrine in hot water, then using a warm knife, free the sides of the terrine and turn out on to a flat board. Warm the blade of a sharp, serrated-edged knife (or use an electric carving knife), and slice the terrine.

Serve the vinaigrette separately.

Variations
Fillets of monkfish, cooked mussels, or baby squid could be added to the terrine.

For four people

Preparation time: 30 minutes

Cooking time: 15 minutes

Chilling time: 5–6 hours

Planning ahead: The dish can be prepared 1 day in advance.

FOR THE MARINADE:
3 tablespoons olive oil
100ml (3½fl oz) white wine
3 tablespoons white wine vinegar
1 garlic clove, peeled and halved
1 bay leaf
8 coriander seeds, crushed
1 sprig of thyme
1 star anise (optional)
½ sachet saffron powder
1 level teaspoon salt
1 teaspoon freshly ground pepper
500ml (18fl oz) water
10g (¼oz) fresh coriander leaves (optional)

FOR THE VEGETABLES:
8 baby onions, peeled
1 carrot (about 100g/4oz),
peeled and quartered lengthways
1 small celery stalk,
cut into sticks 3mm × 4cm (⅛ × 1½in)
1 yellow and 1 red pepper, halved,
seeded, then each half cut into 4
24 small button mushrooms,
washed briefly and patted dry
100g (4oz) cauliflower florets
2 large courgettes, washed and cut
into 2mm × 4cm (⅛ × 1½in) sticks
7 gelatine leaves,
softened in cold water
10g (¼oz) fresh coriander leaves,
chopped
juice of ½ lemon
1 level teaspoon sugar

TO SERVE:
1 quantity plain Vinaigrette
(see page 44)

Terrine de Poireaux Façon Trama

Pressed terrine of leeks served with mustard sauce

For ten to twelve people

Preparation and cooking time: 40 minutes

Resting time: 12 hours

Special equipment:
A terrine, 28cm (11in) long, 10cm (4in) wide and 9cm (3½in) deep;
a wooden board to fit inside the terrine;
a 3kg (7lb) weight.

Planning ahead: The terrine can be prepared up to 3 days in advance.

5kg (11lb) medium leeks
4 litres (7 pints) water
salt and freshly ground pepper

FOR THE VINAIGRETTE:
1 tablespoon white wine vinegar
3 tablespoons sunflower oil

TO SERVE:
2 quantities Mustard Vinaigrette
(see page 45)

WINE

In the valley of Petit Serrant (Anjou, in the Loire Valley), there is a small vineyard of just 7 hectares (about 17 acres). Savennières Coulée-de-Serrant is now one of the leading wines of the region, made from the Chenin grape. Its freshness and its vegetable flavour will accompany the terrine of leeks perfectly.

Preparing and cooking the leeks
Cut the root base off each leek, then cut off the tougher green ends so that each piece of leek is the same length as the terrine (approximately 26cm/10–11in). Remove the first two layers of leaves from the leeks, and slice the leeks lengthways two-thirds down the middle. Wash in three changes of tepid water, drain and reserve.

In a large saucepan bring the water with about 80g (3¼oz) salt to the boil. Add half the leeks and cook, covered, for about 14–17 minutes, according to their size. With a slotted spoon remove the leeks and plunge in cold water to prevent further cooking. Cook the remaining leeks in the same water for the same length of time, then refresh.

Drain the leeks well, then press and squeeze them in a tea towel to extract excess water. Taste and season with salt and pepper.

Building the terrine
Cover the inside of the terrine with two layers of cling film, leaving an overlap of 13cm (5in) on each side.

Place a layer of leeks in the terrine with the white part at one end, then place in a second layer of leeks with the green part on top of the white so that white and green are superimposed. Continue building the terrine in this way until it is about 2cm (¾in) higher than the rim of the terrine. Wrap with the overlapping cling film.

Pressing the terrine
Place the wooden board on the terrine, and put the weight on top of it. This will compress the layers of leeks together and extract moisture. Refrigerate for a minimum of 12 hours.

Making the vinaigrette
Mix the vinegar and oil, then taste and season with salt and pepper.

Serving
Remove the weight and invert the terrine on to the board, turning it out carefully. With the serrated edge of an electric carving knife, cut slices 1cm (½in) thick; place each slice on a plate and remove the individual bands of cling film.

Brush the slices with the vinaigrette and surround each with 2 tablespoons of mustard vinaigrette.

CHEF'S NOTES

This terrine will not be a success if made with leeks that are too large; medium size are the best to use. Make sure they have not seeded and that they are not woody in the centre.

The water for cooking the leeks must be at a very fast boil. When adding the leeks, cover for the first 5 minutes so it will regain boiling point quickly. Leeks are from the onion family and if undercooked, will have a very coarse onion taste.

The cling film is left around the terrine to help the carving, as the layers of leeks are very fragile.

Variations
Langoustines or lobster tail can be added to the leek layers; very finely chopped chervil would also be delicious.

Salade de Topinambours et Avocats

Salad of artichokes and avocado

Jerusalem artichokes are considered the 'ugly-duckling' of the vegetable family! Their shape is twisted and they are very knobbly and difficult to peel, but despite all this, they still remain one of my favourite vegetables. This is a good dish for an autumn dinner party.

Preparing the vinaigrette
Make the vinaigrette (see page 43). Divide it between two bowls.

Preparing and cooking the artichokes
Wash and peel the artichokes, cutting off the knobbly bits in order to obtain a cylindrical shape about 3cm (1¼in) in diameter. Poach the artichokes in lightly salted, barely simmering water for 15–20 minutes according to size.

When cooked, drain and slice them 5mm (¼in) thick. Mix with half the vinaigrette and the chopped shallots. Taste and season with salt and pepper. Reserve.

Preparing the avocados
Cut the avocados in half and remove the stones. Peel off the skin and cut the flesh into 5mm (¼in) slices. Add to the remaining vinaigrette in the second bowl.

Serving
Arrange the avocado slices in a circle overlapping each other, on four large plates. Place a mound of artichoke slices in the middle, and sprinkle with the chopped chives. Serve to your guests.

CHEF'S NOTES
Because of their texture, the artichokes have to be monitored very carefully during cooking; if you allow the water to boil they will disintegrate, so cook them very gently, checking their texture continually.

Variations
A salad of warm artichokes by themselves would be delicious, or it could be accompanied by a simple salad of cucumber.

For four people

Preparation and cooking time: 30 minutes

16 Jerusalem artichokes
salt and freshly ground pepper
3 shallots, peeled and finely chopped
2 firm, just ripe avocados
1 tiny bundle of chives, washed,
shaken and finely chopped

TO SERVE:
4 tablespoons Hazelnut Oil Vinaigrette
(see page 43)

 *WINE*

A purist would say no wine, for neither avocado, Jerusalem artichokes nor the vinaigrette invite a serious wine. But your guests might get the wrong impression of the quality of your 'hosting' – so a little wine from the Loire such as a Muscadet or Sancerre will do fine.

Pâté de Campagne

Country pâté

For ten to twelve people

Preparation time: 40 minutes

Marinating time: 24 hours

Cooking time: 1¾ hours

Maturing time: 2 days

Special equipment:
1 terrine, 24cm (9½in) long, 9cm (3½in) wide and 10cm (4in) deep, with lid.

Planning ahead: This terrine must be prepared at least 2 days in advance so that its flavour can mature.

500g (18oz) loin of pork, skinned
500g (18oz) belly pork,
boned and skinned
150g (5oz) each of pig's liver
and chicken livers, very fresh,
with gall bladder removed
2 whole eggs
1 tablespoon plain flour
salt and freshly ground pepper
freshly grated nutmeg

FOR THE MARINADE:
50ml (2fl oz) Madeira
4 tablespoons Cognac
100ml (3½fl oz) dry white wine
2 sprigs of thyme
1 sprig of tarragon (optional)
1 bay leaf

FOR THE GARNISH:
200g (7oz) chicken livers,
gall bladder removed·
1 tablespoon vegetable oil
20g (¾oz) unsalted butter

FOR LINING THE TERRINE:
14 streaky bacon rashers, rind removed

 WINE

Crozes-Hermitage, a white wine from the northern Rhône Valley, is like this dish, a reflection of French tradition. Both are ideal for taking on a *casse-croûte* or picnic.

One of the first pâtés made at the old Quat' Saisons when it was a popular bistro.

Preparing the terrine filling
Mix all the ingredients of the marinade together in a large bowl. Reserve.

Chop the meats and livers into small cubes (2.5cm/1in), and place in the marinade. Cover with cling film and leave in a cool place for 24 hours, turning over once or twice.

Remove the thyme, tarragon and bay leaf and drain the meats from the marinade. Pass the meats through the medium-sized disc of a mincer, collecting them in a large bowl. Mix in the whole eggs and the flour. Season with salt, pepper and grated nutmeg.

Cooking the garnish
Pan-fry the chicken livers in the hot oil and butter mixture for 30 seconds. Allow to cool down, then reserve.

Lining the terrine
Between two sheets of cling film, beat the bacon rashers until they are very thin. Line the terrine with them, covering the sides and bottom so they overlap. Leave them hanging over the edges so that you can eventually cover the top of the pâté entirely.

Preheat the oven to 350°F (180°C) Gas 4.

Building the pâté
Place half of the minced meat filling into the terrine. Season the whole pan-fried chicken livers and place them in the middle of the terrine, then cover with the remaining filling.

Tap the terrine on the table in order to compress the filling, then cover with the overlapping bacon slices. Cover with the lid.

Cooking the pâté
Place the terrine into a *bain-marie* and fill with enough hot water to come half-way up the terrine. Cook in the preheated oven for 1¾ hours. Remove from the oven and allow to cool down for 2–3 hours, then refrigerate for a minimum of 2 days.

Serving
Remove the lid, filter off the juices which will have escaped during cooking, and turn the pâté out on to a carving board. Carve 12 slices. Either arrange these on a serving dish with salad accompanied by gherkins, pickled onions, etc, or alternatively, on individual plates together with a green salad.

CHEF'S NOTES
The terrine is best after having matured for 2–3 days. It can be kept for a maximum of 5 days.

If you are lucky enough to have a wonderful bakery around, carve large slices off a country loaf, toast them, and serve with the pâté.

Pâté de Campagne

Terrine de Lentilles et Faisan

Lentil and pheasant terrine

Lentils have always been traditionally the staple diet of the poor, to the point of being totally neglected and forgotten. Here is one way to rediscover the surprising ways in which you can use lentils.

For ten people

Soaking time: 2 hours

Preparation and cooking time: 2 hours

Resting time: 12 hours

Special equipment:
1 terrine, 24cm (9½in) long, 9cm (3½in) wide, and 10cm (4in) deep, with lid;
a wooden board the same size as the terrine;
a 1kg (2¼lb) weight.

Planning ahead: The lentils must be soaked 2 hours prior to cooking the dish.

FOR THE LENTILS:
300g (11oz) lentils
1 litre (1¾ pints) water
1 onion, peeled and quartered
2 cloves
50g (2oz) smoked bacon, rinded
1 bouquet garni (made with
1 bay leaf, 2 sprigs of thyme,
10g (¼oz) parsley stalks (see page 30)
1 tablespoon salt

FOR THE PHEASANT:
1 young pheasant
¼ onion, peeled and chopped
10g (¼oz) unsalted butter
100ml (3½fl oz) white wine
350ml (12fl oz) water
2 juniper berries, crushed
1 garlic clove, peeled
1 sage leaf
salt and freshly ground pepper

FOR THE JELLY:
250ml (8fl oz) pheasant stock
4 gelatine leaves
(soaked in cold water to soften)

FOR LINING THE TERRINE:
6 large green cabbage leaves

TO SERVE:
250ml (8fl oz) Mustard Vinaigrette
(see page 45)

Preparing and cooking the lentils
Cover the lentils with tepid water and leave to soak for 2 hours.

Drain the lentils and place them in a saucepan together with the measured cold water, the onion, the cloves, smoked bacon, *bouquet garni* and salt. Bring to the boil, then cook very gently for about 30 minutes. Strain, remove onion, cloves and *bouquet garni*, and reserve.

Preparing and cooking the pheasant
Remove the wish bone, pass pheasant over a flame to remove feather stubs, then tie.

In a casserole, sweat the chopped onion for 1 minute in the butter, then add the white wine and bring to the boil. Add the water, juniper berries, garlic, sage and salt and pepper. Bring to the boil again.

Place the pheasant, breast side up, in the braising stock and cook for 30–40 minutes, covered, according to size.

Remove the pheasant, and strain the cooking stock, reserving 250ml (8fl oz).

Cut the legs off the pheasant and remove flesh from thighs, legs and breast. Season and reserve.

Making the jelly
Add the softened gelatine leaves to the hot strained pheasant stock. Stir well and reserve.

Lining and building the terrine
Blanch the cabbage leaves in plenty of boiling salted water then refresh, pat dry and reserve.

Line the bottom and sides of the terrine with cling film, leaving an overlap of 10–15cm (4–6in) on each side. Cover the bottom and sides of the terrine with the cabbage leaves.

Half fill the terrine with the lentils. Arrange the pheasant flesh in the middle and cover with the remaining lentils.

Pour the jelly into the terrine and fold over the cabbage leaves and cling film. Place the wooden board on top of the terrine together with the weight. Refrigerate for 12 hours.

Serving
Remove the weight and the board, and open up the cling film. Turn the terrine out and remove the cling film. Using a serrated knife, carve into slices 2cm (¾in) thick. Serve to your guests, handing the vinaigrette separately.

Terrine de Lentilles et Faisan

CHEF'S NOTES
It is better to buy a young hen pheasant as the flesh will be more tender. It should be hung for 8–9 days in a cool place to enable the flesh to develop flavour.

Variations
Some strips of lightly smoked ham can be placed between the lentils, and the pheasant can be replaced by guinea fowl or partridge.

If you are a vegetarian, or you want to simplify the recipe, you can omit the pheasant completely and replace it with vegetables. Mix together 100ml (3½fl oz) white wine vinegar, 400ml (14fl oz) water and some salt and pepper. Boil 24 whole peeled shallots in this for 30 minutes, drain and reserve. Cook 2 trimmed and washed leeks in the same liquid for 12 minutes, drain and reserve, followed by 24 washed *shiitake* mushrooms – cook for 1 minute only at full boil, then drain and reserve. Use 250ml (8fl oz) of the stock for the gelatine, then proceed with the recipe exactly as above.

 WINE

A dry white Bordeaux wine, especially one from the region of Graves noted for its fine, floral and fruity scents, will provide a pleasant accompaniment for this dish.

Hot Hors d'Oeuvres

Although most of the preparation for the following recipes can be done in advance, the finishing touches are not done until the last moment. All this makes the meal more difficult, and also prevents you from being with your guests. However, you simply choose an easier main course like a casserole perhaps, which just needs reheating, to be followed by a pre-prepared cold dessert. (Of course, if you *want* to avoid some of those guests that you have to invite and have little affinity with, you could prepare a hot hors d'oeuvre, a difficult main course and a hot dessert: you will then be spending most of your time in the kitchen. Quite painless, but tactful!)

Most of these hot hors d'oeuvres can be served as a main course.

For four people

Preparation time: 20 minutes

Cooking time: 30 minutes

*8 tiny courgettes with their
flowers still attached
120g (4½oz) fresh white crab meat
20g (¾oz) fresh brown crab meat
salt and freshly ground pepper
1 tablespoon olive oil
1 teaspoon unsalted butter
2 tablespoons water*

FOR THE JUICE:
*2 shallots, peeled and chopped
40g (1½oz) cold unsalted butter
1 small tomato, seeds and all, chopped
50ml (2fl oz) dry white wine
100ml (3½fl oz) water
4 cardamom seeds, crushed,
or 4 pinches ground cardamom
¼ teaspoon caraway seeds, crushed,
or 1 pinch ground caraway
1 tablespoon fresh brown crab meat
2 tablespoons whipping cream
a pinch of cayenne pepper*

Courgettes en Fleur Farcies, Jus de Cardamome et Graines de Cumin

*Crab-stuffed courgette flowers
with cardamom and caraway sauce*

This hot *hors d'oeuvre* dish is a perfect expression of spring. The filling should inspire you, but can be changed to diced tomatoes with basil or ratatouille, etc. The sauce can be replaced by a raw Tomato *Coulis* (see page 122). If you do not find any delightful vegetables in the shops, then go to the nearest pick-your-own farm and enjoy a healthy morning or afternoon out with your family.

Preparing the courgettes
Cut the flowers off at the base. Open up the flowers and wash under running water (small insects very often choose these magnificent flowers as their country home!). Blanch the flowers in plenty of boiling salted water for 5 seconds. Drain with a slotted spoon, refresh in cold water, then delicately squeeze water out.

Mix the white and brown crab meat, taste, and season with salt and freshly ground pepper. Open up the flowers and fill them with the crab meat. Twist the top of the flower so the filling is nicely contained. Reserve.

Blanch the courgettes themselves in plenty of boiling salted water for 3 or 4 minutes. Drain with a slotted spoon, and refresh in cold water. Season with salt and pepper and reserve.

Preparing the juice
Sweat the chopped shallot in 10g (¼oz) of the butter (dice the remainder) then add the tomato. Add the white wine, bring to the boil and reduce by one-third. Add the water, the cardamom, caraway and brown crab meat. Simmer for 1 minute, then force through a sieve into a small casserole. Whisk in the cream and remaining diced butter until you have a well-emulsified sauce. Taste and correct seasoning with salt and pepper, and add a pinch of cayenne pepper. Keep the juice warm.

Courgettes en Fleur Farcies, Jus de Cardamome et Graines de Cumin

Finishing the dish
Pan-fry the courgette flowers in the olive oil for 2 minutes on each side. Warm the courgettes through in the butter and water. Season with salt and pepper.

Serving
Warm a large serving dish and arrange the stuffed flowers and courgettes on it. Pour the sauce over and serve to your guests.

CHEF'S NOTES
Of course you can buy frozen crab, but it is not the same as fresh, and I am sure your fishmonger, if asked nicely, will boil the crab for you and extract the flesh. All for very little money — and if the request is made nicely enough, perhaps for nothing at all!

Variations
Diced, blanched ginger could be added to the crab, and will add a fiery flavour to the dish, or herbs such as basil or coriander.

 WINE

A southern French dry white with a little spice will complement this dish very well.

Mousse d'Asperges au Jus de Cerfeuil

Asparagus mousse with chervil

Preheat the oven to 340°F (170°C) Gas 3–4.

Preparing and cooking the asparagus mousse
Butter the insides of four ramekins and refrigerate for 5 minutes, so that the butter solidifies.

Cook the asparagus in plenty of boiling salted water for about 4–5 minutes according to the size of the spears. Refresh in cold water and drain. Chop the asparagus and then purée in a food processor with the eggs, egg yolks and chervil.

Add the milk and cream and pass the mixture through a fine sieve. Taste and season with salt and pepper.

Divide the mixture between the ramekins. Place the ramekins in a roasting tray lined with aluminium foil and fill the tray with enough hot water to come three-quarters up the sides of the ramekins. Cover the tray loosely with a large sheet of aluminium foil, place in the oven and cook for 20–25 minutes.

Cooking the garnish
Cook the asparagus spears in plenty of boiling salted water (cooking time will depend on their size). Lift out with a slotted spoon, refresh and reserve.

Preparing and finishing the juice
Sweat the shallot in the teaspoon of butter then add the wine. Bring to the boil for 30 seconds, then add water or chicken stock and chervil and simmer for 2–3 minutes.

Strain into a small saucepan, add the cream and whisk in the remaining cold diced butter. Add the garnish asparagus. Taste, season with salt and pepper and enliven with lemon juice. Keep warm.

Serving
Prepare four warm plates.

With the blade of a knife, loosen the mousses from the ramekins and turn them out on to the middle of each plate, leaving the ramekins over the mousses so that they do not go cold.

Arrange the spears of asparagus around the mousse. Pour the juice around each mousse and sprinkle chervil around. Remove ramekins and serve to your guests.

CHEF'S NOTES
Aluminium foil is placed between the roasting tray and the ramekins to prevent excessive heat escaping from the bottom. The foil placed loosely over the mousse is to make sure it does not dry out during cooking. Do not seal completely otherwise steam will not be able to

---

For four people

Preparation time: 30 minutes

Cooking time: 25 minutes

Special equipment:
4 × 7.5cm (3in) ramekins.

Planning ahead: The mousse mixture can be prepared in advance and cooked at the last moment. The asparagus spears for the garnish can also be cooked and refreshed in advance.

a little butter for greasing the moulds
250g (9oz) small asparagus spears,
bitter base of the stems removed
2 eggs, plus 2 egg yolks
1 tablespoon chopped chervil
200ml (7fl oz) milk
200ml (7fl oz) whipping cream
salt and freshly ground pepper

FOR THE JUICE:
1 shallot or ⅛ onion,
peeled and chopped
40g (1½oz) unsalted butter,
chilled and diced, plus 1 teaspoon
4 tablespoons white wine
100ml (3½fl oz) water
or light chicken stock (see page 34)
15g (½oz) chervil leaves,
washed and patted dry, chopped
1 tablespoon whipping cream
juice of ⅛ lemon

FOR THE GARNISH:
20 asparagus spears,
trimmed as above
1 tablespoon chopped chervil

WINE

It is always difficult to associate a wine with asparagus. A Sauvignon grape from St-Julien, Château Talbot, will do very well.

escape. There would be a build-up of heat and the mousses would rise like little soufflés then deflate miserably.

It is difficult to give an exact time for the cooking. It depends on the distribution of heat in your oven, and the size of the ramekins used. The mousse is cooked when it becomes slightly convex (puffed up). If you are not sure, place a needle in the middle of each mousse; this should come out quite hot and dry when the mousse is ready.

Fromage de Chèvre Rôti au Mesclun à l'Huile de Noisette

Small goat cheese, breadcrumbed and roasted, served on a bed of salads, dressed with hazelnut vinaigrette

A delightful spring salad for everyday eating – good for a lunch or a substantial starter.

Preheat the oven to 400°F (200°C) Gas 6.

For the coating
Skin the warm hazelnuts by rubbing them in a tea cloth. Grind them finely in a processor, then mix with the breadcrumbs.
  Beat the egg yolk lightly.

Coating and cooking the cheese
Dip each goat cheese into the beaten egg yolk, then into the breadcrumb mixture. Roast the cheeses on a lightly oiled baking tray in the preheated oven for about 3 minutes on each side until golden. Remove from the oven and reserve.

Serving
Meanwhile, make the vinaigrette and toss with the salad. Arrange salad attractively on each plate and set the warm goat cheese in the middle.

CHEF'S NOTES
Goat cheeses are in season from early spring to August. If you cannot find Cabecou, choose another variety, as long as the cheese is well matured so that the flavours are powerful and the texture creamy. There are some excellent British goat cheeses about.

For four people

Preparation and cooking time: 20 minutes

*4 Cabecou or other
matured goat cheeses
4 tablespoons Hazelnut Oil Vinaigrette
(see page 43)
4 handfuls mixed salad leaves
(chicory, curly endive, radicchio, or
other salads according to season),
washed and dried (see also page 195)*

*FOR THE COATING:
6 hazelnuts, toasted
3 tablespoons fine, dry breadcrumbs
1 egg yolk*

 WINE

Try a Shiraz. Everything you could wish to find will be here, spice, fruit and oak – beautiful.

Nage de Poissons à la Coriandre

Chunks of fish poached in a a herb-scented vegetable stock

I find the concept of this dish exciting, as it moves away from tradition, with a definite oriental influence. A little bit of adventure in your *cuisine* and on the table . . .

Preparing the vegetable garnish
Lightly salt the cucumber sticks and freeze them for 1 hour. Remove, rinse under cold water and reserve.

Cook the fennel and carrot together in plenty of boiling salted water for 5 minutes. Remove with a slotted spoon and refresh in cold water. Add the courgettes to the water and cook for 3 minutes. Remove and refresh.

Drain and reserve all the vegetables, along with the tomato dice.

Cooking the fish
Season the fish with salt and pepper half an hour before cooking.

Bring the *nage* to simmering point and infuse the lemongrass in it (if used). Add the monkfish and cook for 4 minutes. Next, add the turbot or brill and cook for 3 minutes, then the salmon and red mullet for 1 minute.

Strain off the *nage*, keeping about 200ml (7fl oz) as the juice. Add the coriander to this.

To finish off the juice, add the cream, then whisk in the cold diced butter. Taste and correct seasoning with salt and pepper, and acidulate with a dash of lemon juice. Add all the vegetables to this.

Serving
Warm four soup bowls or large dishes and divide the fish between them, arranging in a mound. Scatter vegetables on and around and pour on the juice.

CHEF'S NOTES
The salt is sprinkled on half an hour before so that it penetrates the fish.

Cooking time will vary according to the size of the fish pieces.

Variations
More than one variety of fish can be substituted with scallop, John Dory, halibut, fillets of small sole, lemon sole or plaice.

The coriander can be replaced by chives, chervil or basil.

Lemon zest could be added on top and, if you feel rich, a heaped tablespoon of Imperial Sevruga caviar gently scattered over the top will be a perfect accompaniment.

For four people

Preparation time: 45 minutes

Cooking time: 10 minutes

Planning ahead: The *nage* can be prepared well in advance. The vegetables can be prepared and cooked in advance.

*90g (3½oz) each of monkfish, turbot or brill and salmon, cut into large chunks
2 red mullet fillets, cut into large pieces
salt and freshly ground pepper
400ml (14fl oz) nage (see page 36)
¼ stalk of lemongrass, chopped (optional)
24 coriander leaves*

FOR THE VEGETABLE GARNISH:
*100g (4oz) cucumber, peeled, halved, seeded and cut into 4cm (1½in) sticks
4 baby heads of fennel, prepared, or 2 outer leaves of fennel, peeled and cut into triangles
1 carrot, peeled and cut into sticks
1 small courgette, cut into sticks
3cm (1¼in) long and 5mm (¼in) wide
1 medium tomato, skinned, seeded and diced*

TO FINISH THE JUICE:
*1 tablespoon whipped cream
25g (1oz) cold unsalted butter, diced
juice of ⅛ lemon*

➲ WINE ➲
A light Chardonnay would do very well, but not one that is too overpowering: try a Montagny, St Véran or Rully.

Nage de Poissons à la Coriandre

Quenelles de Semoule, Sauce Tomate

Gruyère cheese and semolina quenelles baked in tomato sauce

For four people

Preparation time: 30 minutes, plus 2 hours' resting

Cooking time: 1 hour

Planning ahead: The quenelle mixture must be prepared and rested before poaching. The quenelles can be poached and made a few hours in advance, but must be kept cool with a damp cloth over them. The tomato sauce can be prepared a day ahead.

300ml (10fl oz) milk
100g (4oz) semolina
2 egg yolks
50g (2oz) unsalted butter
75g (3oz) Gruyère cheese, grated
salt and freshly ground pepper
freshly grated nutmeg
2 litres (3½ pints) water

FOR THE TOMATO SAUCE:
1 onion, peeled and chopped
3 tablespoons olive oil
1kg (2¼lb) ripe tomatoes,
seeded and chopped
2 garlic cloves, peeled and chopped
3 tablespoons tomato purée
1 sprig of thyme
200ml (7fl oz) water
a pinch of sugar (optional)

FOR GLAZING THE QUENELLES:
20g (¾oz) unsalted butter, melted

WINE

I will refer again to Italy and recommend a Chardonnay from Tuscany. Alternatively, try an aromatic *rosé* from Provence or even a Jurançon dry wine.

Making and poaching the quenelles

In a large pan, bring the milk to the boil then reduce the heat to a gentle simmer. Add the semolina and cook for 5 minutes until it thickens. Remove the pan from the heat and mix in the egg yolks, butter and grated cheese. Taste and season with salt, pepper and 2 pinches of grated nutmeg. Transfer the mixture to a bowl and cover with cling film. Leave to cool, then refrigerate for a minimum of 2 hours.

Divide the mixture into eight and make the quenelles into an oval shape on a lightly floured surface.

In a large saucepan bring the water to simmering point with some salt, then carefully slide in the quenelles. Poach gently for 15 minutes at just below simmering point. Lift the quenelles out gently with a slotted spoon on to a tray lined with absorbent paper, and leave to cool. Remove the paper and cover with a clean, damp tea towel.

Preparing the tomato sauce

Sweat the onion in the olive oil for 4 minutes, then add the chopped tomatoes, garlic, tomato purée, thyme and water and simmer for 20 minutes. Pass through a hand-mouli or purée in a blender, then sieve. Taste and season, adding a pinch of sugar if necessary. Reserve.

Preheat the oven to 325°F (160°C) Gas 3.

Braising the quenelles

Butter the inside of a medium-sized casserole dish. Pour enough tomato sauce in to come one-third up the sides of the dish, and arrange the quenelles in the sauce. Brush the tops of the quenelles lightly with the melted butter, cover with the lid, and braise in the preheated oven for 25–30 minutes.

Serving

Simply place the dish on the table and invite your guests to help themselves. Serve the remaining heated tomato sauce separately.

CHEF'S NOTES

Gruyère cheese is the best type of cheese for this dish, but you could also use Emmenthal or Beaufort. When using Gruyère, however, beware when seasoning the dish as this particular cheese is quite salty.

The quenelles are cooked in two stages: firstly they are poached in the water, and secondly, they are braised in the tomato sauce.

Variations

The tomato sauce can be replaced with a light cream and cheese sauce: simply pour 300ml (10fl oz) double cream into the dish and sprinkle all over with 100g (4oz) grated Gruyère cheese. Do not add any salt.

Quenelles de Semoule, Sauce Tomate

Tarte aux Tomates d'Eté

Summer tomato tart scented with basil

For four people

Preparation time: 30 minutes

Cooking time: 15 minutes

Planning ahead: The puff pastry rounds can be prepared in advance, placed on a pastry sheet and refrigerated.

250g (9oz) bought puff pastry

FOR THE TOPPING:
*1 medium onion, peeled, halved and finely chopped
6 tablespoons olive oil
leaves from 6 thyme sprigs
salt and freshly ground pepper
8 very ripe tomatoes, washed*

FOR THE GARNISH:
*4 tablespoons olive oil, placed in a bowl
8 black olives, stoned and quartered (optional)
16 fresh basil leaves, shredded*

Preparing the puff pastry
Lightly flour the working surface. Cut the puff pastry into four, shape into balls, then roll to thin down to rounds of about 18cm (7in) in diameter and 1–2mm ($\frac{1}{16}$in) thick. Place these rounds on a lightly floured tray and refrigerate for 5 minutes.

Remove the rounds from the refrigerator and cut down to rounds of 16cm (6½in) in diameter. Brush another pastry sheet of approximately 40 × 35cm (16 × 14in) with a little olive oil and place the four pastry rounds on it. Refrigerate again.

With the remaining puff pastry prepare thin strips 1–2mm ($\frac{1}{16}$in) thick by 5mm (¼in) wide. Moisten the edges of the pastry circles with water, using a brush, then curl the thin strips round the circles to make 'sides' for the tarts. Refrigerate.

Preparing the topping
Sweat the onion in the olive oil with the thyme leaves for about 8 minutes, seasoning with salt and pepper. Taste, adjust seasoning if necessary, then cool and reserve.

Remove the eyes of the tomatoes, and halve them across the width. Remove the seeds with the end of a teaspoon, leaving the flesh intact. Cut into rings approximately 3mm (⅛in) thick. Reserve.

Preheat the oven to 450°F (230°C) Gas 8 at least half an hour before baking. Place a lightly oiled pastry sheet in on the lowest shelf for the last 15 minutes to get it really hot.

Preparing and cooking the tomato tarts
Divide the onions between the pastry rounds, spreading them out over the base. Arrange the tomato slices so that they overlap on top of the onions.

Brush the tomatoes and the edges of the pastry rounds with the olive oil from the bowl. Season with salt and pepper.

Quickly remove the hot pastry sheet from the oven, and place the tarts on it, using a palette knife or fish slice. Place on the lowest shelf in the hot oven, and bake for 12 minutes.

Remove the tarts from the oven and sprinkle with the olives (if using) and shredded basil. Cook for a further 3 minutes, then remove from the oven. Rest for 5 minutes.

Serving
Lift each tart on to a serving plate, and serve to your guests.

CHEF'S NOTES
You can now buy very good puff pastry, but look for the best quality, made with *butter*.

The success of this dish depends on the ripeness of the tomatoes. I find that the Roma variety works best, or use small cherry tomatoes.

Tarte aux Tomates d'Été

When you roll the pastry thin, it will become elastic and also difficult to handle, so place it in the fridge for the pastry to relax, cool down and harden; it will then be very easy to cut. If you have a freezer, use it.

The heat of the baking tray will seal and cook the base of the tart. Ensure that the pastry is no thicker than stated, or it could be undercooked and soggy.

Variations
You can vary the topping of the tarts. You could add two boiled and puréed garlic cloves to the onions. Slices of blanched courgettes could be added between the tomato slices. The garnish could include anchovies on top of the tomatoes, and you could use various herbs – the choice is yours, sage, thyme . . .

 WINE

From the Chianti to the Grifi of Tuscany, all these wines will do very well. A Bandol red would also suit.

81

Gratin de Crabe au Pamplemousse Rose

Gratinated Cornish crab meat with pink grapefruit

For four people

Preparation time: 1 hour

Cooking time: 5 minutes

Special equipment:
4 egg dishes or small plates, 14cm (5½in) in diameter.

Planning ahead: It would be advisable to order the crab from your fishmonger well in advance. Ask him to cook it for you and to remove the brown and white crab meat; ask him also to discard the heavy top shell and claws, and to chop the carcasses. It is, of course, asking a lot, and you will need a very professional and helpful fishmonger. If this is not the case, instructions for preparing the crab have been given in the recipe (and you should change fishmonger).

All elements of the dish can be prepared half a day in advance and cooked when needed.

1 crab, 1.25kg (2¾lb) in weight
2 litres (3½pints) water
10g (¼oz) fresh root ginger
salt and cayenne pepper

FOR THE SAUCE:
50ml (2fl oz) olive oil
crab shells, chopped
60g (2¼oz) fennel leaves
3 cardamom seeds
2 tomatoes, seeded and chopped
1 garlic clove, peeled and crushed
1 large sprig of thyme
100ml (3½fl oz) dry white wine
300ml (10fl oz) water
100ml (3½fl oz) whipping cream

FOR THE GARNISH:
1 pink grapefruit

WINE

A dry wine full of fruit, but with some acidity, will match this spicy dish. I would recommend a Pinot Gris d'Alsace or even a Riesling.

Cooking and preparing the crab

Bring the water to the boil, plunge the crab in and cook for 15 minutes. Refresh under cold water.

Place the crab on its back on a board, twist off the claws then twist off the legs (do not pull them). Prise the apron up, pulling at the pointed end near the mouth to remove the body from the shell. Remove the stomach and dead men's fingers (these are soft and spongy and are found at the sides of the body). Pour off any excess water. Strip out the cartilaginous membrane from the shell and discard it.

With a spoon, remove the brown meat from the shell and put it aside. Remove the white meat from the body, claws and legs. Crack the claws and legs with a hammer or lobster cracker. Use a lobster pick or skewer to help you extract all the flesh. Reserve the crab meats together.

Cooking the ginger

Peel the ginger root and dice very finely. Boil in plenty of water for 15 minutes. Refresh, pat dry and mix with the crab meat. Taste and season with salt and cayenne pepper.

Making the sauce

In a large saucepan, heat the olive oil and add the chopped crab shells. Cook for 3–4 minutes over a high heat. Lower the heat to medium and add the fennel, cardamom seeds, tomatoes, garlic and thyme. Sweat for a further 3 minutes, then add the white wine and bring to the boil. Add the water, skim and simmer for 30 minutes.

Strain the stock into another saucepan and boil to reduce down until you are left with 50ml (2fl oz) of concentrated crab juices. Cool and reserve.

Preparing the garnish

Peel and segment the grapefruit. Cut the segments in half lengthways and arrange them around the four dishes. Reserve.

Preheat the grill.

Cooking and serving the dish

In a small saucepan heat the crab meat. Place the dishes under the grill to warm up the grapefruit segments. Place a small mound of crabmeat in each dish, spoon the sauce over, then gratinate briefly under the hot grill (about 2 minutes). Serve to your guests.

CHEF'S NOTES

When cooking the crab, depending on the weight, allow approximately 12 minutes per 1 kg (2¼lb) of crab.

Gratin de Crabe au Pamplemousse Rose

Mousse de Coquilles St Jacques à la Ciboulette

Mousse of scallops served in a chive-scented sauce

For four people

Preparation time: 30 minutes

Cooking time: 15 minutes

Special equipment:
Four small ramekins, 5cm (2in) in diameter and 3cm (1¼in) in height.

Planning ahead: For this dish to be a success, the scallops must be extremely fresh, so it is important to order them well in advance from your fishmonger. Before embarking on this recipe, do read carefully the general notes on mousse-making on page 25.

Ask the fishmonger to open the shells and to give you only the scallop and the white muscle.

The mousse can be prepared, uncooked, up to a day in advance; if this is the case, add 50ml (2fl oz) more cream to the recipe. The sauce can be prepared an hour before the meal, but add the chives only at the last moment.

FOR THE MOUSSE:
150g (5oz) of the freshest scallops, prepared, cleaned and patted dry
1 egg yolk
1 level teaspoon salt
a pinch of cayenne pepper
200ml (7fl oz) whipping cream, chilled

FOR THE CHIVE SAUCE:
40g (1½oz) unsalted butter
2 shallots, peeled and finely chopped
6 small button mushrooms, washed, patted dry and finely chopped
trimmings reserved from the scallops
100ml (3½fl oz) Noilly Prat
3 tablespoons water
2 tablespoons whipping cream
salt and freshly ground pepper
a few drops of lemon juice
1 level tablespoon finely chopped chives

⇒ WINE ⇐

A wine made from the Viognier grape at Candrieu and Château Grillet (in the Rhône Valley) is probably the best marriage. The delicate elegance of one of the world's finest white wines will surprise you.

This is probably the most delicate mousse you could taste, especially if you are able to get those large, sweet-tasting, very fresh scallops.

Preparing the mousse
Purée the scallops in a food processor for 2 minutes, then add the egg yolk and season with salt and cayenne pepper. Remove the bowl from the processor, and place in the freezer for 15 minutes. This will cool the purée down sufficiently for the cream to be safely added.

Return the bowl to the processor, set at medium speed, and gradually incorporate the chilled whipping cream. Taste and correct seasoning.

Lightly butter the inside of the ramekins with a little of the sauce butter, and fill with the mousse.

Preheat the oven to 330°F (160°C) Gas 3.

Cooking the mousses
Place the filled ramekins in a small roasting tray, then pour in enough hot water to come two-thirds up the sides of the ramekins. Bring to simmering point on top of the stove, cover loosely with foil, and then place in the preheated oven. Cook for 15 minutes.

Making the sauce
Meanwhile, melt 15g (½oz) of the butter in a pan (dice and chill the remainder). Sweat the shallot in the butter for 2 minutes, then add the mushrooms and scallop trimmings, and sweat for a further 2 minutes. Add the Noilly Prat and boil to reduce by half. Add the water, followed by the cream. Push through a fine sieve, pressing in order to extract as much juice as possible.

Place the sauce on a low heat, and whisk in the cold diced butter. Taste and season with salt and pepper, enliven with a few drops of lemon juice, then, finally, add the chives.

Serving
Prepare four warm plates. Gently run the blade of a knife around the sides of the ramekins to free the mousses. Shake these gently sideways, and turn out on to the plates. Pour the warm sauce over and around the mousses, and serve to your guests.

CHEF'S NOTES
The trimmings of the scallops are the fibrous muscles which attach the scallops to the shells. The fishmonger will give these to you if you ask. It is not necessary to force the raw mousse mixture through a sieve as the scallops themselves are not fibrous.

If you want to enhance the presentation of the dish, sprinkle a finely diced cooked mushroom on the sauce, or top the scallop mousses with finely cut scallop rounds, poached in the juice for 30 seconds.

Mousse de Coquilles St Jacques à la Ciboulette

Raviolis de Champignons Sauvages
Wild mushroom ravioli

Making the pasta dough
Please read the section on pasta-making on page 26.

Making the filling
Sweat the shallot in the butter for 1 minute until transparent, then add the diced wild mushrooms. Cook over a high heat, stirring continuously, for 1½–2 minutes. Remove from the heat, taste, and season with salt, pepper and a dash of lemon juice. Cool down on a tray.

Thinning down the pasta dough
Divide the pasta dough into 8 pieces (of approximately 30g/1¼oz each) and mould into 5cm (2in) square shapes. Thin down the pieces into ribbons of approximately 35 × 10cm (14 × 4in) and 0.5mm (1/32 in) thickness. Place the ribbons on to a lightly dusted tray and cover with cling film to prevent them from drying out.

Filling the ravioli
Take one ribbon of ravioli dough and brush it lightly with water then, starting 3cm (1¼in) from the edge, place 1 teaspoon filling in mounds at 3cm (1¼in) intervals. There should be six mounds per ribbon. Take a second ribbon and place it on top of the first; press all around the ravioli mounds until the two ribbons are stuck together. With a knife or cutter, cut out the ravioli mounds into circles or squares about 4.5cm (1¾in) wide.

Stretch a piece of cling film over a tray and place the raviolis on it. (This will prevent sticking. Or dust flour on the tray.) Repeat this process for the remaining ribbons; there will be 24 raviolis in all. At this stage, the raviolis can be frozen if not needed immediately. Cover with cling film.

Making the sauce
Sweat the shallot in the butter without colouring, then add the chopped button mushrooms and wild mushrooms. Sweat gently for 2 minutes, stirring from time to time, then add the white wine and reduce down by two-thirds. Add the water and cream and whisk in the cold diced butter until the sauce is well emulsified. Taste, season with salt and pepper, and add a dash of lemon juice.

Liquidise and strain the sauce, pressing with a ladle to extract as much sauce as possible. Reserve in a small saucepan.

Cooking the ravioli
Place 2 litres (3½pints) lightly salted water into a large saucepan and bring to a fast boil. Poach the ravioli for exactly 2 minutes. Lift them from the saucepan using a slotted spoon and place them in a pan holding the butter melted together with the water. Season lightly with salt and freshly ground white pepper.

Raviolis de Champignons Sauvages

Serving
Heat the sauce, divide between the plates, and arrange six raviolis on each plate. Serve to your guests.

CHEF'S NOTES
When making the filling, the diced wild mushrooms must be cooked very briefly over a high heat, stirring all the time, in order to cook them very quickly so as to remove as much water as possible.

The ribbons of pasta will dry out very quickly; it is therefore advisable to cover each one with cling film to prevent this from happening.

You will have some pasta dough left over after cutting the ravioli (approximately 130g/4½oz). This can be used for noodles, tagliatelle, etc. (see page 27). Dry them out and place in a storage jar which will not only be useful to have in your kitchen but will look attractive as well.

Variations
The fillings for ravioli are endless: diced fish, diced courgettes with tomato and basil, crab with ginger, and lobster mousse would all be equally delicious.

Shiitake mushrooms are a Japanese variety, are widely farmed and are available in this country. They could be used instead of wild mushrooms.

Also, if you wish, you could wrap each ravioli in a blanched lettuce leaf.

 WINE
A young Chablis or a Pouilly Fumé will be good partners for this dish, or try a wine from the Jura region.

Millefeuille de Confit de Canard

Flaked duck meat sandwiched in crispy potato galettes, served with a salad

Confit of duck is a speciality from the south-west of France. The duck is cured then gently simmered in duck fat.

Curing the duck legs
Place the duck legs on a small tray, flesh side up, and crumble the thyme and bay leaf over them. Scatter the remaining curing ingredients over them as well. Cover with cling film, refrigerate and leave to cure for 24 hours.

Cooking the duck legs
Wipe all the spices from the duck legs, then in a saucepan bring the duck fat gently to simmering point (do not allow it to boil). Cook the duck legs in the fat for 1½ hours. Leave to cool in the duck fat.
   Preheat the oven to 400°F (200°C) Gas 6.

Cooking the shallot garnish
Place the shallots, duck fat, vinegar and a pinch each of salt and pepper in a sheet of aluminium foil. Wrap completely and bake in the preheated oven for 35 minutes.

Preparing and cooking the potato galettes
You will need twelve galettes. Press the grated potato in a tea cloth to extract all the moisture. Season with a pinch of salt and 2 large pinches of freshly ground white pepper. Melt 25g (1oz) of the butter and mix it with the potatoes.
   Butter a baking tray lightly with the remaining butter and place the pastry ring on the corner of it. Add approximately 15g (½oz) of the grated potato and spread within the ring to about 2 mm ($\frac{1}{16}$in) thickness. Remove ring and proceed in this way for the remaining galettes.
   Place the tray of galettes in the preheated oven and cook for 10 minutes. After 5 minutes, turn the galettes with a palette knife so that they are golden on both sides. Reserve on a tray.

Preparing the cooked duck legs
With a slotted spoon remove the cooked duck legs from the fat, place on absorbent paper and pat dry. (Keep the fat in the fridge and it can be used another time.)
   With a spoon, remove the duck skin. Chop it, then place on to a small tray and roast in the preheated oven until crispy, about 12–15 minutes. Season with salt and pepper and reserve.
   Remove the meat from the duck legs, flake it, and sprinkle with the tablespoon of Xérès vinegar.

For four people

Preparation time: 2½ hours

Cooking time: 1½ hours

Refrigeration time: 24 hours

Special equipment:
1 pastry ring, 10cm (4in) in diameter.

Planning ahead: The duck legs must be cured for 24 hours in advance. The first five stages can be prepared a few hours in advance. Reheat before serving.

2 duck legs
700ml (24fl oz) duck fat
salt and freshly ground pepper
1 tablespoon Xérès vinegar
(see page 18)

FOR CURING THE DUCK LEGS:
2 sprigs of thyme
1 bay leaf
10g (¼oz) mixed black and white peppercorns, crushed
30g (1¼oz) coarse salt
1 garlic clove, peeled and crushed

FOR THE POTATO GALETTE:
200g (7oz) finely grated potato
30g (1¼oz) unsalted butter

FOR THE SHALLOT GARNISH:
20 small shallots
or baby onions, peeled
1 tablespoon duck fat
1 tablespoon Xérès vinegar

FOR THE SALAD GARNISH:
1 handful of prepared salad leaves
(rocket, lamb's lettuce, radicchio, etc.)
2 tablespoons Walnut Oil Vinaigrette
(see page 43)

Millefeuille de Confit de Canard

Building the *millefeuille* and serving

Divide the duck meat, shallots and duck skin into four portions, separately. Place three potato galettes in front of you, then place half of one portion of duck meat over one galette and then add another topped with the other half of the duck meat, finishing with a third galette. Do the same with the remaining galettes. Place the four three-tier galettes on to a tray and warm through in the oven for 2–3 minutes.

Toss the salad leaves in the dressing, and correct seasoning. Arrange the dressed leaves attractively around the plate, then scatter with the duck skin and five shallots per plate. Place the *millefeuille* in the middle of each plate. Serve to your guests.

CHEF'S NOTES

You can buy duck fat in some specialised shops, or you can reserve the chicken or duck fat from whenever you cook a bird. Obviously, to preserve properly, the fat must be clarified, with no juice or solids in it. It would spoil otherwise.

Variations

Of course, to simplify the dish, you can omit the potato galettes. It would still be delicious.

You could also add slivers of duck liver, cooked for 5 minutes in the duck fat then sliced finely and scattered over the salad.

➤ *WINE* ❧

A red wine, Fleurie Cristal, would be a natural partner, or a white wine from the south-west where this dish comes from – Jurançon Sec.

Fricassée de Champignons Sauvages

Fricassee of wild mushrooms

For four people

Preparation time: 20 minutes

Cooking time: 10 minutes

600g (1lb 6oz) chanterelles *or*
girolles *and black trumpets, mixed,*
prepared, roots trimmed,
briefly washed and patted dry
30g (1¼oz) unsalted butter
2 shallots, peeled and finely chopped
a dash of lemon juice
4 tablespoons water
salt and freshly ground pepper

FOR THE SAUCE:
15g (½oz) flat parsley leaves
50ml (2fl oz) water
1 tablespoon whipping cream
40g (1½oz) cold unsalted butter, diced
a few sprigs of chervil, chopped
2 tomatoes, skinned, seeded and diced
into 5mm (¼in) cubes
a dash of lemon juice

FOR THE GARNISH:
1 handful of garlic croûtons
(see page 29)

Blanching the parsley

Throw the parsley leaves into plenty of boiling, salted water and cook for 2 minutes until barely cooked. Refresh under cold water, drain and reserve.

Cooking the wild mushrooms

For the *chanterelles*, heat 20g (¾oz) of the butter in a non-stick frying pan. Sweat the shallots in this for a minute or two, then add the *chanterelles*. Season with salt and pepper, add a dash of lemon juice, then cover and cook for 1 minute. Reserve.

For the black trumpets, bring the 4 tablespoons water and the remaining butter to the boil. Add the black trumpets, cover and cook for 1 minute, then reserve.

Preparing the sauce

Strain all the juices from the *chanterelles only* into a saucepan, add the water, and bring to a gentle boil. Add the cream and whisk in the cold diced butter. Add the chopped chervil, diced tomato and the blanched parsley leaves. Adjust seasoning and enliven the sauce with a dash of lemon juice. Keep warm.

Serving

Reheat the wild mushrooms for 1 minute, then place them together on to a warm serving dish. Pour the sauce around the mushrooms. Serve the warm *croûtons* separately.

CHEF'S NOTES

If undercooked, the parsley will be strong and bitter; if overcooked, it will be slimy and tasteless. Check very carefully during cooking.

Cook the black trumpets separately, since their juices would discolour the sauce.

Variations
Other wild mushrooms or farmed varieties can be substituted such as *shiitake* and *pleurottes*. Dried mushrooms can also be used.

⇒ WINE ⇐

A light, young, smoky Chardonnay will be fine.

Fricassée de Champignons Sauvages

Tarte au Fromage et Blettes à la Franc Comtoise

A Gruyère cheese and Swiss chard tart

For eight people

Preparation time: 30 minutes

Cooking time: 30 minutes

Special equipment:
1 tart tin with a removable base, 28 × 3cm (11 × 1¼in); a baking sheet.

Planning ahead: The shortcrust pastry must be prepared at least 6 hours in advance and refrigerated (see page 20). The tart can be cooked up to half an hour prior to the meal and kept warm.

1 quantity Savoury Shortcrust Pastry, (see page 20)
unsalted butter

FOR THE FILLING:
5 stalks of Swiss chard, peeled and chopped into pieces about 5mm (¼in) thick (net weight about 120g/4½oz)
salt and freshly ground pepper
250ml (8fl oz) milk
250ml (8fl oz) whipping cream
4 whole eggs, lightly beaten
freshly grated nutmeg
200g (7oz) Gruyère cheese, grated

This dish is a tribute to the magnificent region of France I come from, and one day you must make it part of one of your dinner parties!

Preheat the oven to 400°F (200°C) Gas 6.

Preparing the pastry case
Allow the pastry dough to come to room temperature.

Butter the sides of the tin and the base of the baking sheet. Put the latter into the oven to heat through thoroughly.

Lightly flour your work surface, and roll the dough out into a circle 2–3mm (⅛in) thick. Rest it for 2–3 minutes. Place into the tin. Press the sides in well and trim the excess off. Thumb the dough up so that it comes about 2–3mm (⅛in) above the top of the tin. Refrigerate for a minimum of half an hour.

Blind-baking the pastry case
Line the inside of the pastry case with aluminium foil or greaseproof paper and fill with baking beans. Transfer the tin and its contents to the hot baking sheet, and bake in the preheated oven for 10 minutes. Take the sheet and tart out of the oven, remove the foil or paper and beans, and reserve.

Making the filling
Cook the chard stalks for 3 minutes in plenty of boiling salted water, then refresh, pat dry and season with salt and pepper.

Mix the milk, cream and eggs, and season with salt, pepper and a sprinkle of nutmeg.

Filling and baking the tart
Distribute the grated cheese and the chard pieces over the bottom of the tart, and pour the egg and milk mixture in right up to the top. Place the sheet on a hot shelf of the preheated oven, slide into the oven very carefully, and bake the tart for approximately 30 minutes.

Serving
Remove the baking sheet and the tart from the oven and leave to rest for 15 minutes. Remove the ring and gently place the tart on to a round serving dish, using two fish slices. Serve to your guests.

CHEF'S NOTES
Keep the Swiss chard leaves, as these would make a good vegetable accompaniment, cooked as spinach.

Gruyère cheese holds a substantial amount of salt, so take care when seasoning this dish. Gruyère can be replaced by Emmenthal, which is less salty.

Tarte au Fromage et Blettes à la Franc Comtoise

Once you have rolled the dough, it will retract, so it is important to rest it for 2–3 minutes prior to lining the tin.

It is important to preheat your oven well in advance so that the baking sheet and the shelves will be very hot and will cook the pastry through. Place the cheese tart in the hottest part of the oven.

 *WINE*

A crisp dry white wine like a Savennières from the Loire (Anjou) is a nice choice to accompany this dish, or a wine from the same region as the dish – Jura wine.

Mousse de Moules, Jus au Cresson

A mousse of mussels served with watercress-scented juice

For four people

Preparation time: 40 minutes

Chilling time: 1 hour

Cooking time: 18 minutes

Special equipment:
4 small ramekins, 5cm (2in) in diameter, and 3cm (1¼in) in height.

Planning ahead: The mousse can be made 1 day in advance ready for cooking; in this case add 50ml (2fl oz) extra cream to the mousse mixture.

Before embarking on this recipe, please read the general notes on mousse-making on page 25.

FOR THE MUSSELS:
approx. 36 mussels (to obtain
75g/3oz mussel flesh)
2 shallots, peeled and chopped
½ garlic clove, peeled and crushed
1 sprig of thyme
1 teaspoon unsalted butter
3 tablespoons dry white wine
2 tablespoons water

FOR THE MOUSSE:
100g (4oz) scallops with their
corals, washed, patted dry and chilled
1 egg, separated
a pinch of cayenne pepper
150ml (5fl oz) cold whipping cream
salt and freshly ground pepper
butter to grease the ramekins

FOR THE SAUCE:
1 bunch of watercress,
washed and picked over
cooking juices reserved
from the mussels
1 teaspoon whipping cream
15g (½oz) unsalted cold butter,
diced
2 tablespoons peeled,
seeded and diced tomato
a dash of lemon juice

FOR THE GARNISH:
20 mussels

Cooking the mussels

Sweat the shallots, garlic and thyme in the butter for about 30 seconds. Add the white wine and water, bring to the boil, add the mussels, cover and cook over a brisk heat for a maximum of 30 seconds only. (The mussels will open at this stage and should *not* be overcooked.) Strain and reserve the juices. Remove the mussels from their shells and leave to cool (discard the shells and any mussels which do not open). Reserve 75g (3oz) mussel flesh; refrigerate for 10 minutes.

Preparing the mousse

Purée the mussel flesh, scallops and coral in a food processor or liquidiser for 3 minutes until very smooth. Add the egg yolk, half of the egg white and the cayenne pepper, and blend in the cream gradually. Taste and correct seasoning with salt and pepper. Force the mixture through a fine sieve. Reserve.

Preheat the oven to 350°F (180°C) Gas 4, and lightly butter the ramekins.

Cooking the mousse

Divide the mousse mixture equally between the four buttered ramekins, then stand them in a deep baking tray. Pour hot water into the tray until it reaches three-quarters up the sides of the ramekins. On the top of the cooker, bring the water to simmering point, cover the dishes loosely with aluminium foil or greaseproof paper (to prevent drying out), then place in the preheated oven. Cook for 16–18 minutes.

Preparing the sauce and garnish

Plunge the watercress leaves into boiling salted water and boil rapidly for 1 minute, strain and refresh under cold water. Reserve.

Pour the strained mussel cooking juices into a small pan, bring to the boil, add the cream and whisk in the diced butter. Add the diced tomato and the watercress leaves, then taste and correct seasoning; enliven with a dash of lemon juice.

Place the garnish mussels with 1 tablespoon water into a small saucepan, bring to the boil, cover and cook for 2 minutes.

Finishing the dish and serving

Warm four plates. Gently run the blade of a knife around the sides of the ramekins to free the mousses. Shake these gently sideways, and turn out into the centre of each plate. Arrange five of the mussels in their shells around the plates, add the cooking juice from the garnish mussels to the sauce, and spoon this over and around the mousses. Serve to your guests.

Mousse de Moules, Jus au Cresson

CHEF'S NOTES

When you buy mussels, be sure that they are tightly closed and heavy with sea water. Discard any that are open and do not close when tapped sharply.

The aim is to cook the mussels 'rare'. If they are overcooked the mousse would lose its fine texture. After cooking for 30 seconds, the mussels will still be partly raw and will have lost most of their water. They can then be puréed.

 WINE

The best-known white wine from Burgundy – Chablis – will make everyone happy.

95

CHAPTER FOUR

Soups

I was once invited for tea by some acquaintances who were academics in Oxford. As you would expect, books and works of art were prominently displayed, and the conversation over tea was lively. We were shown the house, then lastly the kitchen where a battered microwave was predominant, with great stocks of tinned soups close to it and, of course, a well-used tin opener. Although one can appreciate their prime interests, I thought there was a degree of double standard – a well-fed mind, nourished with the very best ingredients, and a very poor body fed with basic convenience foods.

As we talked further, we spoke briefly about my own subject – about food – and about how easily delicious dishes can be produced at home. A lively demonstration followed: we fetched a few basic ingredients such as a leek, a potato and a tomato, and I made a soup which needed only five minutes' preparation and ten minutes' cooking. I hope my philosophy influenced theirs!

I think soups are at the very heart of basic family cooking, serving as snack, as lunch or as the first course of a more sophisticated meal. They also have the advantage of demanding very little time, and are definitely a good introduction to young potential gastronomes!

Soupe Printanière aux Herbes du Potager

Spring vegetable soup scented with chervil

For four people

Preparation time: 10–15 minutes

Cooking time: 20–25 minutes

Planning ahead: The vegetables can be prepared a day in advance and kept under a wet cloth.

1 shallot
1 medium carrot
1 small potato
1 small turnip,
or 50g (2oz) celeriac
¼ celery stalk
1 small courgette
1 small leek
1 tiny spring cabbage
12 lettuce leaves
1 tomato
800ml (28fl oz) water or light
chicken stock (see page 34)
15g (½oz) unsalted butter
salt and freshly ground pepper
2 tablespoons finely chopped chervil

TO FINISH THE SOUP:
4 tablespoons whipping cream
(optional)
15g (½oz) cold butter (optional)
lemon juice

I still find it amazing that loving mothers and fathers can grab tinned soup and a tin opener when it is so easy to produce beautiful wholesome soup in very little time. This soup can be served every day, or makes a good course for a spring dinner party.

Preparing the vegetables
Peel and dice the shallot, carrot, potato and turnip. Trim and dice the celery and courgette, and trim and finely slice the leek. Cut the spring cabbage into eight pieces. Wash the lettuce leaves, and skin, seed and dice the tomato.

Preparing the soup
Bring the water or chicken stock to the boil.

In a large saucepan, sweat the shallot in the butter for 1 minute, then add the carrot, potato, turnip and celery dice and cook for a further 5 minutes. Do not allow to brown. Add the courgette, leek and cabbage, season lightly, and sweat for another minute. Season lightly again.

Add the boiling stock to the vegetable pan, and simmer for 5–8 minutes. At the last moment add lettuce leaves, diced tomato and chervil and cook for a further minute.

Finishing the soup and serving
Remove the pan from the heat. Stir in the cream if used, and whisk in the cold butter if desired. Enliven the soup with a dash of lemon juice. Pour into a warm dish and serve to your guests.

Variations
Other vegetables could be substituted, such as parsnip, broccoli, etc. Basil or tarragon would also be good complementary flavours.

The cream and butter could be omitted to produce a clear vegetable soup.

Soupe Printanière aux Herbes du Potager

Crème de Courgettes et Laitues

Courgette and lettuce soup

This simple soup for spring reminds me of the plain wholesome cooking of my childhood. It can be enjoyed hot or cold.

Preparing the soup
Bring the chicken stock or water to the boil.

In a saucepan, sweat the onion, garlic and drained diced potato in the butter for about 10 minutes. Add the finely sliced courgettes and the lettuce leaves, and sweat for a further 2 minutes. Add the boiling stock or water and boil for 5 minutes, skimming from time to time.

Add the chopped chervil and liquidise. If you want a very smooth texture, force the soup through a sieve into a clean saucepan.

Finishing the soup and serving
Bring the soup back to simmering point and stir in the cream. Taste, season with salt and pepper, and enliven with lemon juice. Serve to your guests.

CHEF'S NOTES
The cooking of the potato will depend on the variety used. Should it stick, add 100ml (3½fl oz) water.

The cooking time is kept to a minimum in order for the soup to retain its flavour and vivid colour.

For four people

Preparation time: 10 minutes

Cooking time: 15 minutes

*1 litre (1¾ pints) light chicken
stock (see page 34) or water
250g (9oz) onions, peeled and chopped
1 garlic clove, peeled and crushed
50g (2oz) potatoes, peeled, very
finely diced, and rinsed under cold
running water (to remove the starch)
15g (½oz) unsalted butter
300g (11oz) courgettes,
trimmed and finely sliced
1 large or 2 small lettuces,
washed and leaves separated
2 tablespoons finely chopped chervil
100ml (3½fl oz) whipping cream
salt and freshly ground white pepper
lemon juice*

Raymond Blanc in the vegetable garden at Le Manoir aux Quat' Saisons

Consommé de Tomates Parfumé au Basilic

A basil-scented tomato consommé

For four people

Preparation time: 10 minutes

Cooking time: 35 minutes

Special equipment:
Muslin or a clean tea cloth.

Planning ahead: The consommé and garnish may be prepared 1 day in advance and refrigerated until required.

1 large onion, peeled and chopped
3 tablespoons virgin olive oil
1kg (2¼lb) of the ripest,
most scented tomatoes you can find,
washed and quartered
2 garlic cloves, peeled and crushed
15 black peppercorns, crushed
20g (¾oz) salt
1.2 litres (2 pints) water
8 basil leaves, chopped

FOR THE CLARIFICATION:
225g (8oz) ripe tomatoes,
washed and chopped
4 basil leaves
2 egg whites
1 teaspoon sugar (optional)

FOR THE GARNISH:
2 plump, ripe tomatoes
8 basil leaves

A simple mixture of water, fresh herbs and the ripest tomatoes provides a robust and exciting cold soup with the colours and tastes of summer.

Cooking the tomato bouillon
In a large casserole dish, sweat the chopped onion in olive oil for about 5 minutes until translucent, but not coloured. Add the chopped tomatoes (*with* the seeds and skin), the garlic, peppercorns, salt and water. Bring to the boil and skim. Add the basil and cook for a further 5 minutes.

Strain through a fine sieve, pressing down well with a ladle to extract all the flavours and juices. Cool.

Preparing the clarification
Liquidise the tomatoes with the basil leaves and egg whites. Pour into the cold bouillon, whisk well and bring to a gentle boil.

Simmer gently for 10 minutes. Taste and correct seasoning with salt, pepper and the sugar if necessary. Strain into another casserole, through muslin or a tea cloth. Leave to cool, taste again and correct the seasoning.

Cover with cling film and refrigerate.

Preparing the garnish
Remove the eyes of the tomatoes and discard. Plunge the tomatoes into boiling water for 3 seconds, refresh under running cold water and peel the skins off. Cut the tomatoes in half, remove the seeds with a teaspoon, and dice the flesh into 1 cm (½in) squares. Season with salt and pepper. Reserve.

Serving
Divide the diced tomato between four chilled soup bowls and pour the consommé over. Chop the basil leaves and scatter over the consommé. Serve to your guests.

CHEF'S NOTES
The success of this dish depends on the quality of the tomatoes you buy. If they are under-ripe they will be too acidic and not have sufficient flavour. The best are Marmande (beef tomatoes), Roma or cherry tomatoes.

For hints on clarification, see also page 38.

The egg whites will disperse when you whisk them into the cold bouillon. When you gently bring the bouillon to the boil, the egg white will cook, solidify, rise to the surface and trap all the impurities, leaving the bouillon clear.

The difficulty in seasoning a dish which is to be served cold is that when you season a hot dish, the heat heightens the flavours. This is why it is necessary to re-check and adjust the seasoning again when the dish is cold. One answer is to cool a small proportion of the liquid and taste it, then you will know how to season the bulk of the liquid.

Variations
In this case we have used basil, but you can also use fresh coriander or thyme.

Soupe de Pommes Glacée à la Cannelle

Finely sliced apples served in a white wine cordial scented with cinnamon

This is a simple everyday starter dish, ideal for a warm summer day.

Preparing the apples
Peel and cut the apples in half. Remove cores. Cut into sticks, 2mm ($\frac{1}{16}$in) thick and 2cm (¾in) long.

Preparing the soup base
In a casserole, mix the white wine, lemon juice and zest, water, cinnamon, sugar and vanilla pod. Bring to the boil for 1 minute. Remove from the heat and add the apple sticks. Allow to cool, then cover and refrigerate.

Serving
Remove the vanilla pod and cinnamon pieces, and divide the apple between four individual dishes (or place in one large bowl). Sprinkle some freshly ground white pepper on each soup. Serve to your guests.

For four people

Preparation time: 20 minutes

Cooking time: 5 minutes

Planning ahead: This dish can be prepared half a day in advance.

6 Granny Smith apples
250ml (8fl oz) fruity white wine
(Muscadet or Gewürztraminer)
juice of ½ lemon
finely grated zest of ¼ lemon
300ml (10fl oz) water
1 small cinnamon stick,
about 10g (¼oz), cut into 4
175g (6oz) caster sugar
½ vanilla pod, cut lengthways
(optional)
freshly ground white pepper

Soupe de Cerises en Aigre Doux

*Cherry soup scented with cinnamon and lemon
and enriched with soured cream*

This dish is an interpretation of a famous Hungarian recipe which I greatly enjoyed when visiting Budapest with my Hungarian-born wife. A perfect introduction to a hot summer evening meal.

Wash and remove stalks and stones from the cherries, reserving the latter. Crush the stones (with a pestle and mortar or heavy cleaver, for instance), then place them in a casserole with the wine, lemon peel, lemon juice and cinnamon. Chop 200g (7oz) of the cherries and mix with the wine. Bring to the boil for 1 minute, remove from the heat, and leave to marinate for 4 hours at room temperature.

Strain the soup into another saucepan forcing the mixture down with a ladle to obtain as much juice as possible. Add the remaining cherries to the liquid, and return to simmering point for 2 minutes. Remove from the heat, allow to cool down, then refrigerate.

Mix the soured cream into the cherry soup. Taste, then season with a pinch of salt and white pepper. Divide the soup between four china bowls, and serve to your guests.

CHEF'S NOTES
The best cherries for this soup are the sour Morello cherries. If you cannot obtain them, use any other variety. But you must substitute the following ingredients accordingly: 200ml (7fl oz) Banyuls wine and 200ml (7fl oz) any white wine, and the juice of a *whole* lemon.

For four people

Marinating time: 4 hours

Preparation and cooking time: 20 minutes

Planning ahead: The soup can be made a day in advance. Keep refrigerated, covered tightly with cling film.

500g (18 oz) Morello cherries
400ml (14fl oz) Banyuls wine
or *tawny port*
or *½ quantity cherry brandy*
peel of ¼ lemon
juice of ½ lemon
¼ cinnamon stick
150ml (5fl oz) soured cream
salt and freshly ground white pepper

 *WINE*

This cold soup is wonderfully refreshing and has lots of texture, so a little glass of Hungarian Riesling (known as Olasz) or, if you are lucky enough to get your hands on this marvellous wine, the gem of Hungary – Tokay.

Soupe de Cerises en Aigre Doux

Potage de Potiron

Pumpkin soup

For four people

Preparation time: 20 minutes

Cooking time: 40 minutes

Planning ahead: The pumpkin and soup can be done in advance.

1 ripe pumpkin, stalk on,
about 3–4kg (7–9lb) in weight
1 onion, peeled and chopped
15–20g (½–¾oz) unsalted butter
200ml (7fl oz) white dessert wine
400ml (14fl oz) milk
400ml (14fl oz) double cream
1 tablespoon Kirsch (optional)
salt and freshly ground pepper
freshly grated nutmeg

FOR THE GARNISH:
20 slices, cut from a French baguette,
about 5mm (¼in) thick,
lightly buttered, then toasted
100g (4oz) Gruyère cheese,
finely grated
3 egg yolks
2 tablespoons whipping cream
1 teaspoon Kirsch (optional)

The perfect dish for Hallowe'en night.

Preparing the pumpkin
Slice the top off the pumpkin, making a lid (see photograph), and, using a spoon, remove and discard all the seeds. Scoop out most of the flesh ensuring that the shell is not damaged. Put the lid and the pumpkin shell aside.

Preparing the soup
Sweat the onion in the butter for 3 minutes without colouring, then add the pumpkin flesh and cook for 3–4 minutes. Add the white wine and boil to reduce by half. Add the milk and cream and simmer for 15–20 minutes over a low heat. Liquidise and force through a sieve into a clean saucepan. Add the Kirsch (if using). Taste and season with salt, pepper and a pinch of freshly grated nutmeg. Bring to the boil. Reserve, keeping warm.

Preheat the grill, and preheat the oven to 350°F (180°C) Gas 4.

Preparing the garnish
Mix the grated cheese with the egg yolks, cream and Kirsch (if using) and place a little mound of the mixture on each croûton. Grill until they are lightly browned.

Serving
Place the pumpkin tureen and lid separately on a tray and warm up in the preheated oven for about 15 minutes. Remove from the oven, pour the hot soup into the pumpkin tureen, cover with the lid and place on a large plate. Serve to your guests, with the cheese croûtons separately.

CHEF'S NOTES
The pumpkin has to be ripe, otherwise the dish would be tasteless.

Potage de Potiron

Soupe de Poissons

Fish soup

For four people

Preparation time: 20 minutes

Cooking time: 30 minutes

Planning ahead: Order the fish from your fishmonger well in advance, and ask him to scale and gut it for you, and also to chop the bones into small pieces.

The soup and garnish can be made 1 day in advance.

800g (1¾lb) fish (1lb conger eel,
1 whiting, 1 small grey mullet),
scaled and boned
fish bones, chopped small
1 small onion, peeled and chopped
1 small carrot, peeled and chopped
4 garlic cloves,
unpeeled and lightly crushed
2 tomatoes, chopped
1 lemongrass stalk, chopped (optional)
50g (2oz) fennel leaves,
washed and chopped
2 packets saffron powder (see page 18)
100ml (3½fl oz) olive oil
1 tablespoon tomato purée
200ml (7fl oz) white wine,
boiled for 2 minutes
then cooled
1 bouquet garni (made from 1 bay leaf,
4 sprigs of thyme and 2 parsley
stalks, see page 30)
1.5 litres (2½pints) water
1 tablespoon Pernod
salt and freshly ground pepper
2 pinches cayenne pepper

FOR THE GARNISH:
20 garlic croûtons *(see page 29)*
1 quantity Rouille *(see page 41)*

Making the soup

In a large saucepan, sweat all the vegetables together with the lemongrass (if used), herb and saffron powder in olive oil for 2 minutes. Add the fish, chopped bones and tomato purée, stirring all the time, and sweat for a further 2 minutes. Add the wine and *bouquet garni*, and cover with water. Add the Pernod, bring to the boil, skim and simmer for 30 minutes.

Cool the soup down, then remove the *bouquet garni*. Grind the fish bones and the other ingredients in a liquidiser or food processor. Force the soup through a fine sieve, pressing with a ladle to extract as much liquid as possible (approximately 1 litre/1¾pints). Reserve.

Finishing the soup and serving

In a saucepan, bring the soup to the boil, then skim off any fat. Taste and heighten seasoning with salt, pepper and cayenne pepper. Pour into a large tureen. Serve the garlic *croûtons* and *rouille* separately.

CHEF'S NOTES

If you want to make a 'low-budget' soup, it is possible to use only the fish bones and the taste would still be quite delicious. (I may add that this is common practice in small bistros and restaurants.) On the other hand, if you wish to improve the quality of the soup, a couple of rock fish such as red mullet or gurnet or the addition of a few small baby crabs would be welcomed.

Soupe d'Aiglefin

Smoked haddock soup

Haddock is fascinating, and its texture and delicate smokiness fit so well in home cooking. I use it a lot. Here you will have a delicious soup, perfect for a cold winter's night.

Making the soup
In a large saucepan, sweat together the onion and peppers in the butter without colouring for about 10 minutes. Add the curry powder and white wine and cook for another 2 minutes. Bring to the boil, add the milk, cream and the fish, and simmer for about 15 minutes. Cool down and liquidise, then force the soup through a very fine sieve, pressing with a ladle to extract as much liquid as possible. Reserve.

Preparing the garnish
Whip the cream lightly, then add a pinch each of salt and pepper, along with the chives.

Serving
Bring the soup to the boil, taste and correct seasoning with pepper and a dash of lemon juice. Pour into a large tureen and top with the whipped cream garnish. Add the toasted almonds and serve the garlic croûtons separately.

For four people

Preparation time: 30 minutes

Cooking time: 30 minutes

Planning ahead: The soup can be prepared a few hours in advance.

500g (18oz) smoked haddock, skinned and chopped
1 onion, peeled and chopped
2 yellow peppers, halved, seeded and chopped
30g (1¼oz) unsalted butter
1 teaspoon curry powder
100ml (3½fl oz) white wine
700ml (24fl oz) milk
300ml (10fl oz) whipping cream
salt and freshly ground pepper
1 teaspoon lemon juice

FOR THE GARNISH:
100ml (3½fl oz) whipping cream
1 tablespoon chives, finely chopped
20g (¾oz) flaked almonds, toasted
20 Garlic Croûtons (see page 29)

CHAPTER FIVE

Fish and Shellfish

Fish

Years ago, after having had an animated conversation about fishmongers and having expressed my indignation about the poor quality of fish, the then *Good Food Guide* editor, Christopher Driver, felt he had to check whether my comments were justified. Actually, he was very shocked by the nightmarish sight of the fish sold under the guise of fresh – long rows of flabby, sunken and glazed-eyed bodies. Although there is still some malpractice, with a lot of partly frozen fish sold as fresh, there has been an incredible improvement in the quality and variety of the fish on offer. Equally the fresh fish caught by small boats in both Norfolk and Cornwall are becoming more and more available. This fish commands a small premium, but all is worth while if you want to have the best. With luck and our help, these small craftsmen will continue to flourish.

Farmed Fish

Fish farming now accounts for about 30 per cent of the market. At the beginning, the methods used were sound, but we are now witnessing the same problems as in the intensive farming to which cattle, poultry, etc. are subjected. Fish farms are virtually battery farms in the sea. The fish now live in the same cramped conditions as battery chickens, confined in cages with very little space to move; fed with pellets containing antibiotics, the fish cannot exercise and develop muscle (farmed trout is a perfect example of tasteless failure). Unless this industry takes positive steps and shows some initiative, the image of fish farming will be totally tarnished.

My culinary curiosity actually led me to compare the difference between farmed and wild turbot and salmon and, in most cases, the wild ones were better than the farmed ones. I was astonished, however, by the quality of the farmed product in some cases. Unfortunately, one is not able to distinguish one from the other, since there is no labelling system whatsoever. So choose carefully.

How to Recognise Fresh Fish

In Japan fish is only considered fresh when it jumps over the counter; our criteria are rather less stringent and we must rely on other indications of freshness. The appearance of a fish should be attractive; the eyes should be clear and bright – a glazed eye indicates that the fish has long departed from the land of the living. The scales should be shiny, steely and undamaged, the gills should be bright red, and the flesh firm to the touch. There should be no unattractive odour. If the fish looks or smells unpleasant, do not buy it – and tell your fishmonger why; quality and service will only improve through positive critical comments.

Cooking Fish

First of all, the fish must be of the freshest in order to get the best result.

Avoid strong heat throughout the cooking process, except briefly for sealing or browning. Fish have fragile connective tissues with little fat content, so they must be subjected only to gentle heat and should be barely cooked – just to the point when the protein coagulates. If fish is cooked at too high a temperature, or for too long, it will produce an all-too-familiar sight – dried out and disintegrating flesh.

To keep fish moist and firm it is generally cooked in two stages (like meat): cooking and resting. During the cooking, the heat penetrates the flesh, the fibres tense up, and the fish is cooked only to medium rare. During the resting process, done in a warm place and covered, the residual heat will gradually penetrate and cook the flesh and allow the muscle tissues to relax. The flesh retains its taste and firmness and the delicious juices released can be added to the sauce.

How to Tell When Fish is Cooked

This is mostly a case of experience, but here are a few ways:

Test by pressing the thickest part of the fillet with the inside of your finger; if the flesh is still springy and translucent, the fish is undercooked; if there is very little shrinkage and the flesh is smooth and opaque and feels firm and slightly supple with no sign of flakiness, it is correctly cooked. Overcooked fish will shrink and flake and have a dry taste and texture.

Shellfish

The finest seafood in Europe comes from the least polluted seas, from Ireland and Scotland where one can get the best native oysters and shellfish, and from the east coast. Pacific oysters are farmed in Brancaster and Morston in Norfolk. Whitstable remains the gem of the oyster world. From Dover to Cornwall and the Isle of Man, lobsters, shrimps, scallops, clams, crabs and mussels are regularly landed during the summer fishing seasons.

How to Recognise Fresh Shellfish
The shells of fresh shellfish must be tightly closed, or snap firmly shut at the slightest touch; if not the shellfish are probably dead and you should not buy them. Dying shellfish close slowly and not tightly. Do not buy these either. Really fresh shellfish should be heavy with sea water. Less than fresh shellfish are not only unpalatable gastronomically – they can also cause food poisoning.

Crustaceans like lobsters and crabs should be bought alive, or the serum which holds the flesh together will slowly flow out and the flesh will deteriorate very quickly.

Tartare d'Aiglefin à l'Emince d'Avocat

Tartare of haddock garnished with avocado

Preparing the tartare

Chop the haddock finely, into 3mm (⅛in) cubes, then reserve.

Salt the cucumber dice lightly, then marinate for about 15 minutes. Rinse under cold running water, then drain. Reserve.

Boil the potato dice in the salted water for 2–3 minutes until barely tender, then drain. Season with salt and pepper, and reserve.

In a large bowl, mix together the haddock, all the diced vegetables, and the chopped parsley. Reserve.

Preparing the mayonnaise

Make, using the listed ingredients, but following the instructions on page 40.

Preparing the vinaigrette

Mix the ingredients together. Taste and correct seasoning with salt and pepper, then reserve.

Preparing the topping and garnish

Mix together the soured cream, horseradish, lemon juice and cayenne. Taste, season with salt, and reserve.

Halve the avocado lengthways. Remove the stone, peel and cut across in 2–3cm (¾–1¼in) slices. Mix slices with the vinaigrette and reserve.

Building the tartare

Mix the mayonnaise with the haddock mixture, then taste and add freshly ground pepper.

Place the pastry ring or cutter in the middle of one plate, and spoon a quarter of the tartare mixture into it. Press down, and smooth the top. Spread a heaped teaspoon of soured cream on top, using a spatula. Loosen the tartare mixture around the inside of the ring with the blade of a knife, and lift off the ring. Repeat on the three other plates.

Serving

Arrange the avocado slices overlapping around the base of each tartare. Make a small mound of the diced tomatoes in the middle of the tartare, and top with a fresh chervil leaf, if using. Serve to your guests.

CHEF'S NOTES

Buy the best haddock for this dish, undyed if possible.

Wash the parsley, pat dry with kitchen paper, and chop finely. Do not 'wring' in a cloth as you will end up with dried-out fibres.

Do not salt the dish as the haddock will be salty enough already.

For four people

Preparation time: 30 minutes

Cooking time: 30 minutes

Special equipment:
1 pastry ring or cutter, about 5–6cm (2–2½in) wide, 4cm (1½in) high.

Planning ahead: The tartare can be prepared a day in advance, and the dish assembled 1 or 2 hours in advance.

*250g (9oz) undyed,
lightly smoked haddock
¼ cucumber, peeled,
seeded and finely diced
salt and freshly ground pepper
1 medium potato, peeled and diced
into tiny cubes of 3mm (⅛in)
500ml (18fl oz) water
¼ sweet red pepper,
halved, seeded and diced
1 shallot, peeled and finely diced
1 tablespoon chopped parsley*

FOR THE BINDING MAYONNAISE:
*1 egg yolk
1 teaspoon Dijon mustard
salt and freshly ground pepper
120ml (4fl oz) groundnut
or grapeseed oil
1 teaspoon lemon juice*

FOR THE VINAIGRETTE:
*1 teaspoon white wine vinegar
1½ tablespoons groundnut oil*

FOR THE TOPPING AND GARNISH:
*2 tablespoons soured cream
1 teaspoon freshly grated horseradish
a squeeze of lemon juice
a sprinkle of cayenne pepper
1 firm avocado
1 tomato, skinned, seeded and diced
(optional)
4 chervil leaves (optional)*

Tartare d'Aiglefin à l'Émince d'Avocat

Variations

You can easily replace the haddock with smoked mackerel or trout.

If you want to simplify the dish, omit the avocado garnish and horseradish topping, and spoon the tartare mixture directly on to a plate. This would make the dish more homely and suitable for everyday cooking.

 WINE

A crisp Chenin Blanc will be fine wherever it comes from – Vouvray Sauvenier or a Pine Ridge Chenin from California.

Cabillaud à la Boulangère

Fillet of cod, braised with onions and potatoes

For years cod was sneered at, and only used because of its low cost. At last, the delicacy of the cod's flesh is acknowledged, and now the once humble fish features on a great number of quality restaurant menus. . . . Sadly, the direct effect is also that its price has greatly increased.

Preheat the oven to 450°F (230°C) Gas 8.

Preparing the potatoes 'boulangère'
Pat dry potatoes, trim them to give them a cylindrical shape, then cut into 3mm (⅛in) slices. Rinse and drain them. Season with salt and pepper.

Grease the dish with a little of the butter, and fill with alternate layers of onions and garlic mixed together, potatoes and herbs. Season each layer. Finish with a layer of potato. Pour over the chicken stock or water, to half the height of the dish. Dot the remaining butter on the surface of the potatoes.

Bring the stock to simmering point on top of the stove, then place in the preheated oven for 30 minutes, until the potatoes are barely cooked.

Preparing the cod
Heat oil and butter until lightly brown in a large non-stick frying pan, and pan-fry the fish fillets on both sides for 5 minutes until lightly brown. Season with salt and pepper.

Baking the fish
Place the fish on top of the 'boulangère', and cover with the lid. Bake for 8 minutes.

Serving
Serve directly from the dish. Add a pinch of salt, a turn of pepper and a dash of lemon juice to the fish.

Variations
Plaice (30 seconds searing, then 5 minutes' cooking in the oven) and halibut (same cooking time as the cod) can also be used.

Cabillaud à la Boulangère

Escalope de Saumon Sauvage Poêlée à l'Oseille

Fillet of wild salmon, pan-fried and served
with a delicate sauce laced with sorrel

For four people

Preparation and cooking time: 30 minutes

Planning ahead: The sauce can be prepared half an hour in advance and kept warm.

Ask your fishmonger to remove all the bones from the salmon. The fish must be cooked at the last moment.

4 × 120g (4½oz) slices of wild
salmon, 1cm (½in) thick, skinned
1 teaspoon unsalted butter
salt and freshly ground pepper
lemon juice

FOR THE SAUCE:
30g (1¼oz) unsalted butter
2 shallots, peeled and chopped
100g (4oz) mushrooms, chopped
100ml (3½fl oz) Noilly Prat
50ml (2fl oz) cold water
1 tablespoon whipping cream
40 sorrel leaves,
stalks removed and washed

FOR THE GARNISH:
1 tablespoon finely chopped chives

Monsieur Troisgros, the owner at Roanne, created this dish. The acidity of the sorrel matches the richness of the salmon so well.

Making the sauce

In a large frying pan, sweat the shallots in a teaspoon of the butter without colouring them (chill and dice the remainder of the butter). Add the mushrooms and continue to sweat for 1 minute. Add the Noilly Prat, boil for 1 minute and finally add the water.

Strain through a sieve into a small saucepan, pressing the mushrooms and onions to extract as much liquid as possible. Bring the stock to the boil, add the cream and whisk in the cold diced butter. Taste, season with salt and pepper and enliven the sauce with a dash of lemon juice. Keep warm.

Cooking the sorrel

Cook the sorrel leaves for 5 seconds in plenty of boiling water. Drain well, season and add the leaves to the sauce. Reserve.

Preheat the oven to 400°F (200°C) Gas 6, or preheat the grill to very hot.

Cooking the salmon

Heat the butter in a large non-stick frying pan and sear the salmon fillets (without colouring them) for 5 seconds on each side. Season with salt and pepper and place under the preheated grill for 1 minute or in the preheated oven for 2 minutes.

Serving

Divide the sauce and sorrel leaves between four warmed plates, and place a salmon fillet in the middle of each. Add a dash of lemon juice and a pinch each of salt and pepper. Sprinkle with chives and serve to your guests.

CHEF'S NOTES

Lettuce, watercress or spinach leaves can replace or be added to the ingredients. The addition of diced tomatoes would add colour and texture to the sauce.

The sorrel is cooked separately then added to the sauce. That 5 seconds is just enough time; further cooking would result in a purée of sorrel.

Although the fish cooking time seems very short, it is essential not to overcook the salmon, in order to prevent it from becoming dry and flaky.

Variations

A white wine sauce can also be served with this dish (see page 42).

WINE

The fish has quite a rich texture, so I would recommend a Loire white wine such as a Pouilly Fumé or Reuilly with this dish.

Escalope de Saumon Poêlée à la Peau

Pan-fried fillets of wild salmon with lemon butter sauce

The simplicity of this dish is appealing, but the taste and especially the textures should please you. The moist, rich flesh with the crispness of the skin makes this dish.

Preparing the garnish
Cook the watercress leaves in boiling water for 30 seconds, refresh in cold water, then drain and reserve. Keep warm.

Preheat the oven to 400°F (200°C) Gas 6, or preheat the grill to very hot.

Preparing the lemon butter sauce
In a saucepan, bring the water and cream to the boil then whisk in the cold diced butter. Taste and correct seasoning, then add the lemon juice. Reserve and keep warm.

Cooking the salmon
Over a medium heat in a large non-stick frying pan, heat the butter and oil until it turns a light brown colour. Add the salmon fillets, skin side down, and cook for 6–7 minutes until the skin is crisp. Turn the fillets over and cook for 30 seconds. Turn fillets on to the skin side again, and season with salt and pepper.

Place in the oven for a further 2 minutes, or under the hot grill for 1 minute. Add a dash of lemon juice to each fillet.

Serving
Reheat the sauce and whisk to homogenise. Add the reserved watercress leaves. Place the fillets of salmon, skin side up, in the middle of each plate and divide the sauce and watercress leaves around. Serve to your guests.

CHEF'S NOTES
The idea of this dish is to give the salmon skin a crisp texture by cooking it slowly, therefore the initial heat must not be too high.

The watercress leaves should be added at the last moment to the sauce, otherwise the delicate green would turn grey due to the presence of lemon juice in the sauce.

Variations
Fillets of cod and trout can be cooked the same way and are equally delicious. The watercress leaves can be replaced by braised lettuce or sorrel.

The sauce could be replaced by the same quantity of brown chicken stock (see page 35) with 30g (1¼oz) Beurre Noisette (see page 40) added to it, plus a dash of lemon juice.

For four people

Preparation time: 15 minutes

Cooking time: 7 minutes

Planning ahead: Ask your fishmonger meticulously to scale the fillet of salmon, cut it into four portions, and to criss-cross score the skin (just deep enough to penetrate the skin, but not the flesh).

The sauce can be prepared in advance.

4 × 150g (5oz) fillets of salmon, skin left on
15g (½oz) unsalted butter
1 tablespoon olive oil
salt and freshly ground pepper
1 teaspoon lemon juice

FOR THE LEMON BUTTER SAUCE:
2 tablespoons water
1 tablespoon whipping cream
60g (2¼oz) cold butter, diced
1 teaspoon lemon juice

FOR THE GARNISH:
80g (3¼oz) watercress leaves, washed, stalks removed

 WINE

A delicate Sauvignon.

Filets de Limande à l'Oseille et Sauce Vin Blanc

Poached fillets of lemon sole, served on a bed of sorrel with a white wine sauce

For four people

Preparation time: 15 minutes·

Cooking time: 15 minutes

Special equipment:
1 large ovenproof, lidded sauté pan, 20cm (8in) in diameter.

2 × 750g (1½lb) lemon sole, filleted
1 teaspoon melted unsalted butter
salt and freshly ground pepper
1 teaspoon lemon juice

FOR THE SAUCE:
2 shallots, peeled and sliced
65g (2½oz) unsalted butter
75g (3oz) button mushrooms, washed, patted dry and sliced
150ml (5fl oz) dry white wine
100ml (3½fl oz) water
4 tablespoons whipping cream
1 teaspoon lemon juice

FOR THE GARNISH:
1.2 litres (2 pints) water
75g (3oz) sorrel leaves, washed and picked
2 ripe tomatoes, skinned, seeded and diced
15g (½oz) chives, washed and finely chopped

Preparing the fillets of sole

Score the sole lightly on the skin side in a criss-cross pattern with a sharp knife to prevent the fish shrinking during cooking. Brush with the melted butter and season with salt and pepper. Fold the fillets in half, skin-side inwards. Reserve.

Preheat the oven to 375°F (190°C) Gas 5.

Preparing the sorrel garnish

Bring the water to the boil and throw in the sorrel. Cook for 4–5 seconds, drain through a colander, and reserve. Season with some salt.

Cooking the sole and the sauce

In the ovenproof sauté pan, sweat the shallots in 15g (½oz) of the butter for 2 minutes without colouring. (Dice and chill the remaining butter.) Add the sliced mushrooms, and sweat for a further 2 minutes. Add the white wine, bring to the boil and reduce for 1 minute. Add the water and mix.

Lay the folded fillets of sole on the base of the pan in a single layer. Cover with the lid and place in the preheated oven for 6–8 minutes according to the thickness of the fillets.

Remove the fish on to a plate, using a slotted spoon, then cover and keep warm.

Strain the cooking liquid into another casserole, add the cream and bring to the boil. Whisk the cold diced butter in, a little at a time, until the sauce reaches a smooth and velvety consistency. Taste, season with salt and pepper, and sharpen with a dash of lemon juice.

Finishing the dish and serving

Butter a warm serving dish lightly. Arrange the fillets of sole down the centre of the dish and reheat in the oven for 1 minute.

Meanwhile, bring the sauce back to simmering point, and add the sorrel and diced tomatoes. Pour this over the sole, then sprinkle the finely chopped chives over the fish and sauce. Serve to your guests.

CHEF'S NOTES
The sorrel is slightly blanched to diminish some of its acidity.

Variation
The lemon sole could be substituted by turbot, sole, brill or plaice fillets; naturally, cooking times will vary accordingly.

WINE

Definitely a Chardonnay here. From Chablis to the magnificent Chassagne-Montrachet or Puligny-Montrachet, or, for the experimental, a Petaluma Chardonnay from Australia.

Filets de Limande à l'Oseille et Sauce Vin Blanc

Filets de St Pierre Poêlés et Aubergines Confites au Miel, Coulis de Tomates Crues

Pan-fried John Dory with aubergines marinated in honey and vinegar, served with a tomato coulis

For four people

Marinating time: 24 hours

Preparation time: 30 minutes

Cooking time: 10 minutes

Planning ahead: The aubergines must be prepared 1 day in advance, and the tomato *coulis* can be prepared a few hours in advance.

4 × 140g (4¾oz) fillets
of John Dory
salt and freshly ground pepper
2 tablespoons olive oil
lemon juice

FOR THE CANDIED AUBERGINES:
2 small aubergines
100ml (3½fl oz) olive oil
3 tablespoons white wine vinegar
2 teaspoons honey (preferably acacia)
4 tablespoons water
8 basil leaves
2 sprigs of thyme

FOR THE TOMATO COULIS:
50ml (2fl oz) olive oil
6 basil leaves
1 sprig of thyme
2 strips of orange zest
1 strip of lemon zest
6 medium tomatoes,
very ripe (Roma if possible)
10g (¼oz) butter
a pinch of sugar (optional)

Preparing the candied aubergines

Cut the aubergines into 3mm (⅛in) slices (about 12 per person). Season the aubergine slices with salt and pepper and pan-fry them until lightly coloured for 30 seconds on each side in hot olive oil in a non-stick pan. Separately, boil vinegar and honey for a few seconds, then add the water and leave to one side.

Place the aubergines on to a tray, pour the honey/vinegar mixture over, and mix well. Allow to cool then sprinkle with basil leaves and thyme, cover with cling film, refrigerate and marinate for 24 hours minimum.

Preparing the tomato *coulis*

Warm the olive oil gently in a small saucepan with the basil leaves, thyme, orange and lemon zest for 5 minutes. The oil must not boil, or it would fry the herbs. The aim is for the herbs and zests to release their flavours.

Chop the whole tomatoes, then liquidise and strain them through a very fine sieve into a small casserole. Warm the tomatoes through without boiling, then whisk in the strained olive oil and the butter. Taste, season with salt and pepper, and add a pinch of sugar if necessary. Reserve.

Preheat the oven to 350°F (180°C) Gas 4 and/or preheat the grill.

Finishing the dish

Remove the thyme sprigs and basil leaves from the marinated aubergines. Place aubergines on a tray and reheat in the oven for 5 minutes.

Season and pan-fry the John Dory in hot olive oil for 15 seconds on each side, then place under a hot grill for 1 minute, or cook in the preheated oven for 3 minutes.

Serving

Have ready four warm plates or one large serving dish. Arrange the aubergines overlapping in the middle of each plate. Place the fish on top of this, add a dash of lemon juice, and divide the raw tomato *coulis* around. Serve to your guests.

CHEF'S NOTES

Ask your fishmonger to give you the bones of the John Dory, and they will make a delicious fish soup (see page 108).

A large aubergine is like a large courgette or large anything. At this stage of its life, it becomes coarse, hollow and seedy; the firmness of

Filets de St Pierre Poêlés et Aubergines Confites au Miel, Coulis de Tomates Crues

youth has gone, to be replaced by a loose-textured flesh. You can tell by tapping it; if it sounds hollow, reject it. Always buy young aubergines, do not be fooled by size.

Do not be tempted to boil the tomato *coulis*. This would spoil it, and you would lose all the freshness of the sauce; if allowed to boil, it would become like a . . . tinned soup.

Variations
The John Dory can be replaced by red mullet or monkfish medallions, or by the less expensive fillets of plaice or lemon sole.

 WINE

A dry Jurançon wine will be a good accompaniment for this dish.

Homard Braisé dans son Jus aux Légumes d'Été

Homard Braisé dans son Jus aux Légumes d'Eté

Braised lobster in its own juice with summer vegetables

Order the lobsters well in advance from your fishmonger. They must be alive. . . . This is actually the only difficulty in this dish, and you will need a little courage!

Cooking the vegetable garnish
Place the carrot in plenty of boiling salted water and cook for 5 minutes. With a slotted spoon, remove from the saucepan and refresh under cold water; drain and reserve.

Follow the same procedure for the courgette and leek, but cook the courgette for 2 minutes and the leek for 1 minute only.

Preparing and blanching the lobsters
Leave the elastic bands holding the lobsters' claws in place. Press each lobster down on a tray then insert the point of a strong sharp knife right through the 'cross' marking on its head.

Twist and separate the lobster tail from the head and twist and separate the claws from the head. Remove the elastic bands.

Cook the lobster legs for 2 minutes in plenty of boiling water, then the tail and claws for 1 minute. Remove with a slotted spoon, refresh and drain. Reserve.

Shelling the lobster tails, claws and legs
Straighten the tails, holding them in your hand. Using scissors, cut along the insides of the tails. Peel off the flaps and extract the tails from the shells.

Crack open the claws and legs, and free the meat as delicately as possible to enable it to keep its shape.

At this stage, the lobsters will be cooked rare. Reserve.

Preheat the oven to 350°F (180°C) Gas 4.

Pot-roasting the lobster
In a cast-iron casserole dish big enough to hold the lobster, heat the oil until very hot, then add the meat. Sear on top of the cooker for 1 minute, season with salt and pepper, then add the water, cover the pan and cook in the oven for a further 7 minutes. Remove from the oven and relax the meat for 5 minutes. Correct seasoning.

Making the juice
Strain the cooking juices from the casserole into a small saucepan, then add the olive oil and cooked vegetable garnish. Bring to boiling point for 1 minute, then add the diced tomato. Turn off the heat and add the water, lemon juice and chives. Taste and season with salt and pepper.

Serving
Warm four plates.

For four people

Preparation time: 30 minutes

Cooking time: 15 minutes

4 lobsters, 450g (1lb) each in weight
4 tablespoons olive oil
salt and freshly ground pepper
4 tablespoons water

FOR THE VEGETABLE GARNISH:
2 medium carrots, peeled and cut into sticks,
5mm × 4cm (¼ × 1½in)
2 medium courgettes, washed, unpeeled,
and cut into similarly sized sticks
1 medium leek, trimmed and cut into
ribbons, 5mm × 7.5cm (¼ × 3in)

FOR THE JUICE:
100ml (3½fl oz) olive oil
2 ripe tomatoes, skinned, seeded and diced
4 tablespoons water
juice of ⅛ lemon
1 tablespoon finely chopped chives

Arrange the lobster meat in the middle of each plate, scatter the vegetables around and spoon the juice over. Serve to your guests.

CHEF'S NOTES

When pot-roasting the lobsters, the olive oil has got to be really hot. This sears the lobster meat and will enhance the flavour. Do not colour, though, as the flavour will be too strong.

The lobster is cooked in two stages: the short blanching of 1 minute will cook the lobster rare, to enable the shell to be easily removed; the pot roasting of 7 minutes will ensure that the lobster is cooked through.

During the cooking process, the meat will tense up, but the resting time will allow it to become more tender and will also release cooking juices which can then be used to enhance the juice.

The heads of the lobsters, and the shells from tail and legs (but not the bony claws) can be used for a light lobster soup or a lobster sauce.

Escalopes de Barbue aux Parfums d'Herbes

Fillets of brill served with a herb-scented juice

Preheat the oven to 350°F (180°C) Gas 4.

Preparing the brill fillets
Place the brill fillets on a plate. In a pan, melt the butter, then add the lemon juice and salt and pepper. Brush over the fillets, then refrigerate.

Cooking the brill
In a sauté pan, sweat the shallots in the butter for 2–3 minutes without colouring. Add the sliced mushrooms and sweat for a further minute. Pour in the Noilly Prat or wine and boil for 30 seconds to remove the alcohol and some of the acidity. Add the water.

Arrange the brill on the bed of shallots and mushrooms, and partially cover the pan (the gap is so that the steam can escape). Cook in the preheated oven for 7–8 minutes according to the thickness of the fillets.

Remove from the oven, and strain the juices into a small pan. Cover the fish and allow time to rest.

Finishing the sauce
Bring the cooking juices to the boil, then add the cream and whisk in the cold diced butter. Taste, then season with salt, pepper and lift the juice with a dash of lemon juice. Add the finely chopped herbs.

Serving
Warm four plates. Using a fish slice, place a brill fillet in the centre of each plate, then pour the sauce over the fillets. Serve to your guests.

Variations
Many types of fish can be prepared in this way – turbot, John Dory, halibut, sole, cod and plaice.

There are so many variations to this dish according to the time of year: in the spring, the garnish could be asparagus spears; in the summer diced tomatoes and seed mustard; in the autumn wild mushrooms; and in the winter *julienne* sticks of leeks, etc. The choice of herbs is yours.

For four people

Preparation and cooking time: 25 minutes

4 × 140g (4¾oz) brill fillets, skinned
15g (½ oz) unsalted butter
a dash of lemon juice
salt and freshly ground pepper

FOR COOKING THE BRILL:
4 shallots, peeled
and roughly chopped
15g (½oz) unsalted butter
8 button mushrooms,
washed and finely sliced
100ml (3½fl oz) Noilly Prat
or dry white wine
4 tablespoons water

FOR FINISHING THE SAUCE:
1 tablespoon whipping cream
30g (1¼oz) cold unsalted butter,
diced
a dash of lemon juice
1 tablespoon mixed chopped chervil,
tarragon and chives

 WINE

A dry Jurançon, for example Domaine Cauhape, will be a superb complement for brill.

Blanc de Daurade et Petits Calmars au Jus de Citronelle

*Pan-fried sea bream fillet and baby squid
with lemongrass sauce*

For four people

Preparation time: 25 minutes

Cooking time: 45 minutes

Planning ahead: Order the sea bream and baby squid from your fishmonger well in advance. The sauce can be prepared 1 day in advance.

2 sea bream, about 750g (1½lb) in weight,
scaled, gutted and filleted
1 tablespoon unsalted butter
1 tablespoon olive oil
lime juice
salt and freshly ground pepper

FOR THE SQUID:
8 baby squid prepared
2 tablespoons olive oil

FOR THE SAUCE:
½ garlic clove, peeled and chopped
50g (2oz) chopped celery
100g (4oz) chopped fennel
50g (2oz) chopped onion
50ml (2fl oz) olive oil
bones and heads of the sea bream,
chopped
1 sprig of lemon thyme
grated dried zest of 1 orange
1 small piece of dried lemongrass,
chopped finely
100ml (3½fl oz) white wine

TO FINISH THE SAUCE:
1 tablespoon whipping cream
30g (1¼oz) unsalted butter
lime juice

FOR THE GARNISH:
1 tablespoon chopped fresh lemon thyme
1 tablespoon honey
100ml (3½fl oz) water
1 whole onion, (about 150g/5oz),
peeled and cut into 1cm (½in) dice
1 teaspoon unsalted butter
finely chopped chives

Preparing the sauce

Sweat the chopped vegetables (garlic, celery, fennel and onion) in the olive oil for 5 minutes, then add the sea bream bones and heads, lemon thyme, orange zest and lemongrass. Add the white wine and boil to reduce down by half. Barely cover with water and simmer, skimming off impurities, for a further 10 minutes. Cool down and liquidise, then strain through a fine sieve into a small casserole, and reserve.

Preparing the garnish

Place the chopped thyme into a small saucepan with the honey. Bring the water to the boil, pour it over the thyme and honey, and leave to infuse for 10 minutes. Reserve.

Sweat the onion in the butter for 5 minutes without colouring. Season with salt and pepper, strain in the thyme infusion and simmer for a further 10 minutes. Reserve.

Cooking the sea bream fillets

Heat the butter and oil together in a non-stick pan until a hazelnut colour. Sear the fillets on the flesh side for 15 seconds, then turn over and cook on the skin side for about 10 minutes until crisp. Season with salt and pepper and sprinkle a little lime juice over.

Preparing and cooking the baby squid

The squid will be in two parts, namely the tentacles and the body. Cut the bodies in half lengthwise and make a 'criss-cross' in each half with the point of a knife 1mm (¹⁄₁₆in) deep. Heat the olive oil in a sauté pan and sear the tentacles and the bodies for 30 seconds only, stirring all the time. Season with salt and pepper and reserve.

Finishing the sauce

Reheat the sauce and whisk in the cream and cold diced butter. Taste, season with salt and pepper, and enliven with a dash of lime juice. Keep warm.

Serving

Reheat the squid, sea bream fillets and onion garnish.

Prepare four warm plates and place the sea bream fillets in the middle of each plate, skin side up, divide and scatter the baby squid and onions around. Spoon the sauce around. Sprinkle with finely chopped chives and serve to your guests.

CHEF'S NOTES

If possible, try to get gilt-head sea bream which has light pink scales. The red sea bream is the most common variety and is good, but the former is the very best.

Blanc de Daurade et Petits Calmars au Jus de Citronelle

The sea bream fillets are mostly cooked on the skin side so that you obtain a beautiful crisp texture which will be extremely enjoyable. It should be cooked over a medium heat.

The baby squid must be cooked very briefly over a high heat; if they are cooked for too long they will be very rubbery in texture.

Variations
If you want to simplify the dish, omit the baby squid.

Various fish can replace the sea bream fillets – red mullet (in this case, cook for 1 minute only on each side), John Dory and sea bass.

➬ WINE ➬

A white wine from Provence will enhance this dish.

129

For four people

Preparation and cooking time: 35 minutes

Planning ahead: The sauce base can be prepared a day in advance. The fish can also be prepared well in advance.

1kg (2¼lb) monkfish on the bone
2 tablespoons olive oil
salt and freshly ground pepper
lemon juice

FOR THE SAUCE BASE:
2 shallots, peeled and chopped
2 large teaspoons unsalted butter
100ml (3½fl oz) white wine vinegar
100ml (3½fl oz) white wine
150ml (5fl oz) water
chopped bones and trimmings from the fish (throw the dark skin away)

TO FINISH THE SAUCE:
2 tablespoons whipping cream
1 teaspoon mustard seeds
(or 1 teaspoon moutarde à l'ancienne)
40g (1½oz) cold unsalted butter, diced
12 tarragon leaves
5g (⅛oz) chopped chives
1 teaspoon lemon juice

Queue de Lotte Rôtie à la Moutarde et Estragon

Roasted fillet of monkfish
served with a mustard and tarragon sauce

Preheat the oven to 400°F (200°C) Gas 6.

Preparing the monkfish
Peel off the dark skin from the fish and discard. Trim the outer skin and reserve for the stock. Bone out the fish, and chop the bone.

You will have two fillets of about 350g (12oz) each, and the trimmings and chopped bone should weigh in at about 200g (7oz).

Tie the fillets so they keep their shape during cooking. Place on a tray, cover with cling film and refrigerate.

Preparing the sauce base
Place the shallot in a saucepan and sweat in the butter for 2–3 minutes. Add the white wine vinegar and reduce completely. Add the white wine and reduce by half then add the water and the chopped bones and trimmings. Bring to the boil, skim and simmer for 10 minutes. Strain into a small casserole, and reserve.

Cooking the monkfish fillets
Sear the fillets all over in the hot olive oil for 1 minute. Season with salt and pepper, then cook in the preheated oven for 7 minutes.

Remove from the oven, spoon out any fat and reserve the fillets, loosely covered with aluminium foil, in a warm place.

Finishing the sauce
During the cooking of the monkfish, bring the sauce base stock to the boil. Add the cream and mustard, then gradually whisk in the cold diced butter. Add the tarragon and chives. Taste, season and keep warm.

Finishing and serving the dish
Remove the string from the monkfish fillets. Reheat in the oven for 2 minutes. Cut six medallions from each fillet and season with salt and pepper. Add a dash of lemon juice, arrange on warm plates (three per plate), and pour the sauce over. Serve to your guests.

CHEF'S NOTES
Monkfish is one of the easiest fish to bone, as it has only one central piece of cartilage 'bone'. Of course, it would make it even easier if your fishmonger were to do it for you!

When making the base for the sauce, be sure to reduce the vinegar completely or it will be too acidic.

Variations
There are various ways of changing this dish: you could use diced tomatoes, chopped coriander or chervil instead of the tarragon, or a *julienne* of vegetables.

WINE

A white wine from the Côtes du Rhône, especially one made from the Viognier grape will complement the dish very well.

Queue de Lotte Rôtie à la Moutarde et Estragon

Médaillons de Lotte et Moules au Safran

*Pan-fried monkfish fillets served
with mussels and saffron sauce*

For four people

Preparation time: 15 minutes

Cooking time: 12 minutes

Planning ahead: This dish can be prepared up to 2 days in advance.

*1 large monkfish fillet,
about 500g (18 oz) in weight,
which can be cut into 4 médaillons
1kg (2¼lb) mussels
3 tablespoons olive oil
salt and freshly ground pepper
4 shallots or ¼ onion,
peeled and finely chopped
1 packet saffron powder or
1 pinch saffron strands
10g (¼oz) unsalted butter
60g (2¼oz) button mushrooms,
washed, patted dry and sliced
150ml (5fl oz) dry white wine
2 tablespoons water*

TO FINISH THE SAUCE:
*25ml (1fl oz) whipping cream
25g (1oz) cold unsalted butter, diced
½ teaspoon lemon juice
1 small bunch chives,
washed and finely chopped*

Preparing the monkfish *médaillons*
Tie the fillet equally along its length with four pieces of string. Cut in between the strings in three places to divide the fillet into four even *médaillons*. Refrigerate until required.

Preparing the mussels
Wash the mussels under running cold water, scrape the shells and remove the beards. Rinse in plenty of cold water, and discard any which remain open.

Preheat the oven to 400°F (200°C) Gas 6.

Cooking the monkfish *médaillons*
Heat the olive oil in a non-stick saucepan, then add the *médaillons*. Sear and colour lightly for about 30 seconds. Season with salt and pepper and cook in the preheated oven for about 7–8 minutes.

Remove the *médaillons*, discard the olive oil, and reserve the fish in a warm place, covered loosely with a sheet of buttered paper to prevent them drying out.

Braising the mussels
During the cooking of the monkfish, in a cast-iron saucepan sweat the chopped shallots and the saffron in the butter for 2 minutes. Add the mushrooms, and sweat for a further 30 seconds. Add the white wine, boil for 30 seconds, then add the water. Toss in the mussels, cover with a lid, and cook for 1 minute until the mussels just open. Draw off the heat and strain the juices into a casserole. Remove the mussels, shell them and reserve. Discard any that remain closed.

Making and finishing the sauce
Reduce the mussel juice to 150ml (5fl oz), then add the cream and whisk in the cold diced butter. Taste, correct seasoning and add lemon juice to taste. Finally, add the shelled mussels.

Serving
Place the monkfish *médaillons* in the middle of a flat serving dish, and place in the hot oven or under a preheated grill for a minute. Remove the serving platter from the heat and pour the sauce and mussels over. Sprinkle with chopped chives.

CHEF'S NOTES
The fillet should come from a large monkfish, as you want to cut it into *médaillons*. A *médaillon* is a cut from the fillet of certain fish or all meats, and is thickish and round in shape.

The mussels must be extremely fresh, heavy with sea water, and they

Médaillons de Lotte et Moules au Safran

should be firmly closed. The cooking time of 1 minute will be just enough to barely cook the mussels. Do not be tempted to overcook at this stage or they will become leathery and chewy.

You could also reserve 12 cooked mussels in their shells to arrange around the dish.

Variation
You could lightly brush each *médaillon* with mustard and top with Provençal breadcrumbs (see page 28). Place under the grill for 1 minute.

 WINE

The sauce has a good texture and strong flavours, so choose a lively wine from the Loire Valley such as Sancerre, Gros Plant or Muscadet.

133

Huîtres aux Concombres et Ciboulettes

Warm oysters served in their shells with a julienne *of cucumber and a cucumber butter sauce*

For four people

Preparation and cooking time: 20 minutes

Freezing time: 2 hours

Planning ahead: Order the oysters well in advance, and ask the fishmonger to open them for you (see Chef's Notes). They will keep will in their juice in the fridge for 12 hours. Order the seaweed too if using.

The first two stages can be prepared a few hours in advance. The sauce can be prepared 30 minutes prior to the meal.

24 oysters, size 2 or 3,
removed from their shells
oyster juices
seaweed for garnish (optional)

FOR THE CUCUMBER *JULIENNE:*
1 cucumber, washed
1 teaspoon salt

FOR THE CUCUMBER BUTTER SAUCE:
2 large shallots,
peeled and finely chopped
50g (2oz) cucumber peelings,
chopped
1 teaspoon unsalted butter
3 tablespoons white wine
1 tablespoon white wine vinegar
1 tablespoon whipping cream
2 tablespoons oyster juices
150g (5oz) cold unsalted butter,
diced
juice of ¼ lemon
a few grains of salt and
freshly ground white pepper
1 small bunch of chives, washed,
shaken dry and finely chopped

A purist may disapprove of this recipe since he would prefer to use oysters in their natural state – raw. I have found that for a lot of my guests, the texture of raw oysters is a stumbling block; by cooking them lightly, the texture is firmed up, which makes it more appealing. This dish would definitely belong to a very festive day such as Christmas or New Year.

Preparing the oyster shells (and seaweed if used)
Wash the bottom half of the shells. Wash the seaweed in plenty of cold water, blanch in boiling water for 3–4 minutes, then drain well. Arrange on each plate, and place six shells in a circle on top. Reserve in a cold place.

Preparing the cucumber *julienne*
Peel the cucumber, saving 50g (2oz) of the peelings for the sauce. Cut the cucumber flesh into 8cm (3¼in) long pieces, then slice into ribbons 2–3mm (⅛in) thick. Place in a bowl, sprinkle with the salt, and freeze for 1–2 hours.

Defrost cucumber under running water. Drain well and reserve.

Preparing the cucumber butter sauce
See also the instructions for Beurre Blanc on page 39.

In a small saucepan over a medium heat, sweat the shallots and chopped cucumber peelings in the butter for 1 minute. Add the wine and vinegar and boil to reduce to 1 teaspoon of liquid. Reduce the heat, and add the cream and oyster juices. Gradually whisk in the cold diced butter.

Liquidise the sauce and strain it into a small casserole. Taste, add the lemon juice and correct seasoning. Keep warm, whisking from time to time so the sauce does not separate.

Finishing the dish and cooking the oysters
Warm the cucumber *julienne* in a small saucepan. Warm the plates with the oyster shells and seaweed for a few seconds. Add the chopped chives to the cucumber butter sauce.

Bring the juices of the oysters to near boiling point, add the oysters and cook for 10 seconds only, in a covered pan.

Serving
Divide the cucumber between the shells, place the oysters on top, and coat with the cucumber butter sauce. Serve to your guests.

CHEF'S NOTES
Choose oysters that are plump and heavy with sea water and which

are tightly closed. I find that the native Irish oysters are the very best; Colchester oysters are also delicious.

The most difficult step in this dish is to open the oysters. The best and easiest way is to have it done for you, so ask your kind fishmonger. Take along a small container, so that the fish can be kept in their juices, and ask to be given the bottom half of the shell to put the oysters in. (You could also ask for some seaweed, which would make a beautiful bed on which to serve the dish.)

The cucumber *julienne* is 'cooked' by the freezing: its flavour is kept intact and its colour becomes a translucent green.

Only add the chives to the sauce towards the end; if added too early the acid present in the sauce will discolour them and ruin the flavour.

Assembling this dish is quite complicated too. To simplify this, mix the cucumber butter sauce, oysters and cucumber *julienne* together and serve in shell bowls; sprinkle with chives.

Variations
If you cannot obtain seaweed, place the oyster shells on a bed of coarse sea salt instead.
 The cucumber can be replaced by watercress, or edible seaweed.

 WINE

One of the best Chablis will honour this festive dish.

Coquilles St Jacques Façon Oudille

A whole scallop enclosed in its own shell

For four people

Preparation time: 25 minutes

Cooking time: 10 minutes

Planning ahead: Order the scallops in advance from your fishmonger and ask him to open them up for you, clean them and keep the shells. The coral can be discarded as it is not needed for this recipe.

4 large, extremely fresh scallops, with top and bottom shells
200g (7oz) bought puff pastry
10g (¼oz) unsalted butter
a dash of lemon juice
salt and freshly ground pepper
1 egg, beaten

FOR THE GARNISH:
80g (3¼oz) each of leeks, carrots and courgettes
10g (¼oz) unsalted butter
100ml (3½fl oz) water
1 teaspoon chopped chervil
10g (¼oz) chives, finely chopped

TO SERVE:
200g (7oz) rock salt or seaweed

WINE

A white wine from the Rhône Valley, such as St Péray, St Joseph Blanc or Hermitage Blanc.

This dish was created by Monsieur Oudille, former Head Chef of Michel Guérard's restaurant, and it is one of my very favourites. The scallops are placed on a *julienne* of vegetables, then baked in their puff-pastry-sealed shells. The flavours are absolutely stunning – so clean and fresh – and the dish is also very easy! M. Oudille now owns his own restaurant – in Grenade-sur-l'Adour, in the Landes – and a visit is highly recommended.

Preparing the puff pastry
Roll the pastry out to 35cm (14in) long, 14cm (5½in) wide and 2–3mm (⅛in) thick. Refrigerate, then cut into four strips, approximately 3cm (1¼in) in width. These strips of pastry will be used to seal the top and bottom shells.

Preparing and cooking the vegetable garnish
Cut the base of the root and the coarse top off the leek and discard; also discard the first two layers of the leeks. Cut the remaining leek into *julienne* sticks 8cm × 3mm (3¼ × ⅛in). Wash and reserve. Peel and wash the carrots, then cut into similarly sized *julienne* sticks. Reserve. Leaving the skin on, cut the courgettes into similarly sized *julienne* sticks. Wash and reserve.

Place the butter and water into a saucepan, add a pinch of salt and the carrot, and cook for 2 minutes. Add the leek and cook for 1 minute, then the courgette and cook for 45 seconds.

Strain the liquid into another saucepan and cool. Refresh the *julienne* of vegetables under cold water and reserve. When the liquid is cold, add the chopped chervil and chives.

Preparing the scallops
In a small saucepan, melt the butter, add the lemon juice, and season with salt and pepper. Brush the scallops all over with this lemon butter, then refrigerate. The butter will solidify. Reserve.

Building the dish
Place half of the vegetable *julienne* in the bottom of each shell, place a scallop on top, and sprinkle with a turn of freshly ground pepper. Top with the remainder of the vegetable *julienne*. Cover with the top shell.

Brush beaten egg all over the top shell and the edge of the bottom shell, then wrap a strip of pastry all around and press the edges together. The shells should be totally sealed. Brush the pastry all over with egg and reserve in the refrigerator.

Preheat the oven to 400°F (200°C) Gas 6.

Baking and serving the scallops

Place the scallops on a baking sheet, ensuring that they are level, and cook in the preheated oven for 12 minutes.

During the cooking, arrange the rock salt or seaweed on the plates.

Remove the scallops from the oven, place the shells in the centre of each plate and serve to your guests. Leave the pleasure of opening the shell to your guests (have side plates on the table to take the removed top shell).

CHEF'S NOTES

This dish is so clean and natural, it is vital that the scallops are the freshest possible.

The puff pastry can be replaced by shortcrust pastry (see page 20).

If using seaweed, order from your fishmonger well in advance. Blanch it in boiling water for 3–4 minutes so the colour changes to a very attractive emerald green.

Sole Rôtie au Jus de Viande Parfumé au Thym et Romarin

Roasted slip sole with a chicken juice
scented with thyme and rosemary

Preparing the garnish (optional)

Deep-fry the flat parsley and basil or tarragon leaves in hot oil at 300°F (150°C) for 1 minute. Drain on absorbent paper and season delicately with salt and pepper. Reserve.

Preheat the oven to 425°F (220°C) Gas 7.

Cooking the sole

Pat the sole dry in a tea towel. In a large non-stick roasting pan, heat the oil and butter. When the fat starts foaming and is lightly golden, lay the sole in the pan and cook for 2 minutes. Season with salt and pepper, turn the fish over, and cook for a further 2 minutes. Place in the preheated oven for a further 6 minutes.

Finishing the sauce and serving

Slide the sole on to a warm flat serving dish (reserve the cooking juices), decorate with the fried parsley and basil or tarragon (if used), and keep warm.

Pour the brown chicken stock into the juices in the roasting pan. Add the thyme and rosemary and whisk over heat until the juices, butter and stock are well blended. Boil for 30 seconds. Taste, correct seasoning and sharpen the sauce with the lemon juice. Strain into a sauce boat. Serve to your guests.

Variations

The stock can be replaced by the same amount of juices collected from roasting a joint. Tiny roasted onions make a delicious accompaniment.

For four people

Preparation time: 15 minutes

Cooking time: 20 minutes

Planning ahead: Order the sole (slip soles are young fish) from your fishmonger in advance and ask him to cut the heads off, remove the brown and white skin and to trim the sides.

4 small slip sole,
250g (9oz) each in weight
salt and freshly ground pepper
1 tablespoon olive oil (see page 17)
40g (1½oz) unsalted butter

FOR THE SAUCE:
150ml (5fl oz) brown chicken stock
(see page 35)
cooking juices and butter from the sole
1 sprig each of thyme and rosemary
juice of ¼ lemon

FOR THE GARNISH (optional):
3 tablespoons flat parsley leaves
12 basil or tarragon leaves
500ml (18fl oz) oil for deep-frying

 WINE

A white Cassis from Provence will be fine. A full-bodied white from the Côtes de Beaune will be perfection.

Aile de Raie
au Beurre d'Anchois

Poached wings of skate with anchovy and herb butter

Cooking the garnish

Simmer the potato dice in plenty of lightly salted water for 3–4 minutes. Drain and reserve.

In a small pan mix the shallots and white wine vinegar and boil to reduce down completely. Add the white wine and boil for 2–3 seconds, then draw away from the heat and add the butter and diced potatoes. Taste and season with salt and pepper when cold. (Reserve the parsley, adding it just before serving.)

Preparing the anchovy butter

Purée the butter and anchovies in a liquidiser until totally smooth. Reserve and leave to cool in a small bowl. Refrigerate.

Poaching the skate

Place the water, 30g (1¼oz) salt, the *bouquet garni*, crushed peppercorns and vinegar in a large saucepan. Bring to simmering point and skim. Add the skate wings and simmer for about 6 minutes. Turn off the heat. Leave the skate wings in the stock.

Preparing the sauce

Put the measured skate stock into a small casserole, bring to boiling point, then add the cream and whisk in the cold anchovy butter. Add the capers, taste, season with salt and heighten the taste with a dash of lemon juice (about 1 teaspoon). Lastly add the diced tomato and blanched parsley leaves. Keep warm.

Serving

With a slotted spoon, lift the skate wings out of the stock and peel off both the white and black skins. Season with salt and pepper and add a dash of lemon juice. Place a piece of skate in the centre of each warm plate and arrange the potatoes around. Spoon the sauce on to the skate.

For four people

Preparation and cooking time: 1 hour

Planning ahead: Order the skate well in advance. It should be very fresh, and the flesh white and firm with no smell whatsoever. Ask your fishmonger to prepare the skate wings for you.

The skate can be poached 30 minutes in advance and left in its cooking stock (in this case reduce the cooking time to 4 minutes). The sauce can also be prepared 30 minutes in advance and kept warm.

4 very fresh wings of skate,
about 200g (7oz) each in weight,
fins trimmed, washed and patted dry
1.5 litres (2½ pints) water
salt and freshly ground pepper
1 bouquet garni (see page 30)
20 black peppercorns, crushed
50ml (2fl oz) white wine vinegar
lemon juice

FOR THE GARNISH:
400g (14oz) potatoes (Desirée or King Edward), peeled and diced into 1cm (½in) cubes
2 shallots, peeled and finely chopped
1 tablespoon white wine vinegar
3 tablespoons white wine
20g (¾oz) unsalted butter
2 tablespoons finely chopped parsley

FOR THE SAUCE:
10g (¼oz) whole parsley leaves, blanched for 30 seconds and refreshed
50ml (2fl oz) skate stock
1 tablespoon whipping cream
20g (¾oz) small capers, rinsed under cold water
1 tomato, skinned, seeded and diced

FOR THE ANCHOVY BUTTER:
50g (2oz) unsalted butter
15g (½oz) canned anchovies, drained

⇒ WINE ⇐

A little wine from Burgundy such as a young St Véran, Montagny or Rully will be just right.

CHAPTER SIX

Meat, Poultry and Game

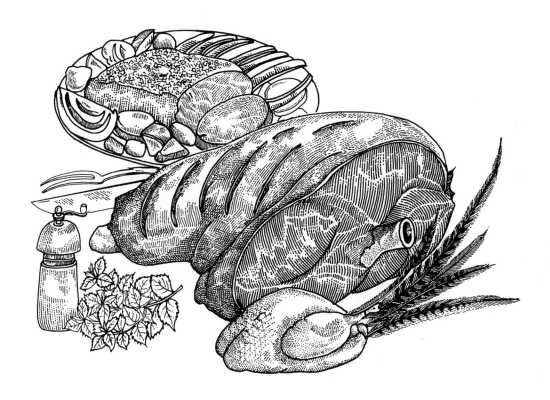

Meat

In the old days farmers used to grow field beans to provide protein for their cattle, then the cheaper soya bean meals were imported; next came an even cheaper protein, that utilising the waste of the abattoir. Intensive farming has turned many herbivorous animals into carnivores, thus ensuring fast growth and better profits. All this is very morbid. How could mankind design such an unnatural, horrible and inhumane way of production? We have had many food scares, and more will undoubtedly come in the meat and fish industries. It is high time that we returned to more traditional methods of farming. Luckily some farmers have already done so and these can be proud of producing such fine quality meat, especially lamb and beef.

Quality of Meat

In this country butchers have led customers to believe that meat should be of an attractive bright red colour, and this practice has yet to be challenged. In order to achieve flavour and tenderness, the meat should be hung, but of course the average butcher is not very keen to do this as he would have to invest in a large cold room, would also have to hold a valuable stock, and during the process of hanging, the water loss would transform itself into a weight, therefore monetary, loss. Obviously at this stage everyone would sympathise with the poor butcher. Personally, I would sympathise with the cook.

The displaying of meat in most butchers' shops is atrocious and would be likely to tempt you to become a vegetarian! The meat is covered with thick layers of fat, blood is leaking all over the place, and no thought at all is given to attractive presentation.

As for service, the problem is even greater. A consumer asking for meat to be boned, fat to be trimmed off, or a joint to be prepared is often ignored. This still occurs in Britain because the consumer has little knowledge of the high standard of service one should expect from the butcher. As I said in the introduction, asking for quality and service is actually helping your butcher to rediscover his craft and professionalism.

Maturing of Meat

Too often the cook will buy what she thinks a beautiful looking joint, then during the cooking disaster will strike! The joint will shrink, will have little taste and will also be very chewy. The cook will then believe that she is not competent and that she has failed in the simplest of skills, and hence will lose face and her confidence. Of course she will blame herself. But have you ever thought of blaming your butcher?

For the Sunday roast to be a success, the joint needs to be hung properly so that the meat will mature and, when cooked, be very tender. During the maturation process, the meat will become more tender and the flavour will be enhanced (as will your confidence).

That vivid red meat has *not* been hung. Meat that has been hung will not be nearly as attractive in appearance. It will have turned a darker red, and the white fat will have turned slightly grey. These unprepossessing signs are actually the signs of well-hung meat.

We have all become very health conscious nowadays, and quite rightly so, but I believe we are becoming obsessed with it. For meat to be tasty, a very thin layer of fat is necessary; this will 'feed' the meat during cooking and thus prevent it from drying out.

Roasting Meat

Specific methods are mentioned in specific recipes.

When appropriate, always try and ask for the bones when roasting meat, as they help make the most delicious juice. Have them chopped finely in order that they may release their juices quickly. Then brown them lightly in a pan on top of the cooker. Lay the meat on the browned bones in the roasting tray and, during the cooking time, the bones will acquire a rich dark brown colour which will lend taste and colour to the juice. The chopped bones can also act as a support for the meat, preventing it coming in contact with the bottom of the roasting tray and forming a dry skin.

The resting time is essential when roasting a joint. During the cooking the meat will tense up and, if carved immediately, will be very tough. The resting time will allow the heat to travel slowly through to the middle of the joint, ensuring that it is cooked perfectly and that the slices will be beautifully pink. The meat should be rested in a warm place at about 140°–158°F (60°–70°C), or left in the switched-off oven.

Poultry

Poultry, more than any other food animal, suffers from intensive production, and I will not go into the atrocious details as they have become well known.

I am still at a loss to understand why farmers in Great Britain have not taken up the challenge and opportunity to produce real free-range chickens, ducks, guinea fowl, turkeys, etc. Why, if one wants the best chicken, does one have to buy a French chicken from Bresse or the Landes to ensure the best quality? (By the way, French labelling is an authentic mark of quality control, unlike its British counterpart.) If these birds were produced in Britain, it would bring a high level of income and the customer would benefit both in freshness and price, and the fact that he had a choice. And the industry could pride itself in producing such quality.

Yet, apart from a few notable exceptions, nothing of significance has occurred. At the moment, I would advise you to buy the French birds if you want to give the best to your family. An authentic free-range chicken has had space in which to develop its muscles unlike its battery counterpart, so after cooking the flesh will be firm. I recently had some guests at Le Manoir who complained that the chicken was tough; they were obviously used to the 'cotton-wool' texture of the British product.

Game

Britain abounds in game. There is a staggering variety available – wild duck, woodcock, teal, grouse, snipe, hare – yet, despite this abundance, game farming has become big business, and in most cases farming spoils the quality. The delicate pink flesh of the French red-legged partridge, for instance, has, through cross-breeding, become strong and resistant to disease – but at the expense of taste and texture, since it ends up much like chicken. Far better to opt for its English counterpart, the grey-legged partridge, which is much more like the real thing.

Hanging Game
Game usually has a distinctive, rather strong taste. Most must be hung for 1–3 days, so that the flesh relaxes, but, generally speaking, if it is hung for too long, the flavour becomes coarse and over-assertive. You will have to rely on the sense and knowledge of your butcher and/or game dealer.

The only game I hang for more than 3 days is venison, pheasant, and partridge. Grouse is so strong to start with that hanging would make it overwhelmingly pungent. Pheasant, on the other hand, which has a white flesh and a rather faint taste, needs to hang for 8–10 days before being drawn and plucked, or it will taste like chicken. During hanging, the flesh develops a mature, distinctive flavour.

Choosing and Cooking Game
Try to avoid farmed game which is much cheaper, but not worth buying, (with the exception of venison). Fresh game should have an attractive appearance and hardly any smell; any odour should not be unpleasant. The skin should be dry, not moist. Never buy birds which were shot in the breast, as the flesh will be inedible.

All game birds are delicious simply roasted. Deglaze the caramelised juices in the pan with a little water, and you can hardly go wrong! Furred game like venison or hare always needs a complementary sauce.

Côtelette de Porc Poêlée aux Morilles

Pan-fried pork chop with dry sherry and morels

Morels are the first wild mushrooms to appear in early spring and are very evocative of my native Franche-Comté. The taste of fresh morels is very delicate, and because they are looked upon as a delicacy the price they fetch is quite high. It may be difficult to find them, so I would suggest you buy them dried from any delicatessen. The taste of dried morels is much stronger than fresh ones, but just as good.

Preparing the morels
Soak dried morels in water for a minimum of 4 hours, then drain them and cut in half. Wash them thoroughly, then drain again and pat dry.

Wash fresh morels in two or three changes of water. Handling them very delicately, pat dry and cut into halves or quarters, according to size.

Preheat the oven to 400°F (200°C) Gas 6.

Cooking the pork chops
Pan-fry the chops in a small roasting tin for 3 minutes on each side in very hot oil and butter until each side is beautifully brown. Season with salt and pepper.

Remove the fat from the tin, and place the tin and chops in the preheated oven for 6–8 minutes.

Place the chops on a plate, cover loosely with buttered paper, and reserve in a warm place.

Preparing the sauce
Put the butter in a pan and sweat the morels for 3 minutes. Add the sherry and boil to reduce by half, then add the cream. Boil until the sauce is of a velvety consistency.

Taste, correct seasoning with salt and pepper, and lift the sauce with a dash of lemon juice.

Serving
Place the chops on a serving dish and reheat in the oven for 2–3 minutes. Pour any juices released by the chops into the sauce. Pour the sauce over and around the chops, and serve to your guests.

Variations
Obviously the dish can be made with veal cutlet, chicken or guinea fowl, instead of pork. Alter the timings accordingly.

In this recipe I use dry sherry instead of the traditional Arbois wine; but, if you have it in your cellar, well, do not hesitate to use it!

Côtelette de Porc Poêlée aux Morilles

Escalope de Veau à l'Orange

Veal escalope, served with an orange sauce

For four people

Preparation time: 25 minutes

Cooking time: 15 minutes

Planning ahead: The orange juice can be reduced before starting the dish.

4 × 120g (4½oz) veal escalopes,
cut from the cushion or rump
1 tablespoon groundnut oil
15g (½oz) unsalted butter
salt and freshly ground pepper

FOR THE SAUCE:
4 oranges
50ml (2fl oz) dark rum
200ml (7fl oz) whipping cream

Preparing the veal escalopes
Place each escalope between two sheets of plastic and flatten them gently with a meat bat to a thickness of about 4–5mm (¼in). Put to one side.

Preparing the oranges for the sauce
Remove the peel from one of the oranges with a potato peeler, then cut it into fine *julienne* sticks. Blanch them in plenty of boiling water for 6–8 minutes, then refresh under cold water and reserve.

Slice the white pith from the peeled orange, and cut orange into segments. Put aside.

Squeeze the remaining oranges, strain juice and reserve.

Pan-frying the escalopes
As the escalopes are quite large, use two non-stick frying pans. Divide the butter and oil between them, then heat until a golden colour. Pan-fry the veal escalopes for about 2 minutes on each side. Season with salt and pepper, and reserve them on a flat serving dish. Keep warm.

Preheat the grill.

Making the sauce
Pour off any fat from both pans, then divide the rum between them. Scrape the caramelised juices which have formed at the bottom of the pans with a wooden spoon, and bring the rum to the boil for about 5 seconds. Divide the orange juice between the pans, mix and heat, then pour the contents of both frying pans into a saucepan. Bring to the boil, skim, then reduce by half.

Add the whipping cream, and boil to reduce until you obtain a well-textured sauce. Towards the end add the *julienne* strips of orange peel.

Taste, and adjust seasoning with salt and pepper. Mix into the sauce the juices which have escaped from the veal escalopes. Keep warm.

Serving
Warm the reserved orange segments.

Arrange the escalopes on a large heatproof serving dish, then place under the hot grill for 2 minutes.

Pour the sauce over the escalopes, and garnish the dish with orange segments. Serve to your guests.

Variation
Fillets of pork or pork chops could be substituted for the veal escalopes.

⋐ WINE ⋑

Try a Sauvignon from Australia (Padthaway, North Coonawarra) which has the nose of ripe peaches, but with lemon and orange flavours and a little honey. This wine is not typical of a Sauvignon, but is well made and quite an interesting experience.

Escalope de Veau à l'Orange

Poussins Rôtis aux Parfums d'Estragon

*Baby chickens, simply roasted,
served with tarragon-scented juice*

For four people

Preparation time: 30 minutes

Cooking time: 30 minutes

Planning ahead: Prepare the brown chicken juice well in advance.

2 oven-ready poussins (baby chickens),
about 600g (1lb 6oz) each
1 tablespoon groundnut oil
15g (½oz) unsalted butter
salt and freshly ground pepper

FOR THE SAUCE:
4 tablespoons red wine vinegar
100ml (3½fl oz) dry white wine
200ml (7fl oz) brown chicken stock
(see page 35)
24 tarragon leaves, blanched
for 30 seconds, then chopped
1 teaspoon chopped chervil

Preparing the baby chickens
Remove the wishbones and trim the wings. Under a flame, singe the surface of the skin to remove feather stubs. Tie the legs together.

Preheat the oven to 400°F (200°C) Gas 6.

Cooking the baby chickens
Heat the oil and butter in a small roasting tray, and lightly colour the chickens all over for about 8 minutes (3 minutes on each thigh, 1 minute on each breast side). Season with salt and pepper.

Roast in the preheated oven for about 15 minutes, placing them on their side for the first 7 minutes, and turning them on to the other side for the rest of the cooking.

Remove from the oven and place chickens, breast side down, on to a small tray. Cover with aluminium foil, and then put aside for about 10 minutes in a warm place.

Preparing the sauce
Remove the fat from the chicken roasting tray, then add the vinegar and boil to reduce completely. Add the white wine, and boil to reduce by half.

Add the brown chicken stock, scraping the bottom of the pan, then taste, and season with salt and pepper. Strain into a small saucepan and add the chopped tarragon and chervil. Boil for 2 minutes then skim off any fat. Reserve.

Serving
Remove the strings from the legs, and carve each baby chicken. Cut the four legs off the birds first and divide into thigh and drumstick; cut the breasts off too. Season all the pieces. Place the carved pieces of chicken on to a warm serving dish, and pour the sauce over them. Serve to your guests.

CHEF'S NOTES
The resting time will allow the flesh to 'relax' and the heat to penetrate the meat slowly, without overcooking it.

When reducing the liquid it is important that most of the vinegar evaporates, otherwise the sauce and the dish would be spoiled – the taste too acidic. However, if the sauce *lacks* acidity, *add* a dash of wine vinegar.

The carcasses of the chickens can be used as a base for a delicious soup.

WINE
A smoky Chardonnay would go well. However, personally I would drink a Rully Clos de Bellecroix 1987 from Domaine de la Folie.

Noix d'Agneau de Lait Rôtie aux Olives

Roasted new season lamb chump with black olive juice

Making the juice

Put the wine in a small saucepan and boil to reduce by half. Reserve.

In a roasting pan, sear and colour all the trimmings and bones of the lamb for about 10–15 minutes, stirring from time to time. Spoon out the rendered fat, and add all the remaining ingredients, plus the reduced wine. Bring to the boil, skim and simmer for 20 minutes. Strain and boil to reduce down to 200ml (7fl oz). Taste, and season with salt and pepper.

Preheat the oven to 425°F (220°C) Gas 7.

Cooking the chumps

Sear and colour the chumps all over in the hot olive oil, season with salt and pepper and roast in the preheated oven for 10 minutes. Spoon out the fat and roast for another 5 minutes. Relax the meat in a warm place, loosely covering with aluminium foil.

Serving

Add the juices released from the chumps to the sauce together with the stoned black olives and bring to the boil. Carve slices of lamb from the chumps and arrange on a serving plate. Spoon the olives and juice around. Serve to your guests.

CHEF'S NOTES

Try not to use olives kept in brine; olives kept in Provençal herbs and olive oil are so much better. A delicatessen would be the most likely place to find them.

For more advice on making the juice, please read the section on sauce making on page 38.

For four people

Preparation time: 20 minutes

Cooking time: 30 minutes

Planning ahead: Ask your butcher to bone out the chumps, trim them, remove excess fat but to leave a thin layer. Ask him also, to chop the trimmings and bones into small pieces (900g/2lb).

The juice can be made 1 day in advance.

2 lamb chumps in the piece, boned
2 tablespoons olive oil
salt and freshly ground pepper

FOR THE JUICE:
100ml (3½fl oz) white wine
900g (2lb) chopped lamb bones
and trimmings
4 ripe tomatoes, chopped
1 garlic clove, peeled and crushed
1 medium shallot, peeled and quartered
1 sprig of rosemary
12 caraway seeds
1 litre (1¾pints) cold water

FOR THE GARNISH:
16 black olives,
stoned and halved lengthways

 WINE

A fruity and spicy red wine from Provence or the Rhône Valley would accompany this dish perfectly. You could also choose a red Chianti or a Rioja.

Jarret de Veau Cuit dans sa Coque d'Argile

Shin of veal cooked in a clay pot

This method of cooking must be one of the oldest. It is also attractive. All the ingredients are placed in a clay pot which is sealed, and then the meat is slowly braised. No flavours can escape, so the concentration of taste in the meat will be enhanced.

Preparing the clay pot
The clay pot is extremely porous and needs to be soaked in plenty of water for about 4 hours before cooking. This will ensure perfect cooking of the veal; if the pot was not soaked, the veal juices would filter into the clay and the meat would completely dry out and, even worse, burn.
    Preheat the oven to 260°F (130°C) Gas ½–1.

Preparing the vegetables
Wash, peel and trim the vegetables as appropriate. Quarter the carrot lengthways; cut the parsnip into four or eight pieces; quarter the turnips, and cut the celery into 4cm (1½in) sticks. Cut each leek in half widthways. Mix all the vegetables together and reserve.

Preparing the shin of veal
In a small saucepan, reduce the wine by one-third, then add the water and reserve.
    Place the shin of veal in plenty of cold water in a large pan, and bring to the boil for 2 minutes; this will remove all the impurities. Lift the veal out with a flat slotted spoon, refresh in cold water, and place in the soaked clay pot. Scatter all the vegetables into the pot, pour in the reserved wine and water, and season lightly with salt and pepper.

Sealing the pot and cooking
Using a spatula, mix the flour and water together to make a paste (this is more like masonry than cooking, but such is our fate!). Smear the paste all around the edge of the pot, then place the lid firmly on top. This will ensure that the pot is totally sealed so that no moisture or flavours can escape. Clean up any excess paste around the edge. There is a little hole in the lid which should also be sealed with the paste.
    Slide the pot into the preheated oven and cook for 3 hours.

Serving
Place four warmed soup bowls on the table. Insert the blade of a knife between the lid and the pot, and force the lid off. Replace the lid, put the pot in the middle of the table and open it in front of your guests.
    With a spoon and fork, detach chunks of meat which will come off the bone easily. Serve the chunks of meat with a little of the cooking juices, some of the vegetables, and accompany with some Dijon mustard, sweet Hungarian gherkins and rock salt.

For four people

Preparation time: 15 minutes

Cooking time: 3 hours

Special equipment:
1 large clay pot 30 × 20cm (12 × 8in) (this can be purchased from any large department store).

Planning ahead: Ask your butcher to prepare the shin of veal attractively, cutting off the knuckle end of the bone and scraping the bone clean of skin, etc.
    The clay pot must be prepared at least 4 hours in advance.

1 shin of veal, on the bone
2 medium carrots
1 large parsnip
2 medium turnips
1 celery stalk
2 medium leeks
100ml (3½fl oz) white wine
200ml (7fl oz) water
salt and freshly ground pepper

FOR SEALING THE LID OF THE POT:
30g (1¼oz) plain flour
3 tablespoons water

Jarret de Veau Cuit dans sa Coque d'Argile

CHEF'S NOTES
Season the shin of veal extremely lightly as there are lots of minerals and natural salts within the vegetables. During the long cooking time these will be released.

Variations
The shin of veal can be replaced by shin of beef or a plump chicken; in this case the cooking time should be altered to 2½ hours and 1½ hours respectively.

It would take a courageous person to eat the bone marrow in view of the recent controversy surrounding beef, but I would definitely be first in the queue!

⇨ WINE ⇦
A white wine from Provence or the Rhône will go well, or a light and youthful red wine from the Loire.

149

Ballottine de Foie d'Agneau en Crépine

A whole spring lamb's liver scented with garden herbs Provençale, simply roasted with a delicate juice

For four people

Cooking time: 45 minutes

Planning ahead: Prepare the brown chicken stock (see page 35) well in advance. The pig's caul must be ordered from your butcher well in advance.

---

1 × 600g (1lb 6oz) lamb's liver
in one piece
1 pig's caul, 30cm (12in) square
12–15 rosemary needles
4 sage leaves
leaves from 3 sprigs of thyme
10g (¼oz) parsley leaves
1 garlic clove, peeled
12 white or black peppercorns,
finely crushed
salt and freshly ground pepper
1 tablespoon olive oil
15g (½oz) unsalted butter

FOR THE JUICE:
150ml (5fl oz) brown chicken stock
(see page 35)
25g (1oz) unsalted butter
1 tablespoon finely chopped parsley

FOR THE GARNISH:
100g (4oz) smoked streaky bacon,
rind removed, cut into lardons
(see page 28)
24 pickling onions, peeled
15g (½oz) unsalted butter
a large pinch of sugar

This dish is particularly delicious when the new season lamb's liver is used.

Preparing the liver
Remove the main nerve from the liver, or ask your butcher to do it for you.

Unfold the pig's caul on your work surface. Chop and mix the herbs and garlic, and sprinkle over the caul, along with the crushed peppercorns. Place the liver in the middle of the caul, season with salt and pepper and wrap it tightly in a cylindrical shape. Tie the liver with four turns of string. Reserve.

Preparing the garnish
Place the lardons in cold water in a saucepan and bring them to simmering point. Cook for 3–4 minutes, then refresh under cold water. Drain and reserve.

Place the pickling onions in a casserole with the butter, a pinch of salt and the sugar, and cook on a low heat, covered, for 15 minutes until the onions are beautifully brown and cooked through. Reserve.

Preheat the oven to 400°F (200°C) Gas 6.

Cooking the liver
In a small roasting tin, sear and colour the liver lightly in the oil and butter for 2–3 minutes, turning it over so it is seared on all sides. Then roast in the oven for 10 minutes.

Spoon the fat out of the pan and cover the liver with aluminium foil. Rest the liver for 10–15 minutes in a warm place.

Making the juice
In a small saucepan bring the brown chicken stock to the boil. In another saucepan, heat the butter until it is foaming and has a light hazelnut colour. Whisk the butter into the chicken stock and, finally, add the chopped parsley. Taste and correct seasoning with salt and pepper.

Serving
Remove the string from the lamb's liver. Carve slices, season with salt and pepper, and arrange them in the middle of warm plates or dishes.

Heat the lardons and onions together and scatter them around the slices. Serve to your guests, handing the juice separately.

CHEF'S NOTES
Pig's caul is the treated lining of the pig's stomach. You can wrap various meats in it for roasting. It will partly melt during the cooking, therefore it does not need to be removed.

Ballottine de Foie d'Agneau en Crépine

Do not be tempted to cook the liver for too long. It will become too well done and very tough.

Variation
Young pig's liver and calf's liver can be cooked in the same way. Adjust cooking times accordingly.

 WINE

A fruity wine from the Loire – Bourgueil or Chinon – would be superb.

For four people

Preparation and cooking time: 1 hour

Planning ahead: Ask your butcher to cut the bird into eight pieces plus the two wings, off the backbones, and also to remove the wish bones. You will also need 300g (11oz) chicken bones, finely chopped, for the stock.

The stock can be prepared 1 day in advance, and the fricassee, half an hour before the meal (it should be kept warm).

1 roasting chicken,
about 1.4kg (3lb) in weight,
cut into 10 pieces,
including the 2 wings
15g (½oz) unsalted butter
1 tablespoon corn oil
salt and freshly ground pepper
50ml (2fl oz) white wine vinegar

FOR THE STOCK:
chopped back bones from the chicken
plus 300g (11oz) of other chicken bones
10g (¼oz) unsalted butter
1 tablespoon corn oil
½ small onion, peeled and chopped
1 garlic clove, peeled and crushed
120ml (4fl oz) dry white wine
4 ripe medium tomatoes, chopped,
leaving the seeds in
1 teaspoon tomato purée
1 sprig of thyme
2 sprigs of tarragon

FOR THE SAUCE:
1 teaspoon Dijon mustard
1 tablespoon whipping cream
40g (1½oz) cold unsalted butter, diced
1 level tablespoon chopped tarragon
1 level tablespoon very finely
chopped chives

WINE

An Australian Chardonnay with the acidity of citrus fruit and an oaky, smoky taste, could be favourable, or why not a Sémillon dry wine from the Barossa Valley.

Fricassée de Volaille au Vinaigre et Estragon

Chicken fricassee with vinegar and tarragon

Preparing the stock

In a large saucepan, sear and lightly colour the chopped chicken bones in the butter and oil for 10 minutes. Add the chopped onion and garlic and sweat for a further 2–3 minutes. Add the white wine and boil to reduce by one-third. Add the chopped tomato and the tomato purée, thyme and tarragon, and cover with water. Bring to the boil, skim and simmer the stock for 20 minutes. Pass through a fine sieve, pressing down with the back of a spoon to extract as much liquid as possible. Cool and then refrigerate. You should have about 200ml (7fl oz).

Preheat the oven to 400°F (200°C) Gas 6.

Cooking the fricassee

In a large cast-iron casserole, heat the butter and oil, and sear the chicken pieces skin side down, turning them over after 2 minutes. Season with salt and pepper, cover and place in the preheated oven for 25 minutes, leaving the lid slightly ajar. Remove from the oven.

Turn the oven down to 325°F (160°C) Gas 3.

Place the casserole on the top of the cooker and spoon out as much fat as possible. Add the vinegar, bring to the boil, and reduce the vinegar until it has totally evaporated. Turn the chicken pieces as you boil, until they are nicely coloured.

Arrange the chicken pieces on a flat serving dish and keep warm in the low oven.

Making the sauce

Add the mustard to the casserole and gradually whisk in the 200ml (7fl oz) stock, scraping the caramelised juices off the bottom. Strain into a saucepan, then add the cream. Whisk in the cold diced butter, then finally add the tarragon and chives.

Serving

Remove the chicken pieces from the oven, pour the sauce over them, and serve to your guests.

CHEF'S NOTES

The best way to remove the fat is to refrigerate the stock; the fat will solidify on the top, and then it is easy to remove. This fat can be kept and used for pastry or roasting.

Fricassée de Volaille au Vinaigre et Estragon

Carré d'Agneau Provençale

Best end of spring lamb coated with a herb-scented crust

Although it's said that spring lamb is the best, this recipe can also be done in the summer or early autumn. I find that summer lamb is the best (around 6 months old), when it has a powerful yet subtle flavour. This main-course dinner-party dish with its Provençal overtones will bring the sunshine to your table.

Preheat the oven to 450°F (230°C) Gas 8.

Preparing the juice
In a roasting tray, sear and colour the chopped bones in hot olive oil for about 6–8 minutes. Add the chopped onion, garlic, rosemary and thyme, and roast in the oven for another 20 minutes.

Place the bones and vegetables in a casserole and reserve. Add the white wine to the tray and boil to reduce by two-thirds. Add the tomato purée and water. Scrape the bottom of the tray to remove any caramelised bits, and pour this liquid into the casserole with the reserved bones. Bring to the boil, skim, and simmer for about 15 minutes.

Strain through a fine sieve and reduce at full boil until you obtain about 150ml (5fl oz). Taste, season with salt and pepper and reserve.

Preparing the lamb coating
Mix all the ingredients together thoroughly. Season with salt and pepper. Turn the temperature of the oven down to 425°F (220°C) Gas 7.

Cooking the lamb
Heat the olive oil in a sauté pan on top of the stove, and sear the meat on the meat side for 1 minute until lightly coloured, then sear on the fat side for another 3 minutes. Lift the lamb on to the four reserved lamb bones and roast in the preheated oven for about 10 minutes.

Remove and season with salt and pepper. Spread mustard all over the meat (not on the bones), then press the meat only in the breadcrumb mixture, so that it is completely covered. Roast again in the oven for another 12–15 minutes. Remove the lamb, reserve and rest on a warm plate, loosely covered with foil, for 2–3 minutes.

Serving
Place the lamb on a chopping board or dish and carve in front of your guests. Garnish as you please (see Chef's Notes), and serve the juice separately.

CHEF'S NOTES
Ask your butcher to give you lamb that has been well hung for at least 10 days for the best flavour and maximum tenderness. (See the introduction to this chapter.)

A beautiful bouquet of watercress could be nicely arranged on a tray, and a Provençal theme followed for vegetables, with such as Pommes Boulangères (see page 116), Ratatouille (see page 198) or French beans.

For four people

Preparation time: 15 minutes

Cooking time: 30 minutes

Planning ahead: The juice and the breadcrumbs can be prepared the day before. Ask your butcher to trim the lamb (French trim), and remove the chine bones and end of ribs. He should cut the fat off the upright rib bones as well. (If he will not, I suggest you change your butcher.) Ask him to keep the bones, and to chop all but four of them up finely.

2 best ends of spring lamb,
about 8 ribs, perfectly trimmed (see above)
2 tablespoons olive oil
salt and freshly ground pepper
4 lamb bones
(to use as a stand for the meat)
1 tablespoon Dijon mustard

FOR THE JUICE:
300g (11oz) reserved lamb bones,
chopped into small pieces
2 tablespoons olive oil
¼ onion, peeled and chopped
1 garlic clove, unpeeled
1 tiny sprig of rosemary
1 sprig of thyme
100ml (3½fl oz) dry white wine
1 teaspoon tomato purée
400ml (14fl oz) water

FOR THE LAMB COATING:
100g (4oz) dried breadcrumbs
2 tablespoons chopped parsley
1 teaspoon chopped dried thyme
a few needles of dried
rosemary, chopped

WINE

A fragrant Provençal red wine would be ideal such as Domaine de la Bernarde, or a young and lightly chilled Bandol *rouge*.

Carré d'Agneau Provençale

Tomates Farcies Façon Maman Blanc

Stuffed tomatoes with minced meat sauce

If you really want to surprise your guests, then serve this dish at a dinner party, as this hearty wholesome food will please even the most sophisticated of palates.

The dish will be all the more delicious if you can get hold of those big ripe Marmande tomatoes.

Preparing the filling
Roughly chop the cold cooked meat, then mince it, using the medium blade of a mincer. Add the sausagemeat, parsley, coriander (if using), garlic and egg. Season with salt and pepper. Mix with a wooden spoon, then taste and correct seasoning. Reserve.

Preparing the beef tomatoes
Slice the tops of the tomatoes off two-thirds up, and scoop out the flesh and seeds. (Reserve these for the tomato sauce.)

Making the tomato sauce
Sweat the chopped onion and garlic for 2–3 minutes in the olive oil, then add the chopped tomatoes, the flesh and seeds from the beef tomatoes, and all the remaining ingredients. Cover and simmer gently for half an hour.

Pass the tomato pulp through a mouli, or purée in a blender and sieve. Taste and correct seasoning with salt and pepper. Reserve.

Preheat the oven to 350°F (180°C) Gas 4.

Filling and cooking the tomatoes
Season the inside of the beef tomatoes then fill right up to the top with the minced meat mixture. Cover with the lid of the tomatoes (and reserve, if not cooking straightaway).

Grease the inside of the dish with 1 teaspoon of the butter, and pour in enough tomato sauce to come one-third up the height of the dish. Arrange the tomatoes in the dish and dab a quarter of the remaining butter on each. Bake in the preheated oven for approximately 30 minutes.

Serving
Reheat the remaining tomato sauce and serve separately.

Variations
This dish can also be cooked using onions. In this case, cook the whole peeled onion first in chicken stock for at least 20 minutes; cool and remove the middle, leaving a 'case', then proceed as above.

For four people

Preparation time: 15 minutes

Cooking time: 30 minutes

Special equipment:
1 Pyrex dish, 28cm (11in) long, 23cm (9in) wide and 7cm (2¾in) deep, or a similarly sized cast-iron casserole.

Planning ahead: The tomatoes can be stuffed well in advance, and the sauce can also be prepared in advance.

4 large ripe beef tomatoes
salt and freshly ground pepper
25g (1oz) unsalted butter

FOR THE FILLING:
300g (11oz) meat taken from a cooked joint (beef, lamb, or pork, the latter being the best)
100g (4oz) raw sausagemeat
2 tablespoons chopped fresh parsley
1 teaspoon chopped fresh coriander (optional)
1 garlic clove, peeled and puréed
1 whole egg

FOR THE TOMATO SAUCE:
½ onion, peeled and finely chopped
2 garlic cloves, peeled and chopped
2 tablespoons olive oil
12 medium ripe tomatoes, chopped (seeds in)
flesh and seeds scooped from the beef tomatoes
2 tablespoons tomato purée
1 bay leaf
1 sprig each of thyme and tarragon

WINE

A little Chianti or red Bandol from Provence will enhance this simple, earthy dish.

Tomates Farcies Façon Maman Blanc

Gigot d'Agneau Rôti aux Parfums d'Herbes

Roast leg of milk-fed lamb scented with herbs

For six people

Preparation and cooking time: 1½ hours

Planning ahead: Ask your butcher well in advance to remove the aitch (hip) bone and the knuckle end of the leg; the thigh bone should also be left cleanly exposed. Keep these bones.

1 leg of spring lamb, 2–2.25kg (4½–5lb) net weight when prepared (with excess fat trimmed and bones removed as above)
50ml (2fl oz) olive oil
600g (1lb 6oz) lamb bones, chopped into small pieces
1 small onion, peeled and chopped roughly into 1cm (½in) dice
1 large carrot, peeled and similarly chopped
2 whole garlic cloves, unpeeled
3 sprigs of thyme
1 beef tomato, cut into 6
500ml (18fl oz) water
1 sprig of rosemary (about 20 needles), finely chopped
leaves from 1 sprig of marjoram, finely chopped (optional)
salt and freshly ground pepper

This dish illustrates the success and magic of a simple 'roast' and instead of reaching out for those bottled sauces, granules and stock cubes, make an aromatic juice from the caramelised juices simply with water!

Preheat the oven to 400°F (200°C) Gas 6.

Roasting the lamb
Heat the olive oil in a 30 × 40cm (12 × 16in) roasting tray on the top of the stove, and sear the lamb bones for approximately 5–8 minutes until lightly coloured. Add the chopped onion and carrot, garlic and thyme.

Place the leg of lamb on top of the bones and vegetables, and roast in the oven for about 40 minutes, basting occasionally.

Remove the tray from the oven, tip it slightly and spoon out all the fat. Add the chopped tomato and the water to the tray.

Turn the oven down to 350°F (180°C) Gas 4.

Sprinkle the finely chopped rosemary and marjoram (if used) over the joint, season with salt and pepper, and roast for another 50 minutes, basting from time to time.

Finishing the juice
Remove the tray from the oven and place the leg of lamb on to another tray. Cover with aluminium foil and leave to rest for 20 minutes. Leave the oven on.

Scrape the bottom of the roasting tray with a spoon to release any caramelised bits, and strain into a small saucepan. You should have about 250ml (8fl oz) of juice. Spoon out any fat, then taste and season with salt and pepper. Reserve.

Finishing the dish and serving
Unwrap the leg of lamb and mix the juices that the lamb has released into the prepared juice. Reheat the leg of lamb in the hot oven for about 10 minutes.

Present the leg of lamb on a carving board if you feel courageous and confident enough to carve it in front of your guests, or carve it, more humbly, in the privacy of your kitchen.

Serve the heated juice separately, and accompany with a ratatouille (see page 198) and pommes boulangère (see page 116).

CHEF'S NOTES
Turn to page 140 for advice on how to choose and buy best-quality meat. See also the advice on roasting.

Do not season the meat before roasting as the fat will melt, run off the meat and carry away the salt. Season the meat half-way through

Gigot d'Agneau Rôti aux Parfums d'Herbes

the cooking time, and also after slicing, since the salt will not permeate the meat throughout.

Baste the joint with the cooking fat several times so that the joint will not dry out (especially one not covered with fat), and will have a nice appearance.

The idea is not to obtain a thick sauce, but a light, very lively and tasty juice. At this stage, according to how much juice has evaporated, you may need to add a little more water.

Variations
The taste of the juice could be enhanced with diced black olives, lemon juice, or a little chopped thyme or basil.

Following this principle, any roast can be cooked in the same way – pork, veal or beef. Simply change the aromatic herbs.

 WINE

A well-matured Bordeaux wine from Pauillac or a Coteaux des Baux will be the best partners for this dish.

159

Cailles Rôties au Vin 'Cherry Brandy' et Ecorces de Pamplemousse Rose

Roasted quails served with a cherry-brandy sauce flavoured with pink grapefruit peel

For four people

Preparation time: 20 minutes

Cooking time: 1 hour

Planning ahead: Order the quail from your butcher well in advance and be sure to ask for the very best and freshest possible.

The garnish and the brown chicken stock can be made in advance.

8 fresh quails, gutted
½ tablespoon olive oil
10g (¼oz) unsalted butter
salt and freshly ground pepper

FOR THE GRAPEFRUIT GARNISH:
1 pink grapefruit
1 litre (1¾pints) water
60g (2¼oz) caster sugar

FOR THE SAUCE:
2 tablepoons red wine vinegar
200ml (7fl oz) red wine (Rhône)
100ml (3½fl oz) cherry brandy
2 strips of grapefruit peel
grapefruit juice
200ml (7fl oz) brown chicken stock (see page 35)
1 tablespoon whipping cream

Preparing the grapefruit garnish

With a sharp knife, slice off the top and bottom of the grapefruit, then the skin, including the pith, all around. Cut the peel into 16 sticks of 5cm (2in) long and 5mm (¼in) thick. (Reserve two larger strips for the sauce.) Simmer the peel sticks for 20 minutes in plenty of water then drain.

Working over a bowl, slice into the peeled grapefruit between the segments, cutting off the membranes. Divide into eight segments and reserve in the bowl. Pour the juice into another bowl and squeeze what's left of the grapefruit to extract all the juices. Taste the segments and, if too bitter, add a small amount of extra sugar.

In a small saucepan, mix together the measured water and caster sugar, and cook over a low heat for 3 minutes. Add the blanched grapefruit peel sticks, and candy for 15 minutes at a gentle simmer.

Preparing the sauce base

In a saucepan boil the red wine vinegar until there is 1 teaspoon left. Pour in the red wine and cherry brandy, add the two strips of grapefruit peel, and boil to reduce by half. Add the reserved strained grapefruit juice, the brown chicken stock and whipping cream, and bring to the boil for 3 minutes. Skim and reserve.

Preheat the oven to 400°F (200°C) Gas 6.

Cooking the quails

Heat the oil and butter together in a roasting tin and brown the quails all over for 3 minutes. Season and roast in the preheated oven for 7–8 minutes.

Remove from the oven, spoon out the fat and leave to rest for 5 minutes. Carve the breasts and legs. Cover with aluminium foil and keep in a warm place.

Finishing the sauce

Chop the carcasses, add them to the sauce base, and simmer for 3–5 minutes. Strain, taste and correct seasoning. Keep warm.

Serving

Arrange the quail breasts and legs in a warm dish and reheat in the oven for approximately 5 minutes.

Reheat the grapefruit peel sticks and segments and arrange around the quail. Pour the sauce over and serve to your guests.

⇒ WINE ⇐

A wine from the Pomerol would make this dish.

Suprêmes de Volaille au Vinaigre et Coulis de Légumes

Chicken supreme served with vinegar and vegetable coulis

Preparing and cooking the *julienne*

Halve the red pepper, remove seeds and cut off the stalk and the ends. Trim the inside and cut in half, across the width. Slice very fine *julienne* sticks lengthways.

Reserve and chop 40g (1½oz) of the pepper trimmings for the sauce.

Sweat the pepper sticks in the butter, add the vinegar, paprika and some salt, cover with a lid, and cook for 3 minutes. Reserve.

Preheat the oven to 450°F (230°C) Gas 8.

Preparing the vegetable sauce

In a small casserole, boil to reduce the vinegar completely, then add the white wine. Boil to reduce by half.

Separately, over a gentle heat sweat the onion and the pepper trimmings in butter for 5 minutes. Add the courgette, tomato, garlic and *bouquet garni*. Cook for a further 3 minutes. Add the reduced vinegar and white wine and chicken stock or water, and simmer for 10 minutes. Add the paprika and allow to cool.

Remove the *bouquet garni* and liquidise the sauce until you have a very fine purée. Force through a fine sieve, then taste and season with salt and pepper. Reserve.

Cooking the chicken

Brush the chicken breasts with a film of mustard. Season with salt, pepper and paprika. Heat the butter over a medium heat in a large sauté pan until it is hazelnut brown in colour. Pan-fry the chicken breasts, without browning, for 3 minutes on each side. Then cook in the preheated oven for 5 minutes.

Serving

Reheat the garnish and the sauce. Place the four breasts of chicken on to a serving dish and spoon the sauce over them. Scatter with the red pepper *julienne* sticks.

CHEF'S NOTES

This sauce does not contain either butter or cream, and is bound together with vegetables which are liquidised. This provides homogeneity to the sauce.

For four people

Preparation time: 20 minutes

Cooking time: 1 hour

Planning ahead: The sauce and the *julienne* of peppers can be prepared in advance.

*4 breasts of chicken
skin and bone removed
10g (¼oz) mustard
salt and freshly ground pepper
2 large pinches of paprika
20g (¾oz) unsalted butter*

FOR THE RED PEPPER *JULIENNE*:
*1 red pepper
5g (⅛oz) unsalted butter
1 teaspoon white wine vinegar
1 pinch of paprika*

FOR THE VEGETABLE SAUCE:
*2 tablespoons white wine vinegar
100ml (3½fl oz) white wine
70g (2¾oz) onions,
peeled and finely chopped
40g (1½oz) red pepper trimmings,
chopped, reserved from the julienne
20g (¾oz) unsalted butter
50g (2oz) courgettes,
trimmed and chopped
1 medium tomato, seeded and chopped
½ garlic clove, peeled and chopped
1 bouquet garni (see page 30)
250ml (8fl oz) light chicken stock
(see page 34) or water
1 large pinch of paprika*

 WINE

A smoky white Burgundy – scented with vanilla and oak – from the Côtes de Beaune.

For four people

Preparation and cooking time: 30 minutes

4 medallions of milk-fed veal, trimmed, each weighing 150g (5oz)
1 teaspoon butter
1 teaspoon groundnut oil
salt and freshly ground pepper
1 tablespoon Calvados (optional)
50ml (2fl oz) white wine
200ml (7fl oz) dry cider
200ml (7fl oz) double cream

FOR THE GARNISH:
2 Granny Smith apples
1 teaspoon butter
1 teaspoon caster sugar

 *WINE*

The easiest choice will be a bottle of good dry farm cider. Or an Arbois white wine made with 100 per cent Sauvignon grapes (Puffenay 1986) which has the scents of apple and cider. The originality of this wine will be a marvellous partner to this original dish.

Médaillons de Veau au Cidre et Pommes

Pan-fried veal medallions served with a cider sauce and caramelised apples

Preheat the oven to 400°F (200°C) Gas 6.

Preparing and cooking the garnish
Peel and quarter the apples, remove the cores, and slice each quarter into three (12 slices per apple).

Heat the butter in a non-stick pan. Lay the apple slices in the pan, sprinkle with sugar and cook and brown lightly for 3 minutes on each side over a medium heat until both sides are coloured. Reserve and keep warm.

Cooking the veal and sauce
Heat the butter and oil in an ovenproof sauté pan until very hot and colour both sides of the fillets for about 3 minutes each. Season with salt and pepper.

Cook in the preheated oven for 7–8 minutes.

Remove the pan from the oven and discard any fat. Reserve the medallions loosely covered with aluminium foil on a plate, keeping them warm.

Add the Calvados to the sauté pan and bring to the boil. Add the white wine and boil to reduce by half. Add the cider and reduce again by half. Stir in the cream and boil for 4–5 minutes until it has thickened. Taste, and correct seasoning with salt and pepper.

Serving
Warm four plates. Reheat the medallions and apples briefly in the oven, then arrange the apple slices, overlapping in a circle, on each plate. Place the veal medallions in the centre of each plate.

Add the juices that the veal has released to the sauce, bring this back to the boil, and spoon over each fillet. Serve to your guests.

CHEF'S NOTES
Granny Smith apples are the best, as they have a good consistency and are lightly acidulated.

Variations
You can replace the veal with fillet of pork, in which case increase the oven cooking time by 4 minutes.

Suprêmes de Pigeon Sauvage Poêlé aux Myrtilles

Pan-fried breasts of wood pigeon,
served with red wine sauce and blueberries

Marinating the pigeon breasts
Mix the ingredients for the marinade together. Turn the breasts of pigeon over in the marinade. Cover with cling film and refrigerate for 24 hours.

Making the sauce
In a large casserole, brown the pigeon carcasses in very hot oil for about 5–6 minutes. Add the diced vegetables and continue to brown for a further 4 minutes. Remove from the heat, spoon out any fat, sprinkle with the flour and stir. Add the port and red wine and top up with water until the pigeon carcasses are completely covered.

Bring to the boil, skim off any impurities, and add the thyme and juniper berry. Simmer for half an hour, then strain and boil to reduce down until the sauce has reached the right consistency (about 200ml/7fl oz in volume). Taste, season with salt and pepper and add the redcurrant jelly, then reserve.

Cooking the blueberry garnish
In a small saucepan mix together the blueberries, sugar and water. Cook over a gentle heat for 3–4 minutes. Reserve and keep warm.

Preheat the oven to 375°F (190°C) Gas 5.

Cooking the pigeon breasts
Heat the oil and butter in a frying pan until very hot. Pat dry, sear and brown the pigeon breasts for 30 seconds on each side. Pat dry, season with salt and pepper and cook in the preheated oven for a further 3 minutes.

Remove the breasts from the oven and rest in a warm place for 2–3 minutes, loosely covered with aluminium foil.

Serving
Reheat the sauce. Warm a large serving dish. Remove the skin from the breasts and put aside. Place the breasts on the serving dish, pour over the sauce and scatter the warm blueberries around. Serve to your guests.

CHEF'S NOTES
The legs of the pigeons are not eaten as they would be far too tough.

According to which wine you are using for the sauce, the acidity may differ.

Pigeons are wild, and will be very lean and muscly. They should not be cooked to more than medium, or the meat will be very tough.

The pigeon skin could be chopped very finely, cooked under a grill and added to the dish itself or to a salad if you so wished.

For four people

Preparation time: 2 hours

Marinating time: 1 day

Cooking time: 40 minutes

Planning ahead: Order the wood pigeons well in advance from your butcher, and ask that they be hung for 6–7 days. Also, ask your butcher to remove the breasts and chop the whole carcasses; the latter will be used in the sauce.

The pigeon breasts should be marinated 1 day in advance. The sauce can also be prepared a day in advance.

4 wood pigeons, breasts removed
1 tablespoon groundnut oil
15g (½oz) unsalted butter
salt and freshly ground pepper

FOR THE MARINADE:
2 tablespoons red wine
1 sprig of thyme
½ bay leaf
½ garlic clove, peeled
1 tablespoon groundnut oil

FOR THE SAUCE:
chopped pigeon carcasses
4 tablespoons groundnut oil
¼ medium onion, peeled and diced
1 medium carrot, peeled and diced
¼ celery stalk, diced
1 tablespoon plain flour
100ml (3½fl oz) port
300ml (10fl oz) full-bodied red wine
1 sprig of thyme
1 juniper berry
1 teaspoon redcurrant jelly

FOR THE GARNISH:
80g (3¼oz) blueberries
1 teaspoon sugar
1 tablespoon water

 WINE

For the lover of claret, a good Pomerol is my advice. You can, as well, find a favourable Spanish Cabernet Sauvignon with odours of red fruit.

Boeuf Braisé au Fumet de Vin Rouge

Casserole of beef in red wine

The earthy flavours of a casserole dish, simple and delicious.

Preheat the oven to 275°F (140°C) Gas 1.

Cooking the dish

In a saucepan, boil the vinegar to reduce it completely, then add the red wine. Reduce to 250ml (8fl oz), add the water and reserve.

Separately, heat the oil in the casserole and colour the diced beef over a strong heat for 8–10 minutes. Add the button mushrooms, onions or shallots and cook for a further 2–3 minutes. Sprinkle over the flour, stir and cook for a further minute. Add the reduced wine, the *bouquet garni*, crushed peppercorns (or pepper), tomatoes and garlic.

Cover and cook in the preheated oven for 2½ hours.

Serving the dish

Remove the dish from the oven, taste, correct the seasoning with salt and pepper, and serve to your guests.

Variations

Wild rice or potato purée are extremely good accompaniments for this dish (see pages 208 and 209).

You could also add 15 caraway or coriander seeds for a different flavour.

For four people

Preparation and cooking time: 2 hours, 50 minutes

Special equipment:
A 23cm (9in) cast-iron casserole with lid.

Planning ahead: The dish can be prepared a day in advance, refrigerated and reheated at the last moment.

800g (1¾lb) chuck steak, diced into 4cm (1½in) cubes
25ml (1fl oz) red wine vinegar
600ml (1pint) full-bodied red wine (Rhône or Rioja)
150ml (5fl oz) water
2 tablespoons groundnut or other non-scented oil (see page 17)
100g (4oz) white button mushrooms, washed and patted dry
20 pickling onions or shallots, peeled
1 dessertspoon plain flour
1 bouquet garni (see page 30)
5 black peppercorns, crushed, or 3 pinches freshly ground black pepper
300g (11oz) Roma or beef tomatoes, skinned, quartered and seeded
4 garlic cloves, peeled and halved
salt

❧ WINE ☙

A full-bodied Claret, a Rhône red or a Californian Cabernet Sauvignon would be the solution here. You can also find in supermarkets some very good Romanian Cabernet Sauvignon, often very reasonably priced.

Coq au Vin

Chicken braised in red wine

Rediscover the wholesome taste of this classical regional dish.

Marinating the chicken
Place the chicken pieces and all the marinade ingredients (except for the red wine) together in a large bowl. In a saucepan, bring the wine to the boil, then skim and leave to cool down. Pour the wine over the chicken pieces and vegetables, cover with cling film, and refrigerate for 24 hours.

Preheat the oven to 350°F (180°C) Gas 4.

Cooking the chicken and making the sauce
Strain the chicken marinade through a colander into a large bowl. Pat the chicken pieces dry and reserve. Place the marinade vegetables plus the peppercorns, etc., into another bowl and reserve.

Sear the chicken pieces in the very hot oil (or clarified butter) for 10 minutes in a casserole dish or sauté pan until they are lightly browned. Season with salt and pepper. Place the chicken pieces on to a plate and spoon the oil out of the casserole.

In the same casserole, melt the *roux* butter, stir in the flour and cook gently, stirring frequently for 5 minutes until the mixture turns golden brown. Turn up the heat and gradually add the red wine marinade to the *roux*, whisking continuously to prevent any lumps forming as it thickens. When all the wine has been added, bring to the boil and skim. Season with salt, add all the marinade vegetables and other ingredients, plus the chicken pieces. Cover with a lid and cook in the preheated oven for 30 minutes.

Cooking the garnish
Pan-fry the mushrooms and lardons in hot butter for 2 minutes. Taste, then season with salt and pepper.

Serving
Arrange the chicken pieces and sauce on a hot serving dish and scatter the vegetables, mushrooms and lardons around. Serve to your guests.

Variations
The sauce could also be flavoured with tarragon, coriander and fine *julienne* strips of blanched orange zest.

Noodles, wild rice or any root vegetable would be a good accompaniment for this dish.

For four people

Preparation time: 20 minutes

Marinating time: 24 hours

Cooking time: 40 minutes

Planning ahead: Ask your butcher to chop the chicken for you. The dish can be prepared and cooked in advance.

*1 × 1.8kg (4lb) chicken,
cut into 10 pieces (2 winglets,
2 breasts cut into 4, 2 thighs, 2 legs)
4 tablespoons cooking oil
(or clarified butter, see page 30)
salt and freshly ground pepper*

FOR THE MARINADE:
*1 small onion, peeled and cut in half,
each half studded with a clove
20 black peppercorns, crushed
4 garlic cloves, peeled and crushed
20g (¾oz) smoked streaky bacon
24 shallots or small onions, peeled
2 carrots, peeled and quartered
2 celery stalks,
trimmed and each cut into 3
750ml (1¼pints) full-bodied red wine*

FOR THE SAUCE *ROUX*:
*25g (1oz) unsalted butter
25g (1oz) plain flour*

FOR THE GARNISHES:
*150g (5oz) button mushrooms,
washed and patted dry
lardons made from 100g (4oz) smoked
streaky bacon, blanched and refreshed
(see page 28)
10g (¼oz) unsalted butter*

 WINE

A light red wine, not too woody, will be fine. Why not a Beaujolais or a good table wine?

Pintadeau Rôti aux Lentilles

*Roasted guinea fowl, served on a bed of
lentils,* lardons *and baby onions*

For four people

Preparation time: 30 minutes

Cooking time: 1 hour, 10 minutes

Planning ahead: The guinea fowl and
the juice can be prepared half a day in
advance; the garnishes can be cooked
then too. The guinea fowl can be
cooked a few hours in advance.

*2 guinea fowl, each weighing
about 700g (1½lb)
salt and freshly ground pepper
1 tablespoon olive oil
15g (½oz) unsalted butter*

FOR THE JUICE:
*chopped winglets from the guinea fowl
1 tablespoon olive oil
1 teaspoon unsalted butter
200ml (7fl oz) brown
chicken stock (see page 35)
100–200ml (3½–7fl oz) water
1 sprig of thyme
½ bay leaf*

FOR THE GARNISHES:
*200g (7oz) lentils, picked,
soaked for 2 hours and drained
100g (4oz) smoked streaky bacon,
rinded and chopped
2 sprigs of thyme
½ bay leaf
1 garlic clove, peeled and crushed
24 small pickling onions, peeled
20g (¾oz) unsalted butter
a pinch of sugar
lardons cut from 100g (4oz) smoked
streaky bacon, blanched and refreshed
(see page 28)*

It is well worth looking for free-range guinea fowl, if possible hung
for about a week. If you succeed, you will certainly have a memorable
meal. I find guinea fowl tastes so much more interesting than chicken.

Preheat the oven to 450°F (230°C) Gas 8.

Preparing the guinea fowl
Remove the wishbones and winglets and reserve these for the juice.
Singe the guinea fowl over a flame to remove the feather stubs, then
truss them.

Preparing the juice
Sear and colour the chopped winglets in hot oil and butter for about
5 minutes. Add the brown chicken stock and pour in enough of the
water to cover. Add the thyme and bay leaf, bring to the boil, skim
and simmer for 30 minutes. Strain, taste, and adjust seasoning. Reserve.

Cooking the garnishes
Lentils Place in a small saucepan, together with the bacon, thyme, bay
leaf and crushed garlic. Barely cover with water, season with salt and
pepper, then simmer for about 20 minutes. Drain off the cooking juices
in a sieve, then taste lentils and adjust seasoning.
Onions In a sauté pan, brown the onions in butter and cook over a
gentle heat for 20 minutes. Season with salt, pepper and a pinch of sugar.

Cooking the guinea fowl
In a roasting pan, sear and lightly brown the guinea fowl in the oil
and butter for about 4 minutes on each thigh side and 2 minutes on
each breast. Season with salt and pepper, turn them on to their backs,
and cook in the preheated oven for 25 minutes.

Remove from the oven, spoon off the fat, cover with aluminium
foil and reserve.

Serving
Carve the guinea fowl, removing legs, thighs and breasts. Season inside
the breasts, place the pieces in a roasting tray and reheat for 5–10
minutes.

Mix the *lardons* and onions together and reheat them and the lentils
separately. Arrange the lentils in the middle of a serving dish, scatter the
onions and *lardons* around and place the cut guinea fowl pieces on the
top. Reheat the juice and serve in a sauce boat. Serve to your guests. Or
you can present the whole bird with its garnishes, as in the photograph.

Pintadeau Rôti aux Lentilles

CHEF'S NOTES

According to the variety of lentil you use, they may take a little longer to cook. Traditionally, lentils are soaked for 12–24 hours, but I find this process to be very detrimental to both flavour and texture. (Imagine those poor little pulses drowning and gasping in chlorinated water for that length of time!)

Do not throw away the carcasses of the guinea fowl, as they can be chopped and infused in the sauce to improve its flavour. You can also make delicious clear soup with them.

⇨ WINE ⇦

A red Pinot Noir from the Côte Chalonnaise (Rully or Mercurey) would be perfect.

Filets de Lièvre Rôtis au Lard

Fillets of hare, wrapped in bacon and roasted, served with red wine and juniper sauce

For four people

Preparation time: 10 minutes

Marinating time: 6 hours

Cooking time: 40 minutes

Planning ahead: Order the saddles of hare well in advance from your butcher and ask him to bone them, trim the fillets perfectly and to chop the bones finely.

The sauce can be prepared well in advance of the meal.

4 fillets of hare, prepared
(from 2 saddles of 900g/2lb each)
salt and freshly ground pepper
6 finely sliced smoked bacon
rashers, rinded
1 tablespoon cooking oil or dripping

FOR THE MARINADE:
100ml (3½fl oz) full-bodied red wine
50ml (2fl oz) port
2 tablespoons Cognac
1 sprig of thyme
1 bay leaf

FOR THE SAUCE:
chopped bones from the hare
50ml (2 fl oz) groundnut oil
¼ medium onion, peeled and diced
1 celery stalk, trimmed and diced
1 small carrot, peeled and diced
20g (¾oz) plain flour
70ml (2¾fl oz) red wine vinegar
400ml (14fl oz) full-bodied red wine
2 juniper berries
100g (4 oz) button mushrooms,
washed, patted dry and chopped
1 teaspoon redcurrant jelly
4 tablespoons whipping cream

Marinating the fillets of hare
Simply mix all the ingredients for the marinade in a small tray. Lay the fillets in the tray, turn them over in the marinade, then cover with cling film and marinate for 4–6 hours in the refrigerator.

Preparing the fillets of hare
Flatten the bacon rashers with a cleaver in order to minimise shrinkage. Reserve.

Remove the hare fillets from the marinade, pat dry and season with salt and pepper. Place three bacon rashers on a board, overlapping each other by about 1cm (½in), and tightly enclose two of the fillets in them. Secure with string around and knot tightly at 2cm (¾in) intervals. Repeat for the remaining fillets. Reserve in the refrigerator.

Preheat the oven to 450°F (230°C) Gas 8.

Making the sauce
In a roasting tray, lightly brown the chopped bones in hot oil for 3–4 minutes, add the diced vegetables, and roast in the preheated oven for 15 minutes. Remove from the oven and carefully drain any fat from the tray. Sprinkle the bones and vegetables with flour and roast for another 5 minutes. Remove from the oven.

During the roasting time, in a saucepan, reduce the red wine vinegar completely. Add the red wine and all the marinade ingredients, and bring to the boil. Skim off any fat and impurities, then add the juniper berries, chopped mushrooms, redcurrant jelly and cream.

Pour this liquid over the bones and vegetables in the roasting tray and simmer over a medium heat for 20 minutes. Strain, then reduce the liquid until about 150ml (5fl oz) sauce is left. Taste, correct seasoning and reserve.

Cooking the fillets of hare
Pan-fry the bacon-wrapped fillets in hot oil for 4 minutes turning them continuously so that they are seared all over. Roast in the preheated oven for 8 minutes.

Remove from the oven, and drain off any fat. Cover loosely with aluminium foil, and leave the fillets to relax for 3–4 minutes.

Serving
Cut the string securing the fillets, then cut each into four medallions. Place in a serving dish or on to individual plates, allowing two medallions per plate. Reheat the sauce and pour over the hare. Serve to your guests.

Filets de Lièvre Rôtis au Lard

CHEF'S NOTES
The saddles of hare must not be hung for more than 2 days as the flavour is strong enough; they should hang just enough for the muscles to relax.

Variations
This recipe can also be made using rabbit.

Chestnuts, chicory and gratin of turnips would be perfect garnishes for this dish (see pages 209 and 207).

 WINE

A red wine from the Rhône Valley, Hermitage or Côte Rôtie will be a good companion to this dish.

Civet de Lièvre aux Marrons

Jugged hare with chestnuts

For four people

Preparation time: 30 minutes

Marinating time: 24 hours

Cooking time: 3 hours

Planning ahead: Order the hare well in advance from your butcher and ask him to cut it into pieces for you.

1 hare, skinned and cut into pieces
25g (1oz) lard
20g (¾oz) plain flour
500ml (18fl oz) cold water
2 teaspoons redcurrant jelly
salt and freshly ground pepper

FOR THE MARINADE:
1 bottle red wine
75g (3oz) each of carrots and onions
50g (2oz) celeriac
25g (1oz) celery
6 black peppercorns
1 bay leaf
2 juniper berries

FOR THE GARNISH:
24 chestnuts, prepared and
cooked (see page 209)
lardons cut from 3 rashers streaky
bacon, blanched and refreshed (see page 28)

Preparing the hare

If your butcher is not very forthcoming, please do the following. Cut the legs from the hare (front and back), remove the bottom of the saddle (the hip bones etc), and the rib cage. Cut the remaining saddle into four pieces. Cut the legs into two pieces each. Place in a dish in one layer.

Marinating the hare

In a saucepan, boil the marinade wine for 5 minutes, then cool down. Meanwhile, peel and finely dice the vegetables, then add to the wine in the pan with the remaining marinade ingredients. Allow to cool to room temperature. Pour over the pieces of hare in the dish and marinate for 24 hours in the refrigerator. Drain well, retaining the liquid, and separate the meat from the vegetables. Pat dry very thoroughly.

Preheat the oven to 280°F (145°C) Gas 1½.

Cooking the hare

In a casserole, fry all the pieces of hare in the hot lard for 5 minutes until they colour. Add the diced vegetables and cook for 2 minutes. Add the flour and cook for a further 2 minutes. Pour in the marinade and mix well. Add the water to cover (if necessary), and the redcurrant jelly. Season with salt and pepper. Cover with a tight-fitting lid and cook gently in the preheated oven for 3 hours, or until tender.

Finishing the dish and serving

When the hare is cooked, remove the meat from the casserole and pass the juices through a fine sieve into a saucepan (discard the vegetables). Boil to reduce the sauce to the correct consistency.

Return the meat and sauce to the casserole, add the chestnuts and *lardons*, and cook on top of the stove for 5 minutes. Correct seasoning and serve from the casserole.

CHEF'S NOTES

Do not be tempted to shorten the cooking time or change the temperature – the hare would become very tough. The slow cooking of the hare at a relatively low temperature will ensure that the flesh will fall off the bones very easily.

The best accompaniments for this dish are pasta or a selection of winter vegetables and a potato purée.

⇒ *WINE* ⇐

A red Côtes du Rhône like Châteauneuf-du-Pape or Gigondas will be fine. Or try a Barbaresco or Barolo from Italy.

Civet de Lièvre aux Marrons

Filets de Chevreuil aux Noix Fraîches

Fillets of venison served with a red wine sauce, scented with walnuts

For four people

Preparation time: 30 minutes

Marinating time: 24 hours

Cooking time: 12–15 minutes

Planning ahead: Order the venison well in advance from your butcher, and ask him to prepare the fillet and chop the bones of the best end from which the fillet comes (see Chef's Notes).

The sauce and the garnish can be prepared in advance.

500g (18oz) fillet of well-matured venison, trimmed
salt and freshly ground pepper
1 teaspoon groundnut oil
1 teaspoon unsalted butter

FOR THE MARINADE:
600ml (1 pint) Hermitage wine, or full-bodied red wine
1 small celery stalk, diced
1 carrot, peeled and diced
1 medium onion, peeled and diced
1 juniper berry, crushed
8–10 black peppercorns, crushed
1 sprig of thyme
½ bay leaf

FOR THE SAUCE:
500g (18oz) bones from the best end of saddle, chopped into small pieces
100ml (3½fl oz) groundnut oil
1 tablespoon plain flour
50ml (2fl oz) red wine vinegar
100ml (3½fl oz) port
100ml (3½fl oz) game or brown chicken stock (optional, see page 35)
200ml (7fl oz) water
1 level teaspoon cornflour or arrowroot diluted in 2 tablespoons water
2 tablespoons whipping cream
15g (½oz) ground walnuts
1 teaspoon redcurrant jelly if necessary

FOR THE GARNISH:
8 shelled walnuts, halved
100g (4oz) diced celery and apple, pan-fried in a little butter (optional)
20 small celery leaves, deep-fried (optional)

I rarely recommend game that has been farmed, but farmed deer is one of the exceptions. During its life, the animal has great space and lives in its natural environment, hence the meat it produces is very good and can be as tasty as its wild counterpart.

Marinating the venison
Bring the wine to the boil, then allow to cool down to room temperature. Place the venison fillet, and the remaining marinade ingredients into a large bowl and pour in the wine. Cover with cling film and marinate for 24 hours.

Strain the wine and reserve, along with all the vegetables, herbs and spices, for the sauce. Pat the venison dry and reserve.

Preheat the oven to 450°F (230°C) Gas 8.

Preparing the sauce
In a roasting tray lightly brown and sear the bones and trimmings in hot oil for about 5 minutes, then add the diced marinade vegetables and cook for a further 5 minutes. Tilt the tray and spoon out the fat. Sprinkle the bones and vegetables with flour. Roast the bones and vegetables in the oven until they are well coloured, approximately 20 minutes. Remove from the oven.

Transfer the bones and trimmings to a saucepan. Deglaze the roasting tray with the red wine vinegar, scraping out all the caramelised juices from the bottom of the tray. Reduce completely. Add the port, red wine from the marinade, game or brown chicken stock (if using) and the water, then pour over the bones in the saucepan. Bring to the boil, skim and reduce until you have about 200ml (7fl oz) juice. Bind it with the diluted arrowroot.

Strain the stock into another saucepan, bring to the boil again and skim off any fat. Add the cream and reduce the sauce down until it has a good consistency, then add the ground walnuts and leave to infuse for about 5 minutes. Taste and correct seasoning. If the sauce is too sharp, add a very small amount of redcurrant jelly; if it is too sweet, add a little dash of red wine or red wine vinegar. Reserve.

Adjust the oven temperature to 400°F (200°C) Gas 6.

Cooking the venison fillet
Season the fillet with salt and pepper. Sear and brown in hot oil and butter for 1 minute, then cook in the oven for about 10–12 minutes.

Remove from the oven and discard any fat. Leave to rest for 10 minutes covered loosely with aluminium foil to keep it warm. Correct seasoning.

Filets de Chevreuil aux Noix Fraîches

Serving

Reheat the deep-fried celery leaves, diced celery and apple (if used). Arrange attractively on a serving plate. Add the halved walnuts.

Carve the fillet into four medallions, place in the middle of the plate, and pour the sauce all around. Serve to your guests.

CHEF'S NOTES

I am afraid this is an expensive dish. When you bone the fillet from the best end, you will lose two-thirds of the weight: 1.5kg (3¼lb) meat and bone comes down to 500g (18oz).

 WINE

For this dish I would recommend a well-matured wine from the Pauillac area (Bordeaux).

Crêpes Franc Comtoise

Ham and mushroom pancakes

This recipe is from my native country, and is a dish that featured on my menu at the Quat' Saisons in Summertown. Simple, unashamedly rich and delicious!

Making the béchamel sauce
In a small saucepan, melt the butter and add the flour, then stir and cook gently for 2–3 minutes until a light golden colour. Cool down a little.

Separately, in another saucepan, bring the milk to the boil then add it, slowly, to the butter and flour mixture, whisking constantly. Bring back to the boil until the sauce thickens, then season with salt, pepper and grated nutmeg. Reserve.

Preparing and cooking the pancakes
Make up the batter as described on page 22, using *half* the quantity and omitting the sugar; cook and reserve the pancakes (about eight).

Making the filling
Over a high heat, melt the butter and sauté the mushrooms for about 1 minute until they are barely cooked. Add the ham and season with salt and pepper.

Preheat the oven to 450°F (230°C) Gas 8.

Filling the pancakes
Combine together the béchamel sauce, mushrooms and ham, then divide between each pancake. Roll them up tightly around the mixture, then place in a well-buttered roasting dish.

Finishing the dish and serving
Pour the cream over the pancakes, then sprinkle the cheese over the top. Cook in the preheated oven for approximately 15–20 minutes, then serve piping hot to your guests.

CHEF'S NOTES
It is not necessary to season the cream with salt due to that already contained in the Gruyère cheese.

For four people

Preparation time: 30 minutes

Cooking time: 15–20 minutes

Special equipment:
A roasting dish, 18cm (7in) wide, and 28cm (11in) long.

Planning ahead: The recipe can be made well in advance, and the finishing stage done at the last moment.

½ quantity of Pancake Batter
(see page 22)

FOR THE BÉCHAMEL SAUCE:
20g (¾oz) unsalted butter
20g (¾oz) plain flour
250ml (8fl oz) milk
salt and freshly ground pepper
freshly grated nutmeg

FOR THE FILLING:
20g (¾oz) unsalted butter
250g (9oz) button mushrooms,
washed, patted dry and sliced
200g (7oz) cooked ham, finely chopped

FOR THE TOPPING:
300ml (10fl oz) double cream
100g (4oz) Gruyère or Emmenthal
cheese, finely grated

⇒ WINE ⇐
A dry white is needed for this dish, such as a dry Jurançon wine or, even better, an Arbois wine from L'Etoile, with its very original taste and scent.

Crêpes Franc Comtoise

For four people

Preparation and cooking time: 1¼ hours

Special equipment:
4 soufflé dishes 10cm (4in) diameter × 7cm (2¾in) high.

Planning ahead: Please read the section on soufflé-making (on page 23) before embarking on this dish.

The tomato sauce can be made in advance, and all the preparations for the meatloaf can also be done in advance.

*300g (11oz) leftover cooked meat
(veal, pork, lamb or beef),
roughly chopped
20g (¾oz) parsley, finely chopped
8 tarragon leaves,
finely chopped (optional)
2 garlic cloves, peeled,
crushed then puréed
4 egg yolks
200ml (7fl oz) milk
salt and freshly ground pepper
7 egg whites
1 teaspoon lemon juice
butter for greasing*

FOR THE TOMATO SAUCE:
*1 small onion, peeled
and finely chopped
1 tablespoon olive oil
1 garlic clove, peeled and crushed
300g (11 oz) tomatoes,
halved, seeded and chopped
4–5 tarragon leaves,
chopped (optional)
1 sprig of thyme
2 heaped tablespoons tomato purée
200ml (7fl oz) water*

FOR THE GARNISH:
1 tablespoon finely chopped parsley

Pain de Viande Soufflé, Sauce Tomate

Meatloaf soufflé, served with a tomato coulis

A good way to use leftovers from a roast.

Preheat the oven to 375°F (190°C) Gas 5.

Making the tomato sauce
In a casserole, sweat the onion in the oil, without browning, for 2–3 minutes. Add the garlic, tomatoes, chopped tarragon (if using), and thyme. Cover and sweat for 5 minutes. Remove the lid, add the tomato purée and the water, and cook slowly for 30 minutes. Taste, season with salt and pepper, and pass through a Moulinex. Reserve in a small casserole.

Making the meatloaf soufflé
Mince the meat through the fine disc of a Moulinex, or place into a food processor for 30 seconds until ground.

Place the mince in a bowl, add the chopped parsley and tarragon (if using), garlic, egg yolks and milk. Season with salt and pepper. Mix thoroughly with a spatula and taste. Add more seasoning if necessary.

Place the egg whites in a bowl and whisk to soft peaks. Add the lemon juice and some salt, and carry on whisking until firm peaks are achieved.

Take one-third of the egg white and combine thoroughly with the meat mixture. Then carefully fold in the remainder of the egg white. Taste, and adjust seasoning if required.

Generously butter the inside of the soufflé dishes and pour in the soufflé mixture.

Cooking the soufflés
Place the dishes into a roasting tin, and add enough water to come one-third up the height of the dishes. Bring the water to the boil on top of the stove, then place into the preheated oven. Cook for 40–45 minutes.

Serving
Reheat the tomato sauce. Remove the soufflés from the oven, passing the blade of a knife along the inside of the dishes to free them. Shake them sideways to loosen them. Turn them out on to a large warm serving dish, and pour the tomato sauce over and around them. Sprinkle the parsley over and serve to your guests.

CHEF'S NOTES
When there is no sugar to 'support' the egg whites, the whites can easily separate and become grainy. The lemon juice is used to bind the egg whites and prevent this.

Pain de Viande Soufflé, Sauce Tomate

Variations

The best meat for this dish is pork.

To add a Provençal touch, add chopped black olives to the mixture.
The meat can be replaced by cooked salmon or any other cooked fish.

 WINE

As the dish is simple and humble for an everyday occasion, so should be the wine – a good red or *rosé* table wine will be fine.

Rôti de Porc aux Pruneaux, Façon Maman Blanc

Roast loin of pork stuffed with prunes

This recipe made my mother a television star in Britain, when a BBC TV crew of seven descended on her kitchen (with one day's notice) to film her cooking it!

Preparing the prune garnish
Remove the stones from the prunes, add Cognac or Armagnac, and stir. Cover with cling film, and marinate for a minimum of 6 hours.

Preparing the loin of pork
Open up the loin of pork, placing the fat side against the table. Season with a pinch of salt and freshly ground pepper and place eight prunes in the middle of the loin. Roll the loin up and secure both ends with skewers, then tie with eight turns of string. Remove the skewers.
Preheat the oven to 425°F (220°C) Gas 7.

Roasting the loin of pork
In a roasting tray, lightly brown the chopped bones in the hot oil and butter for about 5 minutes then place the loin of pork on top of the bones. With a fork prick the tomato (to allow the juices to escape and mix with the meat juices), and add with the garlic and thyme to the roasting tray. Cover loosely with foil and cook in the preheated oven for 1 hour, 10 minutes.
Remove the tray from the oven and place the loin on a plate. Cover loosely with aluminium foil and keep warm. Tip the roasting tray slightly and spoon out the fat (which you can keep for another use).

Preparing the juice and garnish
Add the Madeira to the bones and tomato in the roasting tray and bring to the boil, scraping the caramelised bits from the bottom of the tray. Reduce the Madeira by two-thirds, then add the water and simmer for 5 minutes.
Strain the juice into a casserole, discarding the bones, etc., and skim off any fat. Boil the liquid down to about 200ml (7fl oz).
Add the remaining prunes to the juice and reserve, keeping warm.

Serving
Remove the strings from the loin of pork and carve into 12–16 slices (according to the number of diners). Place these in the middle of a warm serving dish.
Pour the juice and prunes around the cooked slices. Season the slices with salt and pepper, and pour over any juices released by the meat during the resting time. Serve to your guests.

CHEF'S NOTES
Pruneaux d'Agen are the very best prunes. Too often prunes in Britain are too dry or too soft – which means the plums have been badly dried.

For six to eight people

Preparation time: 30 minutes

Marinating time: at least 6 hours

Cooking time: 1 hour, 10 minutes

Planning ahead: The prunes must be soaked 6 hours in advance. The loin of pork can be filled with the prunes half a day in advance, ready to be cooked.

Ask your butcher to bone the loin and trim off the skin and excess fat but to leave a thin layer of fat about 3mm (⅛in) thick. Also, ask him to chop the pork bones into small pieces.

1.2kg (2lb 10oz) boned and
trimmed loin of pork (see above)
salt and freshly ground pepper
chopped bones from the loin
1 tablespoon groundnut oil
15g (½oz) unsalted butter
1 large tomato
1 garlic clove, unpeeled
1 sprig of thyme
200ml (7fl oz) dry Madeira
300ml (10fl oz) water

FOR THE GARNISH:
24 prunes
(pruneaux d'Agen if possible)
6 tablespoons Cognac or Armagnac

WINE

A spicy Riesling or Gewürztraminer or, if you prefer red wine, why not a Brouilly or Fleurie from the Beaujolais area.

Variations

To simplify the dish, pour 120ml (4fl oz) water into the roasting tray during the last 10 minutes of roasting, and omit the Madeira.

The best accompaniment for this dish would be flageolet or French beans with Pommes Sautées (see pages 198, 202 and 197).

Epaule de Chevreuil Braisée au Fumet de Vin Rouge

Shoulder of venison braised in red wine

Preheat the oven to 300°F (150°C) Gas 2.

Marinating the venison

Bring the wine and ruby port to the boil for 1 minute. Skim, then allow to cool down. Place all the ingredients for the marinade together, including the cubes of venison, and pour the cooled wine over them. Cover and marinate for 24 hours in a cool place.

Cooking the venison

Drain the venison through a colander, reserving the marinade liquid and vegetables. Pat the venison pieces dry, then reserve.

In a large cast-iron casserole dish, heat the lard until it is very hot then sear and brown the meat for about 10 minutes; after 5 minutes, add the vegetables from the marinade. Stir from time to time until the meat is very dark brown in colour. Season with salt and ground black pepper.

Spoon out any fat, sprinkle in the flour and cook for a further 3 minutes, stirring from time to time. Pour in the wine from the marinade, boil then skim, then add the garlic clove, bay leaf, thyme and redcurrant jelly.

Bring to the boil, skim and cover the dish, and cook in the preheated oven for a minimum of 2½ hours.

Serving

Remove the casserole, throw in the chocolate flakes, stir, taste and correct seasoning. Serve to your guests either from the casserole dish or in a deep serving dish.

CHEF'S NOTES

Venison is one of the few game meats which need to be hung in order to improve both their taste and texture.

It is essential to dry the diced venison well in order to remove as much moisture as possible; this will ease the searing process. The fat in which the venison is browned must be very hot: if not, moisture would be released from the meat and the dish would stew in its own juices.

Variations

Obviously a lot of ingredients could be added – chestnuts, walnuts, large dice of apples, or peas.

For four people

Preparation time: 15 minutes

Marinating time: 24 hours

Cooking time: 2½ hours

Planning ahead: This dish can be prepared 1 day in advance then refrigerated and reheated very easily. It often tastes better after it has been reheated.

*1kg (2¼ lb) venison shoulder,
boned out,
trimmed and cut into 5cm (2in) cubes
50g (2oz) white lard
salt
12 black peppercorns, ground
25g (1oz) plain flour
1 garlic clove, peeled
1 bay leaf
2 sprigs of thyme
1 teaspoon redcurrant jelly
20g (¾oz) chocolate flakes*

FOR THE MARINADE:
*1 litre (1¾ pints) full-bodied red wine
200ml (7fl oz) ruby port
12 shallots, peeled
1 large carrot, peeled and cut into large cubes
1 celery stalk,
washed and cut into 2cm (¾in) segments*

 WINE

This dish will make happy all those who are passionate about full-bodied claret.

Filet de Boeuf Poêlé à la Croûte de Raifort et Moelle

Pan-fried fillet of Aberdeen Angus beef
topped with a marrow and horseradish crust

For four people

Preparation and cooking time: 40 minutes

Soaking time: 6 hours

Planning ahead: The crust, sauce and garnishes can all be prepared in advance.

4 fillets of beef,
175g (6oz) each in weight
1 teaspoon unsalted butter
1 teaspoon sunflower oil
salt and freshly ground pepper
2 teaspoons Dijon mustard

FOR THE CRUST:
30g (1¼oz) beef marrow,
soaked in cold salted water for
about 6 hours
40g (1½oz) dried bread,
made into crumbs
20g (¾oz) freshly grated horseradish
½ tablespoon Dijon mustard,
mixed with 1 tablespoon whipping cream
12 green peppercorns,
finely crushed with the flat of a knife
(optional)

FOR THE SAUCE:
4 shallots, peeled and chopped
1 teaspoon unsalted butter
400ml (14fl oz) full-bodied red wine
1 sprig of thyme
1 tablespoon whipping cream
100g (4oz) button mushrooms, wiped
4 tarragon leaves, chopped
1 teaspoon arrowroot or cornflour,
diluted in 2 tablespoons water

FOR THE SHALLOT GARNISH:
20 small shallots
or pickling onions, peeled
15g (½oz) unsalted butter
a pinch of caster sugar

FOR THE MUSHROOM GARNISH:
80g (3¼oz) shiitake (or wild)
mushrooms, washed briefly and quartered
1 teaspoon unsalted butter
3 tablespoons water
a dash of lemon juice

Preheat the oven to 400°F (200°C) Gas 6.

Preparing the crust
Poach the marrow in slightly salted water, just simmering, for 3–4 minutes. Drain and dice. Taste and season with salt and pepper. Allow to cool.

Mix the breadcrumbs with the horseradish, mustard and cream mixture and the crushed peppercorns (if using). Season with salt and pepper. Delicately mix in the marrow. Place in a small container and cover with cling film. Reserve.

Cooking the garnishes
For the shallots, melt the butter in a sauté pan, add the shallots or onions, sugar and some salt and pepper, and brown lightly on top of the stove. Cover, then cook in the preheated oven for 20 minutes. Stir from time to time. Reserve.

For the mushrooms, mix the mushrooms, butter, water, lemon juice and some salt and pepper in a small saucepan. Cover and cook over a brisk heat for 30 seconds. Turn off the heat, and reserve until needed.

Raise the temperature of the oven to 425°F (220°C) Gas 7.

Preparing the sauce
Sweat the shallots in the butter for 2–3 minutes. Add the red wine and bring to the boil. Skim then reduce to 150ml (5fl oz). Add the thyme, cream and button mushrooms, and simmer for 3 more minutes. Add the chopped tarragon. Add the arrowroot or cornflour mixture to the sauce and boil for a further 30 seconds. Force the sauce through a fine strainer into a small saucepan. Taste and correct seasoning. Reserve and keep warm.

Cooking the fillets
Melt the butter and oil together in a small sauté pan until a light brown colour. Sear and brown top and bottom of the fillets for 2 minutes, then sear the sides for a few seconds. Season with salt and pepper.

Spread mustard on top of each fillet. Place a little mound of the crust mixture on each fillet, then place in the oven. Roast the fillets for 6 minutes for medium rare, and 9 minutes for medium.

Serving
Reheat the shallots and the mushrooms. Warm four plates. Place a fillet in the centre of each plate and surround with shallots, mushrooms and sauce. Or, more simply, place the four fillets on a warmed serving dish with the shallots and mushrooms, and serve the sauce separately.

CHEF'S NOTES
You deserve the best, ask for the best. Pure Aberdeen Angus is the best, and it should have been hung and matured for 3 weeks.

Cooking time is only approximate as this depends entirely on the thickness of the fillet. If you want the fillet well done, you need to cook it to medium before placing the crust on.

Variations
You can alter the sauce. Proceed in exactly the same way, but omit the arrowroot or cornflour. Instead, add 150ml (5fl oz) brown chicken stock (see page 35) to the reduced wine.

Deep-fried tarragon, chervil and parsley would provide a delicious texture and additional taste, and can be done well in advance (see page 137).

Filet de Porc Poêlé aux Raisins

Pork fillets with sultanas

Marinating the sultanas
Soak the sultanas in hot Darjeeling tea for 6 hours. Strain and keep the remaining tea.
Preheat the oven to 400°F (200°C) Gas 6.

Preparing and cooking the pork fillets
Trim the sinews around the fillets of pork, fold back the tail end, and tie with two turns of string.
In a roasting pan, heat the butter and oil then sear and colour the fillets all over. Season with salt and freshly ground pepper. Roast the fillets in the preheated oven for 15 minutes.
Place the fillets on to a plate, cover loosely with aluminium foil and leave to rest in a warm place.

Making the sauce
Discard the fat from the pan used for the pork and add the Cognac. Boil for a few seconds, then add the dry white wine and reduce by half. Add the tea and cream together, reduce to the right consistency, then add the drained sultanas. Taste, and correct seasoning with salt and freshly ground pepper.

Serving
Warm four plates or a serving dish. Pour the juices released from the pork fillets into the sauce. Slice the fillets and arrange on each plate or serving dish and pour the sauce and sultanas over and around. Serve to your guests.

Variations
Fillet of veal can also be prepared in the same way, but will require 25 minutes' roasting time. One fillet of veal will be enough.

 WINE
A powerful, well-matured red wine, from the Rhône, Burgundy or Bordeaux area according to your tastes.

For four to six people

Marinating time: 6 hours

Preparation time: 10 minutes

Cooking time: 20 minutes

Planning ahead: The sultanas must be soaked for 6 hours in advance.

2 pork fillets
10g (¼oz) unsalted butter
2 teaspoons groundnut oil
salt and freshly ground pepper

FOR THE SULTANAS:
40g (1½oz) sultanas
100ml (3½fl oz) Darjeeling tea

FOR THE SAUCE:
2 tablespoons Cognac
100ml (3½fl oz) dry white wine
4 tablespoons tea from the marinade
250ml (8fl oz) double cream

 WINE
A light Pinot Noir from the Côte Chalonnaise, such as a Rully or Mercurey, would go well.

Rognons de Porc au Poivre Vert et Moutarde

Pan-fried pig's kidneys served with green peppercorns and mustard sauce

For four people

Preparation and cooking time: 1 hour

Planning ahead: The rice can be cooked 1–2 hours in advance.

6 pig's kidneys (very firm and
a delicate cream colour)
15g (½oz) unsalted butter
1 tablespoon groundnut oil
salt and freshly ground pepper
2 tablespoons Armagnac or Cognac
100ml (3½fl oz) dry white wine
400ml (14fl oz) double cream
2 tablespoons Dijon mustard
2 heaped tablespoons green
peppercorns, washed under running
water for half an hour
a dash of lemon juice

FOR THE RICE GARNISH:
150g (5oz) basmati rice,
washed and drained
¼ small onion,
peeled and finely chopped
15g (½oz) unsalted butter
250ml (8fl oz) light chicken stock
(see page 34) or water
2 sprigs of thyme
a dash of lemon juice

WINE

A Côte Rôtie from the Côtes du Rhône has been a delightful experience for me, and I urge you to try it.

This dish reminds me of my very first gastronomic experience. I was a poor student, aged eighteen, had time to kill, and it was 12 o'clock. At that time, all sorts of things start to happen in the French stomach and, by magic, I had some money in my pocket. I decided to treat myself and entered what was thought to be the best local restaurant. It took a little time to familiarise myself with my surroundings, but everyone was very helpful and welcoming, and I soon felt at ease. I ordered dishes which would fit my budget, and the main course, I remember vividly, was pig's kidney with mustard. The food was absolutely brilliant, and I still remember that taste – as well as the presentation which was so different from family *cuisine*. As I didn't know anything about wine, the wine waiter chose for me – a Côte Rôtie, an association that I shall always remember.

Preheat the oven to 350°F (180°C) Gas 4.

Preparing the kidneys
Cut the kidneys in half widthways. Remove the hard membrane. Wash them briefly and pat dry.

Cooking the rice
In an ovenproof pan, sweat the onion in the butter for 3–4 minutes, then add the rice. Stir and cover with the chicken stock or water. Add the thyme, lemon juice and some salt and pepper. Cover the pan and cook in the preheated oven for about 35 minutes. Taste and correct seasoning.

Cooking the kidneys
Put the butter and oil in a large non-stick pan over a strong heat. When the fat turns a light brown colour, add the halved kidneys and pan-fry for about 2 minutes. Season, place on a plate, cover loosely with aluminium foil and keep warm.

Remove the fat from the pan and add the Armagnac or Cognac. Bring to the boil for 1 second then add the white wine and boil for 1 minute. Add the cream and boil for a further 2 minutes, then turn off the heat and mix in the mustard and drained green peppercorns. Taste, season with salt and pepper, and add a dash of lemon juice. Finally add the kidneys to the sauce.

Serving
Prepare four warm plates. Reheat the rice and arrange in a mound in the middle of each plate. Serve the kidneys and sauce around.

CHEF'S NOTES
CHEF'S NOTES
The success of this dish will depend on the quality of the kidneys. Never accept deep red kidneys or those with a flabby texture. They should be firm, light and creamy, with no smell whatsoever.

After 25 minutes, check to see if the rice is cooked. This may take longer according to the variety of rice.

Variations
An alternative to pig's kidneys would be either spring lamb's kidneys or, even better, veal kidneys. If you use the latter, slice them across, after having removed the sinews and nerves.

Filet de Lièvre Poêlé à la Crème de Genièvre

Fillet of hare in a juniper-scented cream

Preheat the oven to 400°F (200°C) Gas 6.

Cooking the hare fillets
Sear and brown the fillets all over in hot oil and butter for about 3 minutes. Add salt and pepper and reserve. Then roast in the preheated oven for 3 further minutes. Remove from the oven, place the fillets on to a plate, loosely cover with aluminium foil and keep in a warm place.

Making the sauce
Spoon out any fat from the roasting tray. Add the gin and boil for 1 second, then add the white wine and reduce by half. Add the cream and ground juniper berries and bring to the boil until you have the right consistency. Taste and season with salt and pepper. Reserve.

Serving
Tip any cooking juices that have been released by the fillets into the sauce. Reheat the fillets for 2 minutes in the oven. Slice the fillets and arrange in the middle of each plate. Spoon the sauce around and serve to your guests.

CHEF'S NOTES
Hare must not be hung for too long otherwise the scent would be too strong.

For four people

Preparation time: 5 minutes

Cooking time: 10–12 minutes

Planning ahead: Order the saddles of hare well in advance. Ask your butcher to trim the fillets, remove the membrane covering them and to bone them out.

4 fillets from 2 saddles of hare
1 tablespoon groundnut oil
1 teaspoon unsalted butter
salt and freshly ground black pepper
2 tablespoons gin
100ml (3½fl oz) white wine
200ml (7fl oz) double cream
4 juniper berries, finely ground

WINE

Again, a Rhône Valley wine, such as a Crozes-Hermitage red or St Joseph red, will be a good accompaniment.

Perdreau Sauvage Rôti

Wild grey-legged partridge served with its own juices

We are lucky in Britain still to be able to get wild game, which in most countries is not possible.

Last year when I visited my parents, my wife and I set out for a long walk in one of the nearby dark forests. It was a warm autumn day, so we decided to sit and rest. We became aware of a strange atmosphere, an unbearable silence. Eventually an old crow gave a few signs that wildlife still existed! At least one species had survived the repeated assaults of the booted Frenchman and his guns. Of course, in France you can shoot whatever you want and in my little village of only 1,000 souls there are 100 guns.

In Britain, because of private land ownership, wildlife is not shot on such a scale and the countryside can look like an animated Walt Disney film with an incredible variety of wildlife.

I specify that you should use wild grey-legged partridge rather than the French red-legged partridge, for the French partridge has been farmed, cross-bred and tastes more like chicken than game. For this dish to succeed you need the genuine article and then you need only to roast it and simply add water to the caramelised juices.

Preheat the oven to 425°F (220°C) Gas 7.

Preparing the partridges and the livers
Shorten the wings and sear the partridges under a flame to remove the feather stubs. Remove any trace of gall from the liver; wash briefly, pat dry and reserve.

Cooking the partridges and making the juice
In a roasting tray sear the wing bones and the partridges in butter and oil for 2 minutes on each side and 2 minutes on the breast (6 minutes in total) until they are beautifully brown.

Season with salt and pepper and roast in the preheated oven for 5–6 minutes according to the size of the partridges. Remove from the oven and place the partridges on a plate, cover loosely with aluminium foil and allow to rest.

In the same roasting tray fry the livers in the remaining butter and oil for one minute, and reserve. Spoon out the excess fat and add the roasting juices and water to the winglets, bring to the boil then simmer for 5 minutes. Taste and season with salt and pepper, then strain through a fine sieve.

Serving
Place the partridges and livers on a serving dish and serve the sauce separately. Pour any cooking juices that have been released by the partridges into the sauce.

CHEF'S NOTES
As this dish is extremely simple, its success will depend on the quality of the ingredients that you will have selected.

You can, if you wish, make a much stronger juice by roasting the partridges, then boning them out, chopping the carcasses and browning them and covering with water and simmering for 10 minutes. Strain and reduce until taste and colour are just right.

Variations
Many other young, top quality game birds could be done this way — pheasant, woodcock, snipe.

Langue de Boeuf à la Moutarde

Braised ox tongue, served with a mustard, caper and gherkin sauce

Soaking the tongue
Trim the tongue, and place in a bowl of cold water under a slow running tap for 4 hours minimum.

Cooking the tongue
Place the tongue in the large casserole, cover with fresh cold water, and boil for 3 minutes. Drain off the water.

Add the chicken stock and *bouquet garni* to the pan, bring to the boil, skim, and simmer for about 2½ hours.

Remove the tongue, place on a tea cloth and peel off the skin. Return the tongue to the stock, and keep warm.

Making the sauce
Place 15g (½oz) of the butter in a large sauté pan; dice the remainder of the butter and chill. Sweat the shallots in the butter in the pan, but do not colour them. Add the wine, then boil to reduce to about 2 tablespoons.

Add the measured amount of cooking juices, and boil again to reduce to 100ml (3½fl oz).

Add the cream, bring to the boil, then add the gherkin *julienne* and capers, tarragon, parsley and mustard. Finally whisk in the cold diced butter.

Taste, and adjust seasoning with salt and pepper, plus a few drops of lemon juice if necessary. Keep warm.

Serving
Reheat the tongue in the cooking stock.

Slice the tongue into slices of about 1cm (½in) thick, and arrange on six individual warmed plates or on a serving dish. Pour the sauce over and around the slices. Serve to your guests.

CHEF'S NOTES
It is important that the capers are well washed, otherwise the sauce would taste too acidic.

The remaining cooking stock can be used to make a delicious soup.

For six people
Soaking time: 4 hours minimum
Preparation time: 20 minutes
Cooking time: 2½ hours
Special equipment:
1 large casserole, about 23cm (9in) in diameter.

Planning ahead: The tongue can be cooked 12 hours in advance, and kept in the stock. The sauce can be prepared 1 hour in advance.

1 ox tongue, about 1.5kg (3¼lb) in weight
1.5 litres (2½ pints) chicken stock (made from stock cubes)
1 bouquet garni (add 2 cloves to the recipe on page 30)

FOR THE SAUCE:
65g (2½oz) unsalted butter
4 shallots, peeled and finely chopped
200ml (7fl oz) dry white wine
200ml (7fl oz) cooking juices from the tongue
200ml (7fl oz) whipping cream
6 small gherkins, cut in fine julienne sticks or dice
1 tablespoon capers, thoroughly washed
8 tarragon leaves, chopped
50g (2oz) parsley, chopped
1 tablespoon Dijon mustard
salt and freshly ground pepper
a few drops of lemon juice (optional)

⇒ WINE ⇐

You could have red or white. If you choose a red, go for a young wine from Beaujolais such as Brouilly or Fleurie, or if white, a very dry wine from the Rhône such as a white Hermitage or Condrieu.

Canetons de Gressingham Rôtis au Jus Parfumé au Jasmin et Raisins de Corinthes

*Roast Gressingham ducklings served
with a jasmine sauce and sultanas*

For four people

Marinating time: 24 hours

Preparation time: 10 minutes

Cooking time: 50 minutes

Planning ahead: Order the Gressingham ducklings well in advance from your butcher.

The sultanas should be marinated for a day before use; the sauce can be made well in advance.

*2 oven-ready Gressingham ducklings
1.6kg (3½lb) each, wishbones removed,
wings and neck cut short
(reserve for the sauce)
1 tablespoon duck fat
(from inside the duck), chopped
salt and freshy ground pepper*

FOR THE SULTANAS:
*100g (4oz) sultanas
200ml (7fl oz) hot jasmine tea*

FOR THE SAUCE:
*wings and necks of ducklings, chopped
700ml (24fl oz) water
10g (¼oz) unsalted butter
10g (¼oz) caster sugar
150ml (5fl oz) orange juice
1 teaspoon soy sauce
100ml (3½fl oz) cherry brandy
10g (¼oz) jasmine tea-leaves
juice of ¼ lime*

The lack of quality in British poultry is very well known. Gressingham and Lunesdale ducks are the only ones worthy of attention. They have a good shape, are meaty with a good flavour and have very little fat content. In my opinion, the Gressingham is the best breed for roasting; it is a cross between a wild and domestic duck, and its flavour is particularly interesting.

Marinating the sultanas
Put the sultanas in a large bowl, and pour the hot jasmine tea over them. Cover, cool down, and refrigerate for 24 hours until the sultanas swell.

Preparing the sauce
Chop the winglets and neck into small pieces. Place in a large pan and sear gently, turning the pieces occasionally, until they are golden brown (about 20 minutes). Remove the excess fat, then cover with the cold water, bring to the boil, skim and simmer for 20 minutes. Pass through a fine sieve and boil to reduce to 200ml (7fl oz).

In a separate pan, melt the butter and sugar together and cook until caramelised. Add the orange juice, soy sauce and boil to reduce by half.

In yet another pan, reduce the cherry brandy by two-thirds, then mix in the reduced duck stock and orange juice mixture. Bring to simmering point, add the jasmine tea-leaves, and leave to infuse for 1 minute. Add the lime juice, taste and correct seasoning with salt and pepper. Strain through a fine sieve to remove the tea-leaves. Reserve.

Preheat the oven to 450°F (230°C) Gas 8.

Preparing and roasting the ducklings
Remove the feather stubs from the ducklings by carefully holding them over a flame. With the point of a very sharp knife, score very light criss-cross lines across the breasts and legs (so the fat will run out easily). Cut the legs off the ducks just above the joint.

Melt the fat in a large roasting tray on the top of the cooker and colour the ducklings for about 5 minutes each side and for 3 minutes on each breast. Season with salt and pepper then roast in the oven on one breast for 10 minutes, then on the other breast for another 10 minutes, and a further 15 minutes on their backs (a total of 35 minutes).

Remove from the oven and discard the fat. Let the ducklings rest on their breasts for 5–10 minutes; carve, and season again.

Canetons de Gressingham Rôtis au Jus Parfumé au Jasmin et Raisins de Corinthes

Serving
Place the ducklings on a large serving dish and reheat in the oven for 5 minutes. Bring the sauce to simmering point and pour over the ducklings. Reheat the sultanas in the jasmine tea, then strain and scatter them over the ducklings. Serve to your guests.

CHEF'S NOTES
If you feel courageous, you could always carve the ducks in front of your guests!

The carcasses of the ducks can be finely chopped and used to make a light soup.

When making the sauce, make sure that the tea is *infused* into the sauce; it must not be boiled, or the sauce will be bitter and far too strong.

Variations
To create a more substantial and textured sauce, add 100ml (3½fl oz) brown chicken stock (see page 35).

 *WINE*

A red Burgundy, and one from the Côte de Beaune in particular, is probably the best choice to marry with this dish.

Pot au Feu

For six to eight people

Preparation time: 30 minutes

Cooking time: 3 hours

500g (18oz) loin of pork,
trimmed of most of the fat
500g (18oz) blade of beef,
trimmed
500g (18oz) leg of lamb, cut short
300g (11oz) smoked streaky bacon,
rind removed
1 shin of veal
1 bouquet garni, tied in muslin
along with 10 black peppercorns
and 1 clove (see page 30)
salt

FOR THE VEGETABLES:
6 large carrots, peeled
2 celery stalks, cut in half widthways
1 fennel bulb, cut in 6
2 medium turnips, peeled and
quartered
3 leeks, washed, cut in
half widthways and tied
24 shallots or small baby onions,
peeled

This is the quintessence of French family *cuisine*, and must be the most celebrated dish in France! It honours the tables of the rich as much as it does those of the poor. Despite its lack of sophistication, it has not only survived time, but is still one of the greatest favourites today, a triumph of simplicity!

Using the same principle, you can also make this dish using beef alone, chicken or boiling fowl.

Blanching the meat
Place all the meat in a large casserole, cover with cold water and bring to the boil for 1 minute. Drain and refresh under cold water.

Cooking the meat and vegetables
In a large cast-iron casserole arrange the meat tightly in one single layer, then cover with water to about 4cm (1½in) above the meat. Add the muslin-wrapped *bouquet garni*. Season with salt and bring to a gentle boil. Skim off any impurities, cover with a lid (leaving a small gap), and simmer gently for 2 hours.

Skim off some of the fat, then add the carrots and cook for 15 minutes. Add the celery, fennel, turnip, leeks and onions and cook for a further 30 minutes. Taste the broth and correct the seasoning.

Serving
You could simply serve the *pot au feu* straight from the dish in which it has been cooked and let your guests help themselves which would lend a convivial feeling to the table, but at the same time this could be a little awkward. An alternative is to carve the meat in the kitchen, place on a serving plate, surround with the vegetables and serve the broth separately in a large bowl.

Serve the *pot au feu* with Dijon mustard and gherkins.

CHEF'S NOTES
The meats are blanched in order to remove most of the impurities. This will keep the broth clear.

The *pot au feu* should be simmered and not boiled, otherwise the meat would become very tough and the broth would be very cloudy. When covering with a lid it is important to leave a gap as this will prevent excess evaporation; if the lid is on tight, the heat would accumulate and the broth would boil.

When skimming the broth, do not skim off all the fat. A little fat will improve and enhance the flavour of the broth.

Variations
The vegetables can vary but if you use cabbage, make sure you cook it separately. For a more substantial dish, you could add a chicken to the pot.

⊰ *WINE* ⊱

A good *vin du pays*, a wine from Beaujolais or the Loire Valley – as long as the wine has a lot of fruit and not too much tannin.

Pot au Feu

Filets de Dinde Farcis aux Marrons

Breasts of turkey stuffed with chestnuts

For eight people

Preparation time: 1 hour

Cooking time: 1½ hours

Planning ahead: Order the turkey front (breasts and wings of the turkey, on the bone) from your butcher well in advance. The boning of the breast can also be done by you or your butcher in advance. The chestnuts and apples can also be prepared beforehand.

1 turkey front, about 3kg (7lb) in weight
8 fresh sweet chestnuts
1 apple
10g (¼oz) unsalted butter
1 teaspoon caster sugar
200g (7oz) sausagemeat
50ml (2fl oz) vegetable oil
100ml (3½fl oz) white wine
1 litre (1¾ pints) cold water

Preparing the chestnuts
Score and deep-fry the chestnuts for 2 minutes as described on page 209. Peel and chop, then reserve.

Preparing the apple
Peel the apple and cut into eight segments. Core each segment. Place the apples, butter and sugar into a hot pan and cook for 2 minutes until they are caramelised. Remove from the pan and allow to cool.

Preparing the turkey
Cut all around the winglets of the turkey close to its body, then chop off the winglets 5cm (2in) below the cut. Remove the wish-bone. Make an incision either side of the breast bone, then remove the two breasts from the carcass and season them. Chop the turkey carcass and winglets into small pieces.

Filling the turkey breasts
Place the turkey breasts skin-side down on a table and, using a sharp knife, make an incision horizontally, cutting four-fifths through the meat to make an envelope.

Place half the sausagemeat inside the centre of each breast then place four apple segments and four chopped chestnuts on top of the sausagemeat. Pull the flap down to close the breast and tie with string.

Preheat the oven to 375°F (190°C) Gas 5.

Cooking the turkey breasts
In a small roasting tray heat the oil and sear the breasts all over for 2 minutes on each side until golden. Remove from the tray and discard the oil. Place the chopped turkey trimmings in the same roasting tray, lay the breasts on top, and season. Roast in the preheated oven for 1 hour.

Finishing the dish
Remove the breasts from the roasting tray and set aside. Keep warm. Deglaze the tray with the white wine, scraping the caramelised juices from the bottom of the tray. Reduce by half, then add the water and bring to the boil. Pour into a saucepan and simmer gently for 30 minutes. Strain through a fine sieve.

Serving
Remove the string from the turkey breasts. Slice the meat and serve to your guests. Add any juices released to the sauce. Serve the sauce separately.

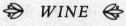

⇒ WINE ⇐
A young Gewürztraminer would be delicious.

Poulet à la Crème et au Riz

*A young chicken simmered in its own broth
with cream, served with basmati rice*

Here is another classic of domestic French cuisine which needs neither great skill nor time.

Cooking the chicken
In a cast-iron casserole arrange the vegetables, and in one single layer add the chicken pieces. Season with salt and pepper.

Add the reduced white wine and the water just to cover. Add the *bouquet garni* and bring to the boil. Skim, cover, then simmer very slowly – a few bubbles should just be breaking on the surface – for about 30–40 minutes, depending on how 'free range' the chicken is.

Skim the fat from the liquid and remove the chicken and vegetables, reserving them separately. You should have about 1.5 litres (2½ pints) broth.

Preparing the sauce
Melt the butter in a saucepan, add the flour and stir to make a *roux*. Add 300ml (10fl oz) broth gradually, stirring continuously to make a smooth sauce.

Add the whipping cream and the finely sliced mushrooms, and stir to blend and cook the mushrooms.

Season to taste with salt and pepper and lift the sauce with lemon juice.

Cooking the rice
Wash the rice in plenty of cold running water for 1 minute, then drain.

In a saucepan melt the butter, then add the rice. Stir so that each grain is coated with butter.

Add 400ml (14fl oz) broth and season with salt and pepper. Bring to the boil, then cover and simmer for 7–8 minutes.

Finishing the dish and serving
Reheat the vegetables in the remaining broth, and reheat the chicken in the sauce.

On a large dish, spoon the rice in the middle, and top with the chicken and sauce. Arrange the drained vegetables around, and serve to your guests.

CHEF'S NOTES
Cooking the chicken will yield about 1.5 litres (2½ pints) broth – you will be using only 700ml (24fl oz). The remainder can be served the next day as a soup.

If you were to choose an old boiling fowl, the cooking time would be about 3 hours. Remove the fat from the fowl first, and do not add the vegetables until about 45 minutes before the end of cooking time.

This rice will cook very quickly, so watch it. In any case, never boil it or the grains will burst and it will become mushy.

For four people

Preparation time: 20 minutes

Cooking time: 1½ hours

Planning ahead: Get the butcher to cut the chicken into 10 pieces: 2 breasts, each halved, 2 wings, and 2 legs, each cut into leg and thigh.

The whole dish can be prepared a few hours in advance.

*1 chicken, about 1.4–1.8kg
(3–4lb) in weight, cleaned and divided
into 10 pieces
200ml (7fl oz) dry white wine,
reduced by half
4 carrots, peeled
1 celery stalk, trimmed and cut into 4
8 small baby onions
or shallots, peeled
2 leeks, washed and
cut in half widthwise
2 level teaspoons salt
10 black peppercorns, crushed
about 2 litres (3½ pints) water
1 bouquet garni (see page 30)*

FOR THE SAUCE:
*25g (1oz) unsalted butter
25g (1oz) plain flour
300ml (10fl oz) cooled broth
from the chicken
200ml (7fl oz) whipping cream
100g (4oz) button mushrooms,
cleaned and finely sliced
juice of ¼ lemon*

FOR THE RICE:
*250g (9oz) basmati rice
30g (1¼oz) unsalted butter
400ml (14fl oz) broth
from the chicken*

 *WINE*

A good dry white table wine will do very well for this simple dish.

CHAPTER SEVEN

Vegetables

Unlike the French, the British have long understood the use of vegetables. Again, unfortunately, a great deal of these vegetables are imported from Europe. The reason still remains a mystery to me.

I once invited executives from the Farmers' Union to try to enthuse them by showing them healthy rows of artichokes, aubergines, French beans, haricot beans, peppers, etc. They showed their appreciation, but the excitement was short-lived. In this country we *can* grow a great number of vegetables which are normally imported from Europe, *and* on a commercial basis. So why should we import artichokes from Brittany, salads from France, and peppers from Holland when all can be grown in Britain? (One can also expand the seasons by using different seeds of particular plant varieties.) As more and more farmers are obliged to diversify, why aren't they taking this opportunity of growing these vegetables instead of importing them?

Freshness

It is possible now to find some very fresh vegetables in the shops. Equally during the spring, summer and autumn seasons, one can go and pick them in the many 'pick-your-own' farms which are now flourishing all across Great Britain. Besides being a delightful outing with family and friends, you will discover the earthy magic of pulling young vegetables from the ground – picking young courgettes still crowned with their golden yellow flowers, gathering beans just as they're ripe. Equally the results will speak for themselves on the plate.

Cooking Vegetables

Vegetables are not an ornamental garnish. They need the same attention as, and should complement perfectly, the main course they accompany.

First, the vegetables should be young – but not *too* young, or their flavour will not have developed. Older vegetables often have a coarse taste and a fibrous or woody texture.

Accompanying vegetables should provide a clean taste to complement the more complex or richer taste of the dish they accompany. Most young vegetables are delicate, so try to preserve or enhance their flavour, texture and colour when choosing your cooking method.

The most common (and most misunderstood) way of cooking vegetables is boiling them in water; under- and over-cooking are the commonest mistakes. See the French bean recipe on page 202.

Preparing Mushrooms

Cultivated button mushrooms Cut off the base of the stalks and wash the mushrooms briefly in plenty of cold water. Pat dry with a tea towel or kitchen towel.

Wild mushrooms Cut off the base of the stalks and scrape the stems and cups very gently with a small paring knife. Only wash – briefly – if grit or dirt is plainly visible. If wild mushrooms are soaked in water and drowned, their taste and texture will be ruined. Morels are the exception: their conical sponge caps hold a lot of earth and sand, so they must be washed in two or three changes of water. Small insects and tiny worms often nest in these tasty fungi, especially the larger ones, so check carefully and discard any affected stalks.

Halve or quarter large mushrooms so that they cook evenly.

Skinning and Seeding Tomatoes

Using a sharp paring knife, cut off the stem and slit the skin. Plunge the tomatoes into plenty of boiling water for 2–5 seconds to loosen the skin (the precise time will vary according to ripeness). Remove with a slotted spoon, refresh in cold water for a few seconds and skin.

Halve the skinned tomatoes, and remove the seeds with a teaspoon. Remove the core too (these, plus the seeds, can be kept for other uses). Cut the flesh into segments or dice.

Preparing Salad Leaves

Discard withered leaves, then cut the base to free the leaves. Wash the leaves in cold water. Fragile leaves such as lettuce should be soaked in water for no longer than 5 minutes; leave firmer leaves like curly endive, radicchio and batavia for up to 10 minutes. They will revive and take up some of their lost moisture.

Wash all salad leaves in at least two changes of water. Use a large quantity of water at first so that all dirt and impurities fall to the bottom, then change the water and repeat with a smaller quantity.

You must dry the leaves well because any excess moisture will interfere with the dressing. Be careful not to bruise them.

To store, wrap in a cloth and refrigerate until ready to use.

Add the dressing at the very last moment, as the vinegar will destroy the texture of the leaves.

Petits Navets Glacés

Glazed baby turnips

Turnips are best when young; they have a pleasant, delicate bitterness. Older turnips can also be cooked this way, but do not use the leaves; halve or quarter them, shape and blanch before cooking.

Trim the tops of the turnips, leaving on about 3cm (1¼in) stalk, and reserve some of the most tender-looking leaves. Wash the turnips and selected leaves and keep them in separate bowls of water.

Stand the turnips upright in a small sauté pan, packed close together. Add the butter, caster sugar and a pinch of salt. Cover with cold water just up to the base of the stalks and bring to the boil. Simmer for about 30 minutes, then check if they are cooked.

Increase the heat and evaporate most of the water, rotating the pan to keep the turnips coated with a film of butter. Keep warm.

For the tops, melt the butter in the water in a small saucepan, and season with a pinch of salt and pepper. Bring to the boil, add the leaves, cover and cook for 2 minutes. Taste and correct the seasoning if necessary.

Arrange the turnips attractively on a flat serving dish and surround with the leaves. Serve immediately to your guests.

Variations

Many root vegetables, such as radishes, baby onions and shallots can be cooked this way.

For four people

Preparation and cooking time: 40 minutes

20 small turnips with their tops
20g (¾oz) unsalted butter
1 level teaspoon caster sugar
salt

FOR COOKING THE TOPS:
1 teaspoon unsalted butter
4 tablespoons water
freshly ground pepper

Fevettes à la Crème et Persil Plat

Young broad beans cooked in cream and parsley

Shell the beans, blanch in boiling water for 5 seconds, then refresh and drain. Make an incision in the skin and squeeze the bright emerald green beans out of their outer skins. Set aside.

Wash the parsley, shake dry, then pick off the leaves. Blanch these in boiling water for 30 seconds, refresh, drain and reserve.

Put the cream and garlic in a medium saucepan, and season with a little salt and pepper. Bring to the boil, add the broad beans and simmer for 1 minute. Add the parsley and simmer for a further 30 seconds.

Taste and correct seasoning if necessary. Serve to your guests.

CHEF'S NOTES
The broad beans must be young. Older broad beans become too starchy and uninteresting.

Blanch the beans for 5 seconds only – just enough to soften the outer skin which must be removed as it is tough and unappetising. (But if you have *very tiny* beans, do not remove the skins as they will be very tender.)

Variations
Young haricot beans can also be cooked this way; increase the simmering time. The broad beans can also be replaced by mangetout.

Pommes Sautées

Sauté potatoes

Dice the potatoes into 1cm (½in) cubes, and simmer them in plenty of boiling salted water for 4–5 minutes until they are barely cooked. Drain the potatoes in a colander. Let the steam escape for a minimum of 5 minutes. Sprinkle with the flour.

In a large, cast-iron sauté pan, heat the oil until it is hot, add the potatoes and colour them lightly for up to 7–10 minutes until they are crisp and golden; at this stage, remove the oil, add the butter, and cook for a further 3 minutes. Taste, and season with salt and pepper. Serve to your guests.

Variations
Obviously, lots of variations are possible with this recipe, simply by adding finely chopped onions or shallots, fresh herbs such as chives and parsley or little *lardons* (see page 28) during the final stage of cooking.

For four people

Preparation time: 10 minutes

Cooking time: 20 minutes

800g (1¾lb) potatoes, peeled
(King Edward or Désirée)
salt and freshly ground pepper
10g (¼oz) plain flour
2 tablespoons groundnut oil
50g (2oz) unsalted butter

Carottes à la Peau

Glazed baby carrots in their skins

Trim the carrot tops, leaving on about 2cm (¾in) of the leaves, then wash the carrots and place in cold water. Taste a little of the raw carrot, to assess its sweetness.

In a large sauté pan melt the butter with a pinch of salt and caster sugar (optional). Bring to simmering point, add carrots, cover with the lid and simmer for 10 minutes.

Remove the lid, add the tarragon and reduce the liquid until the carrots are glazed. Season with a turn of pepper and serve to your guests.

CHEF'S NOTES
It may be less attractive to leave the skin on a young carrot, but the taste is so much better.

For four people

Preparation time: 10 minutes

Cooking time: 10 minutes

20 baby carrots with their tops
30g (1¼oz) unsalted butter
salt and freshly ground pepper
1 pinch of caster sugar (optional)
2 leaves of young tarragon

Ratatouille

Vegetable stew

For four people

Preparation time: 15 minutes

Cooking time: 20 minutes

Planning ahead: The dish can be prepared well in advance.

150g (5oz) onion, peeled
1 medium aubergine, wiped
1 red pepper, seeded
2 medium courgettes,
topped and tailed
2 plum tomatoes, wiped
150ml (5fl oz) olive oil
1 sprig of thyme
salt
1 garlic clove, peeled and puréed

Cut all the vegetables into 1cm (½in) dice.

In a large cast-iron sauté pan, heat the olive oil and sweat the diced onion with the thyme for 5–6 minutes, stirring from time to time. Add the aubergine and pepper dice and cook for a further 5 minutes.

Separately, bring to the boil 1 litre (1¾ pints) water with some salt, and blanch the diced courgettes for 3 minutes. Refresh under cold water, drain and add them to the pan as well. Cook for another 5 minutes, then add the tomatoes and puréed garlic. Cover with a lid and continue to cook for a further 10 minutes. Taste, and correct seasoning if necessary.

Serve to your guests.

CHEF'S NOTES
The ratatouille can also be served as a cold hors d'oeuvre.

Obviously you can add other herbs such as bay leaf, basil or marjoram, etc.

Flageolets

Very young haricot beans

For four people

Preparation and cooking time: 1 hour, 10 minutes

Planning ahead: The beans can be cooked in the stock in advance.

550g (1¼lb) fresh flageolet
beans, podded
30g (1¼oz) unsalted butter
½ garlic clove, peeled and puréed
fresh parsley, chopped
salt and freshly ground pepper

FOR THE STOCK:
1 onion, halved, each half studded
with a clove
1 carrot, peeled
1 sprig of thyme
1 level tablespoon salt
1.5 litres (2½ pints) water

I think flageolet beans (very young haricots) are the best of beans. If you are not lucky enough to have them in your garden, you can find them in the delicatessen, dried.

Place the studded onion halves, carrot, thyme and salt in the water and simmer for 30 minutes.

Add the beans to the stock, and simmer for about 30 minutes. Cooking time will vary according to the maturity of the beans. Taste the beans and, if they are cooked, drain.

In a large casserole, add the butter and melt on medium heat. Add the beans, some stock, garlic and parsley and season with salt and pepper. Cover and simmer for 5 minutes. Serve to your guests.

Variations
This dish will go very well with lamb and pork. You can add some roasting juices to the beans, which will be delicious.

Different beans can be used such as butter beans, white beans, etc. The cooking time will change accordingly.

If you use dried beans, spread them on the table to pick out any stones which might be there. Wash in plenty of water, soak for 2 hours, drain, then follow the recipe as above.

198

An aubergine, just ready for picking

For four people

Preparation and cooking time: 20 minutes

1 English lettuce (round)
200g (7oz) very young peas, after podding
4 tablespoons water
15g (½oz) unsalted butter
salt and freshly ground pepper
a pinch of caster sugar
50g (2oz) lardons (optional, see page 28),
chopped very finely

Fondue de Petits Pois et Laitue

Braised lettuce and peas

Discard the outside leaves of the lettuce, cut off the root, free the leaves and wash them in plenty of water. Drain and reserve.

In a saucepan mix together the water, butter, a pinch each of salt, pepper and sugar. Add the lettuce leaves, cover and cook for 30 seconds. Add the peas and *lardons* (if using), cover and cook for 2 more minutes. Taste and correct seasoning. Serve to your guests.

CHEF'S NOTES
In this recipe, very young peas are used which need hardly any cooking. However, if you use more mature peas, increase the cooking time accordingly.

For four people

Preparation time: 10 minutes

Cooking time: 3 minutes

400g (14oz) spinach leaves
60g (2¼oz) unsalted butter
salt and freshly ground pepper

Epinards au Beurre

Spinach in butter

So often spinach is cooked in masses of boiling water, refreshed, then wrung out in a cloth, then cooked again. This is definitely one of the sacrileges of cooking.

Remove the tough stalks from the centre of the leaves. Wash the leaves in plenty of cold water, twice if necessary, and drain.

In a large saucepan, melt the butter and add the spinach leaves. Season with salt and pepper. Cover and cook at full boil for 2 minutes. Remove the lid, stir and cook for a further minute.

Taste, correct seasoning and serve to your guests.

CHEF'S NOTES
If you are having a dinner party, prepare the spinach ready in a casserole dish with the butter, and cook at the last moment.

Mousse d'Epinards

Spinach mousses

Preheat the oven to 325°F (160°C) Gas 3.

Preparing the spinach and cream
Wash the spinach in two changes of water, drain well and set aside.

Put the garlic in the cream, and simmer for 5 minutes.

Making the mousse mixture
In a pan large enough to hold the spinach, make a *beurre noisette* (see page 40) with the butter. Use a little of this to create a film over the ramekins. Throw the spinach into the pan with the butter, stir, cover and cook for 2 minutes.

Strain the cream into the spinach (discarding the garlic), and boil for a few seconds. Draw off the heat and leave to cool.

In a liquidiser, finely purée the spinach and cream with the eggs, 1 teaspoon salt and 6 turns of pepper for 2–3 minutes. Place in a bowl, taste, correct the seasoning and divide between the lightly greased ramekins.

Cooking the mousses
Line the bottom of a shallow roasting pan with greaseproof paper. Stand the moulds in the pan and add hot water to come three-quarters of the way up the sides of the ramekins.

Loosely cover the pan with pierced buttered foil and cook in the preheated oven for 35–40 minutes.

Serving
Warm four plates.

Invert the ramekins on to the middle of the plates and shake them gently from side to side to release the mousses. Serve to your guests.

CHEF'S NOTES
Some varieties of spinach have little or no flavour. Choose carefully to prevent your mousses from suffering the same fate. Coarse annual spinach is very good.

Variations
Swiss chard, lettuce, leeks and blanched parsley also make delicious mousses.

For four people

Preparation and cooking time: 55 minutes

Special equipment: 4 × 4cm (1½in) ramekins.

Planning ahead: The mousses can be moulded up to 8 hours in advance. They can be cooked half an hour in advance and kept warm in a *bain-marie*.

500g (18oz) spinach leaves, tough stalks removed
1 garlic clove, peeled and sliced
250ml (8fl oz) whipping cream
50g (2oz) unsalted butter
3 eggs
salt and freshly ground pepper

Haricots Verts au Beurre

French beans in butter

For four people

Preparation time: 5 minutes

Cooking time: 5–6 minutes

400g (14oz) French beans, topped and tailed
1.5 litres (2½pints) water
25g (1oz) salt

FOR FINISHING THE DISH:
40g (1½oz) unsalted butter
2 tablespoons water
salt and freshly ground pepper

Bring the water to the boil and add the salt. Cook the beans for 3–3½ minutes, according to the size of the beans. Taste and if ready, drain and plunge them into cold water for 5 minutes, then drain again.

To finish the dish, emulsify the butter and water together. Add the French beans, taste, correct seasoning and cook for 1 minute. Serve to your guests.

CHEF'S NOTES
The concentration of salt in the water appears quite high. Salt will fix the chlorophyll (colour) of the beans and give them their taste.

In the past vegetables were totally overcooked; now the trend is to undercook them, which is equally wrong. The cooking time is proportional to the size of the beans and the texture should be firm, but not crunchy.

During cooking do not place a lid on a pan of green vegetables. There are certain acids contained in vegetables which are released; with the lid on, these acids will attack the colour of the vegetables, which will be lost.

Refreshing beans and other green vegetables in cold water arrests the cooking and preserves taste, colour and texture. This can be done in advance, and it also saves time and effort when serving your complete dish. Just reheat the vegetable in a little butter and serve.

The emulsion of butter and water is important, since water creates steam which heats the vegetables quickly and thoroughly. The water must not evaporate totally or the vegetables will be too greasy; they should simply be coated with a fine film of butter and water emulsion. The final seasoning should be light to allow the taste of the vegetables to come through.

Variations
Swiss chard and mangetout can be cooked in the same way.

Gratin de Potiron

Gratin of pumpkin

This dish can be served on its own or as an accompanying vegetable.

Cooking the pumpkin purée
Place the diced pumpkin and the water in a saucepan, cover and cook for about 20 minutes; remove the lid and boil to evaporate the water. Leave to cool.

Mix together the egg yolks and sugar and whisk well for 2 minutes. Add the cool pumpkin purée and two-thirds of the cheese. Taste and season with pepper.

Preheat the oven to 350°F (180°C) Gas 4.

Preparing the egg whites
Whisk the egg whites until they form soft peaks, then add the lemon juice. Season with pepper then briskly whisk one-third of the egg white into the purée. Carefully fold in the remaining egg white. Taste and correct seasoning.

Cooking the dish and serving
Butter the gratin dish lightly, pour in the purée mixture and sprinkle with the remaining cheese. Dot with the remaining 20g (¾oz) butter and bake in the oven for 15–20 minutes. Serve to your guests.

CHEF'S NOTES
The pumpkin must be ripe to ensure a full flavour.

If you beat the egg whites too much, they will become granular and separate. The addition of the lemon juice prevents this from happening and also counter-balances the sweetness of the pumpkin.

No salt is added to this dish because of the Gruyère.

Variations
You can make a beautiful pumpkin tart in the same way. Omit the cheese, salt and pepper, and increase the sugar to 40g (1½oz). Butter a flan dish lightly and sprinkle with flour before adding the mixture. After cooking, turn the tart out on to a cooling rack, leave to cool, then place on a plate.

You can also add a pinch of powdered cinnamon or a dash of Kirsch liqueur if you wish.

For six people

Preparation time: 15 minutes

Cooking time: 35–40 minutes

Special equipment:
A deep oval earthenware or cast-iron gratin dish, approximately 24 × 30cm (9½ × 12in).

Planning ahead: The pumpkin purée can be made in advance, covered with cling film, and refrigerated.

400g (14oz) ripe pumpkin flesh, seeded and cut into 2 cm (¾in) dice
3 tablespoons water
2 eggs, separated
10g (¼oz) caster sugar
50g (2oz) Gruyère or Emmenthal cheese, finely grated
freshly ground pepper
juice of ¼ lemon
25g (1oz) unsalted butter

WINE

A crisp white wine made from the Chenin grape – from France or America.

Gratin de Blettes

Gratin of Swiss Chard

Swiss chard is not a very well-known vegetable, but to me it is one of the most tasty. Both the large green leaves and stalks are eaten, and the former can simply be prepared as spinach. This vegetable can be found in the garden or shops between July and October.

Peel the stalks if necessary.
    Cut the stalks into small pieces about 2–3cm (¾–1¼in) long, and boil for 4 minutes in plenty of boiling salted water. Drain, pat dry and season.
    Preheat the oven to 350°F (180°C) Gas 4.
    Butter the gratin dish. Place the chard stalks in a casserole. Add the cream and cook at full boil for 3 minutes. Add the cheese and stir, pour into the gratin dish and cook in the preheated oven for 40 minutes. Serve to your guests.

CHEF'S NOTES
Very little salt is needed in this dish, as Gruyère cheese is already salty.

Peeling the Swiss chard will depend on its maturity. The young vegetable will not need peeling, whereas older chard, with more fibrous and longer stalks, will (these will be seen towards the end of the season, in October).

Chips de Céleri-Rave Frits

Golden brown, crispy celeriac chips

A wonderful accompaniment for roast game.

Wash the celeriac, cut off the tops, and peel. Quarter, then cut into the thinnest possible slices.
    Deep-fry four at a time in the hot oil, until they turn a rich golden brown, keeping them well separated with a kitchen fork.
    Lift out the frying basket, shake off excess oil then drain on absorbent paper. Keep warm until ready to serve to your guests.

CHEF'S NOTES
Slice the celeriac as finely and evenly as possible. Thick or uneven slices will burn.

Do not cook all the slices at once: this will lower the temperature of the oil, causing the chips to soak it up and stick together. The edges will darken first, but do not worry; the chips must be cooked through to the middle. Remove them when the oil stops sizzling, indicating that no moisture is left.

Do not season the chips – frying concentrates the already spicy flavour of the celeriac.

Pommes de Terre aux Pistils de Safran

Saffron potatoes

This dish goes very well with all Provençal dishes.

Halve or quarter the larger potatoes. Trim them all into small barrel shapes and keep in cold water.

In a medium sauté pan sweat the potatoes and shallots in the butter for 1 or 2 minutes, then add the saffron, thyme and bay leaf and season with salt and pepper. Shake the pan to make sure all the potatoes are well coated with saffron.

Add the chicken stock or water, cover the pan with buttered paper and the lid, and simmer for about 15 minutes.

Remove the lid and reduce at full boil until the potatoes are glazed.

Remove the thyme and bay leaf, taste one potato, correct the seasoning if necessary, and serve to your guests.

CHEF'S NOTES

Saffron threads are expensive. They have a concentrated but slightly bitter flavour, so must be rehydrated before using to regain their delicacy.

Most varieties of potatoes can be used, even new.

For four people

Preparation and cooking time: 35 minutes

Planning ahead: If using saffron threads, rehydrate them in 2 tablespoons water for 1 hour beforehand. The chicken stock (if used) must be made in advance.

The dish can be prepared 1 hour in advance, then warmed in a hot oven before serving.

550g (1¼lb) potatoes, peeled
2 shallots, peeled and finely chopped
20g (¾oz) unsalted butter
a pinch of saffron threads
or saffron powder
1 sprig of thyme
1 bay leaf
salt and freshly ground pepper
100ml (3½fl oz) light chicken stock
(see page 34)

Echalotes Caramelisées

Caramelised shallots

Melt the butter in a sauté pan, put in the shallots, closely packed together, add a pinch of salt and pepper, and cook uncovered over a moderate heat for about 10 minutes.

Partially cover with a lid and cook over moderate heat for about 30 minutes, stirring occasionally, until the shallots are melting and brown. Taste, correct the seasoning and serve to your guests.

CHEF'S NOTES

When peeling the shallots, remove the tough second layer of skin and cut them just above the roots so they remain whole once cooked.

They can also be baked in a fairly hot oven (400°F/200°C/Gas 6); the cooking time will vary, depending on the size of the shallots.

Variations
Very small onions can also be cooked this way.

For four people

Preparation and cooking time: 50 minutes

Planning ahead: This dish can be cooked in advance and kept warm.

30 shallots, about 350g
(12oz), peeled
20g (¾oz) unsalted butter
salt and freshly ground pepper

Salsifis Glacés

Glazed salsify

For four people

Preparation and cooking time: 40 minutes

Planning ahead: The salsify can be cooked 1 hour in advance.

12 salsify roots
2 litres (3½pints) water
2 tablespoons white wine vinegar
25g (1oz) unsalted butter
a squeeze of lemon juice
300ml (10fl oz) light chicken stock
(see page 34) or water
salt and freshly ground pepper

Wash and scrub the salsify with a hard brush to remove any dirt. Peel and place in the water acidulated with the vinegar to prevent discoloration. Drain and cut into 4cm (1½in) sticks just before cooking.

In a medium saucepan, sweat the salsify in the butter with the lemon juice for 2 minutes. Add the stock or water and season with a pinch each of salt and pepper. Bring to the boil, cover and simmer for about 15 minutes. Remove the lid, and reduce at full boil until the salsify is glazed.

Taste and correct seasoning, then serve to your guests.

CHEF'S NOTES
Wear rubber gloves when handling the salsify or it will stain your fingers.

Variations
You could add a spoonful of whipping cream and some chopped parsley.

Gratin de Topinambours

Gratin of Jerusalem artichokes

For four people

Preparation time: 20 minutes

Cooking time: 20 minutes

Special equipment:
1 gratin dish 20cm (8in) square.

Planning ahead: This dish can be prepared in advance, kept refrigerated and cooked at the last moment.

1.25kg (2¾lb) raw Jerusalem artichokes
(750g/1½lb peeled)
salt and freshly ground pepper
10g (¼oz) unsalted butter
500ml (18fl oz) whipping cream

For me the gratin is the very best accompanying vegetable dish you can have with a beautiful succulent roast.

Preheat the oven to 350°F (180°C) Gas 4.
Wash the Jerusalem artichokes to remove all the earth from them. Peel (you will need a little patience, for artichokes are knobbly and difficult to peel), cut through the knobs, then cut into slices 5mm (¼in) thick. Season with salt and pepper.

Butter the gratin dish and arrange the Jerusalem artichoke slices overlapping in the dish. Season each layer with salt and pepper and pour the cream over the top. Cook in the preheated oven for 20 minutes. Serve to your guests.

CHEF'S NOTES
If you wish, you may dot the top of the gratin with little dots of butter to obtain an even golden colour.

Gratin de Navets

Gratin of turnip

Preheat the oven to 350°F (180°C) Gas 4.

Peel the turnips thinly, then cut into slices 2–3mm (⅛in) thick. Reserve.

Separately simmer the cream with the garlic, thyme, white wine vinegar and a pinch of salt for 3 minutes.

Butter the gratin dish and arrange the sliced turnips overlapping in the dish. Season each layer lightly with salt and pepper.

Strain the warm cream over the dish and cook in the preheated oven for 40 minutes. Serve to your guests.

For four people

Preparation time: 15 minutes

Cooking time: 40 minutes

Special equipment:
1 gratin dish 20cm (8in) square.

Planning ahead: This dish can be prepared 1 hour in advance.

*1kg (2¼lb) turnips
(750g/1½lb peeled)
500ml (18fl oz) whipping cream
1 garlic clove, peeled
1 sprig of thyme
1 dash of white wine vinegar
salt and freshly ground pepper
10g (¼oz) unsalted butter*

Endives Rôties

Roasted chicory

Preheat the oven to 400°F (200°C) Gas 6.

Trim off the roots and remove any withered leaves from the chicory heads. Cut the chicory heads in four lengthways, wash in plenty of cold water, drain and pat dry.

In a cast-iron sauté pan, melt the butter until it is a light golden colour, then add the chicory. Cover with a lid and place in the preheated oven for 20 minutes, turning from time to time. Season with salt and pepper.

When the chicory is beautifully browned, place on a serving plate, give it a few turns of pepper and a sprinkle of lemon juice. Serve to your guests.

CHEF'S NOTES
This vegetable recipe would go particularly well with any game dish.

For four people

Preparation time: 5 minutes

Cooking time: 20 minutes

*4 medium heads of chicory
15g (½oz) unsalted butter
salt and freshly ground pepper
a dash of lemon juice*

Choux de Bruxelles

Brussels sprouts

In Great Britain, Brussels sprouts are picked traditionally after the seventh frost. Furthermore, they are cooked and stewed for a lengthy time. This is one way of cooking them. In this recipe it is essential to use *young* Brussels sprouts as they are absolutely delicious and delicate in taste, and their cooking time is short.

Trim off the bases and remove any withered leaves from the sprouts. Cook them in plenty of boiling salted water for 5–6 minutes, according to size. Refresh under cold water and drain.

At the moment of serving, melt the butter with the water in a saucepan, add the Brussels sprouts, heat through, season with salt and pepper, and serve to your guests.

For four people

Preparation time: 10 minutes

Cooking time: 5 minutes

400g (14oz) small Brussels sprouts
salt and freshly ground pepper
20g (¾oz) unsalted butter
2 tablespoons water

Riz Sauvage au Naturel

Wild rice

Preheat the oven to 350°F (180°C) Gas 4.

In a medium ovenproof pan, sweat the chopped shallot in 2 teaspoons of the butter for 2 minutes without colouring. Stir in the rice and season with a pinch of salt and pepper. Add the water, bring to the boil, and cover with greaseproof paper. Cook in the preheated oven for about 1 hour.

Taste and correct the seasoning. Make a *beurre noisette* with the remaining butter (see page 40), stir it into the rice, and serve to your guests.

CHEF'S NOTES
Wild rice (actually the seeds of a North American aquatic grass) is expensive, but it has a far better flavour than refined, processed rice (see page 17). The cooking time may vary from type to type, so check by tasting towards the end. Do not expect the soft texture of white rice; wild rice should remain firm. Do not cook at a higher temperature as excess heat will make the rice burst open.

For four people

Preparation and cooking time: 1 hour, 10 minutes

Planning ahead: The rice can be cooked several hours in advance.

150g (5oz) wild rice,
washed and drained
1 shallot, peeled and finely chopped
15g (½oz) unsalted butter
salt and freshly ground pepper
200ml (7fl oz) water

Châtaignes

Braised chestnuts

This is the ideal accompaniment for any game dish, and for certain meats such as pork and turkey.

Preheat a deep-fryer to 350°F (180°C).

With the point of a small knife, score a ring all around each chestnut without piercing the flesh. Deep-fry in two batches for 1 minute, then cool for 2–3 minutes. Loosen, remove and discard the shell and the brown skin around the chestnuts.

In a saucepan simmer the chestnuts, stock, celery, sugar, salt and pepper gently for 10–15 minutes. Remove the chestnuts with a slotted spoon on to a serving dish and serve to your guests.

CHEF'S NOTES
Pan-fried segments of apple will be a good addition to the chestnuts.

For four people

Preparation time: 10 minutes

Cooking time: 12 minutes

24 fresh sweet chestnuts
vegetable oil for deep-frying
400ml (14fl oz) light chicken
stock (see page 34)
1 small celery stalk
1 teaspoon sugar
salt and freshly ground pepper

Purée de Pommes de Terre

Potato purée

The type of potato that is used will determine the quality of the purée, but Belle de Fontenay is the very best potato, or Binges could be used. However, King Edward is easily obtainable and produces quite a good purée.

Quarter the potatoes and simmer gently in salted water until they are perfectly cooked. Drain in a colander then purée them through a mouli into a casserole. Place the casserole on a medium heat and stir in the cream, the milk and finally the butter. Taste and season with salt and pepper. Serve to your guests.

CHEF'S NOTES
Timing for cooking is difficult since this depends on the size of the potato. To see how well a potato is cooked use the tip of a sharp knife. The water must not boil, or the outside of the potato will be overcooked and crumbly.

Variations
Butter could be replaced with olive oil. Cream can be omitted if you want a lighter purée and it will still be delicious.

New potatoes can also make a delicious purée: simply peel them, leave them whole and cook as per instructions. Reduce the quantity of milk to 300ml (10fl oz).

For four to six people

Preparation time: 5 minutes

Cooking time: 25 minutes

800g (1¾lb) whole potatoes,
peeled and washed
2 litres (3½pints) cold water
40g (1½oz) salt
100ml (3½fl oz) whipping cream
350–400ml (12–14fl oz) milk
80g (3¼oz) unsalted butter
salt and freshly ground pepper

CHAPTER EIGHT

Desserts

In French families, as children, we were made to sit down all through the meal, and as I remember, this was quite painful. To add insult to injury, we had to remain quiet and not distract from nor interfere with the serious grown-up conversations which centred around the most important subjects – religion, army, politics, etc. Nothing to enlighten the mind of a six-year-old! The thought of the dessert to come made me endure all this.

So the dessert was, and remains, an important part of the meal. A great number of cooks are inhibited about pastry-making, soufflé-making and similar 'difficult' techniques, and avoid even attempting them. This is a shame. The recipes given are easy and clear, and once the few principles are understood, you will succeed. Besides the joy it will give you, it will also give you the confidence to try some more ambitious desserts. Your family and friends will love you even more for it.

A great number of the desserts in this book belong to my childhood, and were made by my mother and grandmother.

For eight people

Preparation time: 50 minutes

Cooking time: 25 minutes

Special equipment:
1 tart tin with removable base, 28 × 3cm (11 × 1¼in); a baking sheet.

Planning ahead: The shortcrust pastry should be prepared at least 6 hours in advance and refrigerated (see page 20). The dish can be prepared a few hours prior to your meal.

1 quantity Sweet Shortcrust Pastry (see page 20)

FOR THE RHUBARB FILLING:
400g (14oz) rhubarb, washed, peeled and chopped into 2cm (¾in) pieces
100g (4oz) sugar
200ml (7fl oz) water

FOR THE LEMON CREAM FILLING:
2 egg yolks
50g (2oz) caster sugar
70ml (2¾fl oz) double cream
finely grated zest of ¼ lemon

 *WINE*

A sweet dessert wine would be perfect, such as a Sauternes, Gewürztraminer, Selections des Grands Nobles, or a more humble Loire wine such as a Quarts de Chaume, Château Belle Rive or a Vouvray Moelleux.

Tarte à la Rhubarbe et Citron

Rhubarb and lemon tart

Preheat the oven to 375°F (190°C) Gas 5.

Preparing the pastry case
Allow the pastry dough to come to room temperature. Butter the sides of the tart tin and the base of the baking sheet. Put the baking sheet into the oven to heat through thoroughly.

Lightly flour your work surface and roll the prepared dough out into a circle of 2–3mm (⅛in) thickness. Rest for 2–3 minutes. Place into the tart tin. Press the sides in well and trim the excess off around the edge. Refrigerate for a minimum of half an hour.

Blind-baking the pastry case
Line the inside of the pastry case with aluminium foil or greaseproof paper and fill with baking beans. Transfer the tart tin and its contents to the hot baking sheet, and bake in the preheated oven for 10 minutes. Remove from the oven, remove the foil or paper and beans, and reserve.

Preparing the rhubarb filling
In a saucepan, bring to the boil the sugar and water, then add the chopped rhubarb and simmer for 1 minute. Strain into a colander and reserve.

Preparing the lemon cream filling
Place the egg yolks and sugar in a bowl and beat for 10 minutes with an electric mixer set on high speed, until the volume has tripled. Mix in the double cream and the finely grated lemon zest.

Cooking the rhubarb tart
Distribute the rhubarb over the bottom of the tart, then spread with the lemon cream filling. Cook in the oven at the same temperature for 25–30 minutes.

Serving
Remove the tart from the oven and sprinkle with extra caster sugar. Cool down, remove from the tin and with two cake slices lift the tart on to a round serving dish. Cool for 1 hour before serving.

Tarte à la Rhubarbe et Citron

Soufflé aux Fruits de la Passion

Passion fruit soufflé

For four people

Preparation and cooking time: 30 minutes

Special equipment:
4 soufflé dishes, 8–9cm (3–3¾in) in diameter, and at least 4cm (1½in) high.

Planning ahead: Please read the soufflé-making section on page 23 before attempting this recipe

12 passion fruits
3 tablespoons water
80g (3¼oz) Pastry Cream
(see page 47)
7 egg whites (size 3)
60g (2¼oz) caster sugar
butter and caster sugar for the moulds
icing sugar for dusting

Often home cooks feel that soufflés are beyond their capabilities, and rarely attempt this dish. To cook a soufflé has a certain magic, but once the basic principles are understood, it becomes really very easy to achieve and it is so rewarding. All the ingredients can be prepared in advance and it will only take you 3–4 minutes to finish before baking. Place the pastry cream and passion fruit juice in one bowl, the egg whites in another. Leave your guests for only a few minutes, just enough time to whisk the egg whites, mix them into the base and into the moulds; then bake them in the oven and return with the glorious soufflés!

Preheat the oven to 375°F (190°C) Gas 5.

Preparing the moulds
Brush the inside of the soufflé dishes with butter and sprinkle with caster sugar. Shake off excess sugar.

Preparing the passion fruits
Cut the passion fruits in half. Spoon out the seeds and juices into a saucepan. Add the water and bring to the boil for 30 seconds. Force through a sieve into a small saucepan.

Preparing the soufflés
In a large bowl mix the passion fruit juice and the pastry cream.

Whisk the egg whites to soft peaks then gradually add the caster sugar and whisk until firm peaks are reached. Whisk one-quarter of the egg white into the passion fruit mixture, then fold the remaining egg white in carefully.

Fill the soufflé dishes with the soufflé mixture, and smooth over the tops with a palette knife. Rub your thumb around the edge of the soufflé to push the mixture away from the edge.

Cooking and serving the soufflés
Cook the soufflés in the lower half of the preheated oven for 10–12 minutes. Dust the tops with icing sugar and serve to your guests.

Variations
A small exotic fruit salad or passion fruit sorbet could be served with this soufflé (see pages 254 and 274).

 *WINE*

A dessert wine such as a Californian Muscat Essensia will be perfect, or a Quarts de Chaume to complement the acidity of the dish.

Crêpes au Beurre d'Oranges Façon Suzette

Orange and Grand Marnier pancakes

Crêpes Suzette may be one of the most classical ways of preparing pancakes, but it still remains one of my favourite desserts. This dish was also my first attempt at cooking (I was seventeen) and, instead of impressing my mother with this delicious and boozy concoction, the dish turned into a small disaster. The pie dish in which the golden pancakes were placed was carelessly put on to a hot plate, and blew up into millions of little pieces. Definitely not an experience which anticipated my choice of profession!

Preparing the sauce
In a saucepan, melt the butter then add the caster sugar. Mix together and cook until a light golden brown. Add the strained orange juice and bring to the boil. Skim and boil until you have about 150ml (5fl oz) liquid left. Cool down and add the Grand Marnier or Cointreau. Reserve.

Making the garnish
Place the *julienne* sticks of orange peel in a pan holding at least 1 litre (1¾ pints) cold water, bring to the boil and skim. Cook for about 6–8 minutes, then strain and refresh under cold water.

In a small saucepan, combine the 100ml (3½fl oz) water and the 50g (2oz) caster sugar, and cook until the sugar has dissolved. Add the drained *julienne* sticks and cook gently to crystallise, about 10 minutes. Reserve.

Marinate the orange segments in the Grand Marnier with the remaining teaspoon of caster sugar.

Cooking the pancakes
Lightly butter the pancake frying pan. Heat until it is very hot, pour in a small ladleful of batter, and rotate so it covers the whole frying-pan surface. Cook for 30–40 seconds, then turn over with a spatula and cook the other side for another 30 seconds. Make 12 pancakes.

Preheat the oven to 450°F (230°C) Gas 8.

Finishing the dish and serving
Allow three orange segments per pancake. Place these in the middle of each pancake, then fold together into a triangular shape. Sprinkle with caster sugar. Place the filled pancakes on a tray and warm up in the hot oven for 2 minutes. Bring the sauce to the boil, arrange three pancakes in the centre of each warm plate, pour the sauce over and scatter the orange *julienne* sticks around. Serve to your guests.

Variations
Caramelised apple segments with a caramel sauce (see page 250) would also be delicious; in this case add 1 tablespoon of Calvados.

For four people

Preparation time: 25 minutes

Cooking time: 40 minutes

Special equipment:
1 pancake frying pan, 5mm (¼in) deep.

Planning ahead: Please read the instructions on how to make pancakes on page 22 before embarking on this recipe.

1 quantity Pancake Batter (see page 22)
butter for greasing
caster sugar for sprinkling

FOR THE SAUCE:
1 tablespoon unsalted butter
100g (4oz) caster sugar
500ml (18fl oz) fresh orange juice
(you'll need about 8 oranges), strained
2 tablespoons Grand Marnier
or Cointreau

FOR THE GARNISH:
peel of 2 oranges,
cut into fine julienne sticks
100ml (3½fl oz) water
50g (2oz) caster sugar,
plus 1 teaspoon
segments from 5 oranges
(a minimum of 40 segments)
1 tablespoon Grand Marnier

 *WINE*

An orange Muscat from California or a glass of champagne.

Gratin de Rhubarbe et Fraises

Rhubarb and strawberry gratin

270g (9½oz) strawberries
300g (11oz) rhubarb
125ml (4½fl oz) water
125g (4½oz) caster sugar
a dash of lemon juice
4 egg yolks
100ml (3½fl oz) whipping cream
icing sugar for dusting

Preparing the fruit
Wash the strawberries briefly in cold water to remove any dirt. Remove from the water and dry in a cloth. Remove the stalks and quarter the strawberries.

Peel the rhubarb sticks and cut each stalk into 2cm (¾in) segments.

Cooking the rhubarb
Mix the water, caster sugar and lemon juice in a casserole. Bring it to the boil and turn down the heat to simmering point. Cook the rhubarb in this for 3–5 minutes, depending on the texture of the rhubarb. Drain through a sieve into a casserole. Reserve the rhubarb on a tray and allow to cool.

Making the *sabayon*
Place the egg yolks in the bowl of an electric mixer and whisk at the highest speed until the egg yolks have tripled in volume.

Meanwhile, cook the rhubarb syrup for 2 minutes.

Lower the speed of the whisk and pour the hot syrup on to the egg yolks, in between the beaters and the sides of the bowl, and whisk the mixture until cold. Whip the cream and fold it delicately with a spatula into the egg yolk-syrup mixture.

Preheat the grill to its hottest.

Finishing the dish and serving
Place the strawberries in the middle of each heatproof plate. Then scatter the rhubarb around the strawberries and spoon the *sabayon* over both fruit. Sprinkle with icing sugar and glaze under the grill for about 30 seconds. Serve to your guests.

CHEF'S NOTES
There is an emulsifier in the egg yolks. The volume of the egg yolks will develop due to the air incorporated by the whisking; the hot syrup poured in will partly cook the egg yolks and make the *sabayon* stable. The operation must be done with great care: if the syrup trickles against the side of the bowl it would solidify, and if it is poured over the beaters it could 'spit' and be very dangerous.

Variations
The rhubarb and strawberries can be replaced by other types of fruit: raspberries, blackcurrants, wild strawberries, etc.

WINE

A good dessert wine will counterbalance the acidity of the rhubarb. Quarts de Chaumes or Monbazillac would be excellent.

Gratin de Rhubarbe et Fraises

Sorbet de Mangue et Citron Vert

Mango and lime sorbet

For six to eight people

Preparation time: 30 minutes

Special equipment:
A *sorbetière* (see page 32).

Planning ahead: The syrup must be and the sorbet can be prepared well in advance. Before serving, chill the glass bowls or glasses in the freezer for 30 minutes.

*2 medium mangoes, peeled and
stoned (will yield 300g/11oz pulp)
150ml (5fl oz) lime juice
(approx. 4–6 limes)
200ml (7fl oz) Stock Syrup (see page 46)*

Liquidise the mango flesh with the lime juice and stock syrup, then strain through a fine sieve into the bowl of the *sorbetière*.

Churn for 15–20 minutes, according to the cooling power of your machine.

Using 2 dessertspoons dipped in hot water, place the sorbet into the frosted glass bowls or glasses and serve to your guests.

CHEF'S NOTES
Choose mangoes that are firm but ripe; if the mangoes are unripe, they will be extremely fibrous and the taste will not be developed.

You could serve this sorbet with Coconut Tuiles (see page 276), which would be delicious.

Poires au Vin Rouge et Grains de Cassis

Poached William pears in red wine and blackcurrants

Preparing the blackcurrants
Place the blackcurrants and sugar in a large saucepan, pour in the water and red wine, bring to the boil and skim off any impurities. Simmer for about 5 minutes, then strain the liquid into another saucepan (which should be large enough to hold the four pears comfortably). Press the blackcurrants with a ladle to extract as much juice as possible.

Preparing the pears
Peel the pears, leaving the stems in, and rub with the wedge of lemon. Place in the saucepan with the blackcurrant juice, stems up. The liquid should cover the pears, but top up with water if needed. Cook very slowly for about 15 minutes.

Turn off the heat, add the garnish blackcurrants, and leave the pears to cool down in the juice. Refrigerate for a minimum of 6 hours.

Serving
Place the pears, juice and blackcurrants in a nice glass bowl and scatter the mint leaves around.

CHEF'S NOTES
The best variety of pear to use is undoubtedly William, so they are well worth shopping around for. Ripe Comice or Conference would be second choice.

The cooking time of the pears may vary according to which type of pear you are using, and also the degree of ripeness. It may, therefore, be necessary to increase the cooking time. Do not allow the wine to boil as this would overcook the pears.

For four people

Preparation time: 15 minutes

Cooking time: 20 minutes

Marinating time: 6 hours

Planning ahead: This dish can be prepared a day in advance and refrigerated. This will improve its flavour.

4 William pears
150g (5oz) blackcurrants
100g (4oz) caster sugar
100ml (3½fl oz) water
300ml (10fl oz) red wine
¼ lemon

FOR THE GARNISH:
120g (4½oz) blackcurrants
18 small mint leaves

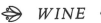
WINE

A fruity red wine, for example Beaujolais.

For four people

Preparation time: 20 minutes

Planning ahead: This dessert should be prepared a minimum of 5–6 hours in advance of your meal.

Alternatively, it can also be prepared a day in advance and refrigerated.

2 peaches
1 small melon
100g (4oz) each of strawberries,
blackcurrants, blackberries
and raspberries
8 mint leaves

FOR THE SAUCE:
200g (7oz) raspberries
200g (7oz) strawberries
100g (4oz) caster sugar
juice of ½ lemon

≫ WINE ≪

To simplify things, I will propose a glass of good sparkling wine or – if possible – champagne.

Soupe de Fruits

Medley of summer fruits,
steeped in a raspberry and strawberry sauce

Preparing the sauce
Trim, wash and drain the fruit. Place all the ingredients in a blender and purée, then force the pulp through a fine sieve into a large mixing bowl.

Preparing the fruit
Wash and drain the fruit and mint leaves. Remove stems.

Cut each peach into eight segments. Discard stones.

Halve the melon, remove the seeds, and divide each half into six. Remove the peel and cut each piece into three (36 pieces in all).

Cut large strawberries in halves and quarters; leave smaller ones whole.

Mix all the fruit together and place in the sauce. Chop the mint leaves very finely and mix with the fruit. Cover with cling film and chill for at least 5 hours.

Serving
Place the fruit and sauce into a glass bowl, and serve – very cold – to your guests.

CHEF'S NOTES
The fruit must be of the best quality and very ripe. If the blackberries are too acidic, sprinkle them with 20g (¾oz) caster sugar and marinate for 2–3 hours.

After chilling, taste and add a little sugar if necessary.

Variations
Various fruits can be added or substituted – wild strawberries, grapes, mango, pears, etc.

A red fruit sorbet can be served with this simple dessert (see page 240).

Soupe de Fruits

Terrine aux Fruits d'Eté au Coulis de Framboises

Terrine of summer fruits with a raspberry sauce

Simple, attractive, lively and the perfect dessert for a hot summer day.

Preparing the jelly
Soften the gelatine leaves in cold water.

Bring the orange juice and caster sugar to the boil in a pan, skim, then remove from the heat. Add the softened gelatine leaves, and the Cointreau if you are using it. Stir for 30 seconds, then strain.

Put a small layer of jelly – about 5mm (¼in) thick – into the terrine, covering the bottom, and allow to set in the fridge for about 20 minutes.

Building the terrine
When the initial layer of jelly is set, mix all the fruits together without bruising them, and place in the terrine so that they come to the top. Press down lightly so that there is as little space as possible between them.

Place the remaining jelly over ice and cool down (until it thickens), then pour over the fruits. Cover the terrine with cling film, and refrigerate for a minimum of 12 hours.

Preparing the raspberry sauce
Purée the fruit with the icing sugar, then force through a fine sieve. Taste and liven up with lemon juice and a bit more sugar if necessary. Reserve.

Serving
Dip the terrine into hot water for a few seconds. Run the blade of a knife which has been dipped into hot water down the sides of the dish, keeping the blade tight against the sides.

Turn the terrine out on to a tea towel. Using a serrated knife which has been dipped into hot water, carve into slices. Arrange on a plate, and surround the slices with the raspberry sauce.

CHEF'S NOTES
The fruit must be at its ripest. Remember to remove stones from the relevant fruit.

Blackberries can be acid. Taste, and if they are, marinate for 1 hour in 20g (¾oz) caster sugar.

The easiest way of carving the terrine would be to use an electric carving knife if you have one.

For eight to ten people

Preparation time: 30 minutes

Special equipment:
A terrine, 23cm (9in) long, 9cm (3½in) wide and 9cm (3½in) deep.

Planning ahead: The terrine must be made a day in advance.

The sauce can also be made in advance.

FOR THE ORANGE JELLY:
7 gelatine leaves
500ml (18fl oz) fresh orange juice
120g (4½oz) caster sugar
1 tablespoon Cointreau (optional)

FOR THE FRUITS:
650g (1½lb) perfectly ripe mixed summer fruit: 150g (5oz) cherries, stoned;
200g (7oz) raspberries;
and 100g (4oz) each of strawberries, blackberries and blackcurrants

FOR THE RASPBERRY SAUCE:
300g (11oz) raspberries
100g (4oz) icing sugar
juice of ¼ lemon

Terrine aux Fruits d'Eté au Coulis de Framboises

Variations

A plum or cherry jelly would also be delicious to bind the terrine instead of orange jelly. Make as for the orange jelly.

> *850g (1lb 14oz) plums or cherries, stoned*
> *75g (3oz) caster sugar*
> *100ml (3½fl oz) water*
> *juice of 1 lemon*
> *7 gelatine leaves, soaked in cold water to soften*

Cook the plums or cherries with the sugar and water for 15 minutes, then add the lemon juice and softened gelatine leaves. Force the pulp through a chinois sieve, then reserve and use as above.

WINE

A sweet Jurançon wine would be just right or indulge in a bottle of good champagne.

Pêches au Vin Blanc

Peaches poached in white wine

A typical summer family treat! Despite the presence of wine the dessert is pretty harmless and the children may join in as the wine has been boiled and all the alcohol evaporated.

Preparing the orange and lemon
Cut the whole orange and half lemon into fine slices (skin included), about 3mm (⅛in) thick. Remove the pips.

Preparing and cooking the peaches
Remove the stalks from the peaches and place them in a single layer in a casserole. Add the water, white wine, sugar and vanilla pod and cover with the orange and lemon slices. The liquid should just cover the fruit.

Cut out a round of greaseproof paper the same size as the casserole and make a hole in the middle.

Bring the syrup and fruit to the boil, then skim. Lower the heat so one single bubble breaks at the top, then place the greaseproof over the top and cook for approximately 20 minutes. Turn off the heat and leave the peaches to cool down in their syrup.

Finishing the dish and serving
With a slotted spoon remove the peaches from the syrup and gently peel off their skins. Place the peaches in a glass bowl, add the orange and lemon slices, and strain the syrup over. Cover and refrigerate for at least 6 hours.

Simply serve the dessert from the bowl on the table.

CHEF'S NOTES
It is very difficult to check when the peaches are actually cooked, and the cooking time will also depend on their ripeness and size. One way of being certain is to look at the stem end: if the peaches are not cooked, air from inside the stem will escape, bubbling out. But when the bubbles cease, the peaches are cooked. In no way should the peaches be *boiled*; simmer them gently so as not to damage the delicate flesh and to obtain a clear syrup.

Variations
This dessert can also be made with red wine or champagne, but you should boil the wine first.

Peaches can be replaced by pears, which should be rubbed with lemon juice to prevent oxidisation.

Two or three mint leaves would also make a nice addition!

For four people

Cooking and preparation time: 1 hour

Planning ahead: This dish can be prepared 1 day in advance, covered and refrigerated.

1 orange
½ lemon
8 ripe peaches (white if possible)
500ml (18fl oz) water
500ml (18fl oz) white wine
200g (7oz) caster sugar
1 vanilla pod (see page 18)

WINE

A dry white wine from the Sauvignon grape to complement the flavour of peach.

Pêches au Vin Blanc

Tarte aux Abricots
Apricot tart

For six people

Preparation time: 40 minutes

Cooking time: 40 minutes

Special equipment:
One pastry ring, 23cm (9in) in diameter, 2.5cm (1in) high.

Planning ahead: The pastry needs at least 6 hours' chilling before use. The tart itself can be prepared and cooked 3–4 hours in advance.

½ quantity Sweet Shortcrust Pastry
(see page 20)
10 ripe, firm apricots
1 teaspoon semolina
2 tablespoons caster sugar
icing sugar to decorate

FOR THE ALMOND CREAM:
50g (2oz) unsalted butter, softened
50g (2oz) icing sugar
50g (2oz) ground almonds
1 whole egg
1 tablespoon whipping cream
1 teaspoon Amaretto
(Italian almond liqueur, optional)

Preparing the pastry base
Place the pastry ring on to a non-stick pastry sheet. On a lightly floured work surface, roll out the dough to about 3mm (⅛in) thickness (it will be approximately 35cm/14in in diameter). Wrap it round the rolling pin and line the inside of the ring with it, using your thumbs to press it down, thus ensuring that the pastry is tucked right into the mould. Cut off the overlapping dough at the top. Prick the dough bottom with a fork. Refrigerate for at least an hour. This will allow the pastry to 'relax' again, and will prevent shrinkage during cooking.

Making the almond cream
Combine all the ingredients in a bowl and mix until well blended. Put aside.
   Preheat the oven to 375°F (190°C) Gas 5.

Building the apricot tart
Spread the almond cream on to the bottom of the tart and sprinkle with semolina.
   Stone and quarter the apricots, then arrange them attractively, rounded side up, on the top of the cream. Sprinkle the caster sugar over the tart.

Baking the tart
Place the tart in the hottest part of the preheated oven and bake for 45 minutes. Remove from the oven and allow to cool down.

Serving
Run the blade of a knife around the inside of the ring, then lift it off. Place the apricot tart on a cooling rack then on to a serving tray, sprinkle the edges with a little icing sugar, and serve to your guests.

Variation
The apricots can be substituted by peaches, plums or cherries, or poached pears.

⇒ WINE ⇐

I'll be selfish, and refer to my birthplace where one of the most wonderful dessert wines is made with Sauvignon grapes which are dried on straw before vinification – *vin de paille du Jura*. This wine will balance the acidity of the apricots, and is well worth looking for.

Tarte aux Abricots and Clafoutis aux Cerises

Clafoutis aux Cerises

Traditional batter cake with black cherries

Preheat the oven to 400°F (200°C) Gas 6.

If using the Kirsch, sprinkle over the cherries and stir. Bring the milk, cream and vanilla to the boil. Turn off the heat and leave to infuse for a few minutes.

Place the eggs and the sugar in a mixing bowl and whisk until creamy. Add the flour and salt and whisk until smooth. Then strain in the vanilla milk, beating to amalgamate.

Generously butter the inside of the dish and sprinkle with caster sugar. Add the cherries, then pour the batter mixture over the cherries.

Cook in the preheated oven for 25 minutes. Remove, allow to cool until warm, and sprinkle over some caster sugar. Serve to your guests.

Variations
Apricots or apples could replace the cherries.

For four to six people
Preparation time: 20 minutes
Cooking time: 30 minutes
Special equipment:
An ovenproof dish about 25cm (10in) long, 23cm (9in) wide and 5cm (2in) high.
Planning ahead: This dish must be prepared 1 hour in advance and served tepid.

500g (18oz) black cherries, stoned
4 tablespoons Kirsch (optional)
100ml (3½fl oz) milk
150ml (5fl oz) whipping cream
½ vanilla pod, or 2 drops
vanilla essence (see page 18)
4 eggs
120g (4½oz) caster sugar
20g (¾oz) plain flour
a pinch of salt
butter and sugar for
greasing and sprinkling

WINE

Sample the delights of a late harvest Gewürztraminer from Alsace; it has a gentle sweetness and lots of fruit and spice.

Mousse au Citron à la Giboulée de Cerises

Lemon mousse garnished with cherries

For eight people

Preparation time: 15 minutes

Cooking time: 1 hour

Special equipment:
8 ramekins (6–7cm/2½–2¾in wide) or 8 rings the same size, or 1 large pastry ring (23cm/9in wide). (If you use a large ring, you will have to divide into portions.)

Planning ahead: The mousse and cherries can be prepared in advance and assembled at the last moment.

FOR THE MOUSSE:
200ml (7fl oz) milk
grated zest and juice of 2 lemons
½ vanilla pod, split in half
(see page 18)
4 egg yolks
65g (2½oz) caster sugar
3½ gelatine leaves
(soaked in cold water to soften)
200ml (7fl oz) whipping cream
3 egg whites

FOR THE CHERRY GARNISH
AND SAUCE:
1kg (2¼lb) cherries, stalks
and stones removed
100g (4oz) caster sugar
2 teaspoons Kirsch

A dessert for a summer dinner party.

Making the base for the mousse
In a small saucepan, bring the milk to the boil with the lemon zest and split vanilla pod. Simmer for 2 minutes.

Separately whisk the egg yolks and add 40g (1½oz) of the sugar. Add three-quarters of the lemon juice.

Pour the milk mixture over the egg yolks, whisking all the time. Transfer to the saucepan and thicken over a medium heat, stirring constantly with a wooden spoon, taking great care that the cream does not boil.

Add the softened gelatine leaves to the mixture, and stir for 10 seconds. Strain into a bowl and leave at room temperature to cool.

Finishing the mousse
Whip the cream lightly and reserve. Whip the egg whites until in soft peaks, then add the remaining caster sugar and lemon juice. Whisk until firm peaks are achieved.

Using a spatula, briskly mix a quarter of the vanilla cream base into the whipped cream. Fold in the remainder. Then incorporate the egg whites into the mixture, folding delicately with a spatula.

Pour the mousse into the large pastry ring or the eight small individual rings or ramekins. Refrigerate for at least 4 hours to set.

Preparing the cherry garnish and sauce
In a saucepan mix the cherries with the sugar, cover and cook for about 5 minutes. Set aside one-third of the cherries for the garnish.

Liquidise the remaining two-thirds, then force through a sieve. Reduce this *coulis* by boiling until the texture has thickened. Taste and add a little more sugar if necessary. Finally add the Kirsch and reserve.

Serving
Dip the bottoms of the ramekins in hot water for 3 seconds. Slide the blade of a warm knife down the side of the moulds to loosen the mousse and upturn the mousse on to the middle of a plate. Or slice a larger mousse into the requisite number of wedges. Pour the sauce around the mousse and decorate with the cherries. Serve to your guests.

CHEF'S NOTES
See instructions for Vanilla Cream (page 46).

If you want to cool cream quickly, place on ice. The vanilla cream must be cold before adding the whipped cream. The whipped cream must be whipped lightly or it will become grainy.

The egg white must have firm peaks but not too firm (unlike meringue),

Mousse au Citron à la Giboulée de Cerises

or it would be difficult to incorporate it into the cream. Work delicately with a spatula, lifting and folding gently. Do not try to obtain a perfect homogeneous mix, or you will lose the lightness of the mousse.

When serving, a dash of lemon juice on the mousse will heighten its flavour.

Variations
Cherries can be replaced by raspberries. Do not cook them; make a raw *coulis* (see page 222) and arrange fruit around.

 WINE

For this we go to Australia which produces sweet wines full of citrus fruit flavours, such as an orange Muscat. A glass of Madeira, the older the better, would be a good choice. Or California produces Essensia, Muscat Fleur d'Oranges, which is sweeter than Australian wines.

Millefeuille de Framboises et leur Coulis

Layers of caramelised pastry leaves and raspberries

Preheat the oven to 375°F (190°C) Gas 5, and preheat the grill to very hot.

Preparing the pastry rounds
Lightly flour the work surface and roll the pastry out to a maximum thickness of 1–2mm ($\frac{1}{16}$in). Place the pastry on one of the pastry trays, cover with the sheet of silicone paper, then top with the other tray. Place the weight in the middle of the top tray, and cook the pastry for about 10 minutes in the preheated oven.

Remove from the oven, take off the weight and the top tray, and cool for 15 minutes.

Cut out twelve rounds with the pastry cutter. Sprinkle each round with lots of icing sugar, and caramelise under the hot grill. Reserve. (This operation will need all your attention as it is very quick!)

Making the sauce
Liquidise the raspberries with the sugar, sieve and taste; add a little more sugar if necessary, then the lemon juice. Reserve.

Preparing the filling
Place the raspberries in a large bowl, sprinkle with the caster sugar and add the raspberry alcohol (if using). Mix together and leave to marinate for about 30 minutes. Whip the cream lightly. Reserve.

Building the *millefeuilles* and serving
Place eight rounds of puff pastry in front of you, and mask each round with a little whipped cream. Arrange marinated raspberries on each of them. Reserve the other four rounds of puff pastry.

Place the four plates in front of you and on each plate, place one round of puff pastry topped with cream and raspberries. Place another layer of puff pastry topped with cream and raspberries on top of this, then add the final layer of pastry with the caramelised top showing.

Spoon the raspberry sauce around each *millefeuille*. Serve to your guests.

CHEF'S NOTES
The method of cooking the pastry is a bit unusual. Placing the rolled pastry between two baking trays with a weight on top prevents the pastry from rising and provides a delightfully flaky sheet which can then be cut when cooked.

According to your oven, the cooking time of the pastry may vary: in a convection oven, it will require only 8–10 minutes, whereas in other ovens it could take approximately 12–15 minutes.

You may need to add a little more sugar to the sauce, depending on the ripeness of the fruit.

For four people

Preparation time: 35 minutes

Cooking time: 20 minutes

Special equipment:
1 round pastry cutter 8cm (3¼in) in diameter;
2 non-stick pastry trays of 30 × 40cm (12 × 16in);
1 large sheet of silicone or good greaseproof paper;
1 × 1kg (2¼lb) weight.

Planning ahead: The puff pastry rounds can be cooked in advance.

200g (7oz) bought puff pastry, the best you can buy (made with butter if possible)
icing sugar

FOR THE SAUCE:
300g (11oz) raspberries, washed and picked over
100g (4oz) caster sugar
juice of ¼ lemon

FOR THE FILLING:
300g (11oz) raspberries, washed and picked over
50g (2oz) caster sugar
1 tablespoon raspberry alcohol (optional)
100ml (3½fl oz) whipping cream

 *WINE*

A dessert wine from Monbazillac or the Jura will fit perfectly.

Salade de Fruits au Kirsch

Fruit salad served with Kirsch

Preparing the fruit
Pineapple Wash and cut the rind off the pineapple. Remove the middle woody part of the pineapple. Reserve the trimmings (the rind and core), and cut the flesh into segments.
Peaches Cut the peaches in half, remove the stones, and cut the flesh into slices.
Pear and apple Peel, quarter, remove the cores and cut each quarter into four slices.
Oranges With a sharp knife, cut off and discard the rind and white pith, and segment the oranges (retaining the membranes and centres).
Raspberries Hull, wash briefly and drain.
Strawberries Hull, wash, drain and cut in halves or quarters according to size.
Banana Peel and cut into slices, 5mm (¼in) thick.
In a large glass bowl, mix all the fruit together.

Cooking the syrup
Place the sugar, orange juice, water and lemon juice in a saucepan and add the pineapple trimmings (the rind and core) and the trimmings from the oranges. Bring to the boil, skim and simmer for about 10 minutes. Strain, pressing with a ladle to extract as much juice as possible.
Leave to cool down until tepid, then add the Kirsch.

Marinating the fruit salad
Pour the tepid syrup over the fruit and refrigerate for at least 6 hours before serving to your guests.

CHEF'S NOTES
When preparing the pineapple and oranges, keep all the trimmings for the syrup.

For the best possible flavour, the syrup must be poured just warm over the fruit so there is an exchange of flavours between the syrup and the fruit. Maceration will ensure that all the flavours have infused.

Variations
Of course, other fruits can be used in this recipe such as wild strawberries, blackcurrants, blackberries, etc.

For six people

Preparation time: 30 minutes

Cooking time: 20 minutes

Chilling time: at least 6 hours

FOR THE FRUITS:
1 pineapple, approx. 150g (5oz) in weight
2 peaches
1 pear
1 apple
2 oranges
100g (4oz) raspberries
100g (4oz) strawberries
1 banana

FOR THE SYRUP:
150g (5oz) caster sugar
150ml (5fl oz) orange juice
150ml (5fl oz) water
juice of 1 lemon
4 tablespoons Kirsch

 WINE

This dessert does not call for an accompanying wine.

Diplomate aux Fruits d'Eté et Coulis d'Abricots

Summer fruit pudding with apricot coulis

This is the longest recipe in the book and it is more than likely that those of you who attempt it will end up hating me, due to the length of time involved. I sincerely hope that the enjoyment it will provide will counterbalance this initial feeling.

Preheat the oven to 425°F (220°C) Gas 7.

Making the sponge biscuit

In a food processor, whip the egg whites until they form soft peaks, then sprinkle in the caster sugar. Adjust the mixer to slow speed and add the egg yolks, whisk for 10 seconds then remove the bowl from the processor. Gently fold in the flour with a spatula.

Line one of the pastry trays with silicone paper. Place the mixture into the piping bag and pipe 6 fingers 10cm (4in) long on to the prepared tray. Cook in the preheated oven for 10 minutes. Remove from the oven and cool down.

Line the second tray with silicone paper and, using a palette knife, spread the remaining biscuit mixture over it 5mm (¼in) thick. Bake in the preheated oven for 5–6 minutes. Remove from the oven and cool down.

Making the almond-scented cream

In a large bowl, whisk together the egg yolks, caster sugar and almond essence.

Separately, in a saucepan, bring the cream to the boil then pour one-third of it into the egg mixture and stir; add the egg/cream mixture to the remaining two-thirds of cream in the saucepan. Cook over a medium heat until the mixture has thickened.

Add the softened gelatine leaves, then strain the mixture through a fine sieve into a bowl. Allow to cool down to room temperature.

Preparing the fruit

Raspberries Liquidise 75g (3oz) of the raspberries with the caster sugar then force through a sieve into a saucepan. Warm the purée and the half gelatine leaf to 104°F (40°C) and gently fold in the remaining raspberries. At this stage it is important to retain the shape of the raspberries. Add the raspberry alcohol (if using). Allow to cool down. Carefully remove the raspberries and purée from the saucepan and place on to a plate. Reserve.

Blackcurrants Place 75g (3oz) of the blackcurrants and the water into a saucepan and bring to the boil. Lower the heat and poach for 5 minutes, then force through a fine sieve into another saucepan. Add the caster sugar, remaining blackcurrants and cook gently for 2 minutes. Add

---

For twelve to fifteen people

Preparation time: 1¼ hours

Refrigeration time: 24 hours

Special equipment:
2 pastry trays 30cm (12in) square;
2 sheets of silicone paper (or good quality greaseproof paper), the same length as the pastry trays;
a large piping bag with 1.3cm (½–¾in) diameter nozzle;
a terrine 24cm (9½in) long, 10cm (4in) wide and 8cm (3¼in) deep;
1 sheet of silicone paper 24 × 35cm (9½ × 14in) to line the terrine.

Planning ahead: Make the stock syrup in advance.

FOR THE SPONGE BISCUIT:
5 egg whites
150g (5oz) caster sugar
5 egg yolks
150g (5oz) plain flour

FOR THE ALMOND-SCENTED CREAM:
8 egg yolks
100g (4oz) caster sugar
3 drops almond essence
500ml (18fl oz) double cream
2 gelatine leaves, softened in cold water

FOR THE FRUIT:
250g (9oz) raspberries
10g (¼oz) caster sugar
½ gelatine leaf, softened in cold water
1 tablespoon raspberry alcohol (optional)

250g (9oz) blackcurrants
50ml (2fl oz) water
10g (¼oz) caster sugar
¼ gelatine leaf, softened in cold water

150g (5oz) wild strawberries (or use small strawberries)
20g (¾oz) caster sugar
a drop of lemon juice

200g (7oz) cherries, stoned, with their juices
50g (2oz) caster sugar
½ gelatine leaf, softened in cold water
20ml (¾fl oz) Kirsch

the softened quarter gelatine leaf, and allow to cool down. Gently remove from the saucepan, place on to a plate, and reserve.

Wild strawberries Place the strawberries in a bowl together with the caster sugar and the lemon juice. Fold the strawberries gently in the sugar until they are completely coated, taking care to retain their shape.

Cherries Strain the juice from the cherries into a saucepan, add the caster sugar and bring to the boil for 15 seconds. Add the cherries and simmer for about 5 minutes. Add the softened half gelatine leaf and the Kirsch. Remove from the saucepan, place on to a plate and leave to cool down. Reserve.

Nectarines In a saucepan bring to the boil the sugar, water and lemon juice. Add the nectarine quarters and cook on each side for 5 minutes. Allow to cool down, then remove the skins. Reserve.

Apricots Bring the stock syrup to the boil and add the lemon juice; place the apricot halves into the syrup and poach them gently for 15 minutes. Leave them to cool down in the syrup. Reserve.

Making the apricot *coulis*

Liquidise the apricot quarters together with the sugar and lemon juice. Pass the *coulis* through a sieve and reserve in the refrigerator.

Lining the terrine

Line the bottom and sides of the terrine with the sheet of silicone paper; there will be an overlap of about 4cm (1½in) on each side.

Remove the sponge biscuit sheet and the six sponge fingers from the silicone paper. Soak the biscuit fingers in the Kirsch and syrup mixture for 1 minute. Reserve.

Cut the large sponge biscuit sheet into two pieces, one 28 × 24cm (11 × 9½in) and the other 24 × 6cm (9½ × 2½in). The second piece will be used for topping the pudding.

Line the bottom and sides of the terrine with the first piece of sponge biscuit. Using a pastry brush, moisten it all over with the Kirsch syrup.

Building the dessert

Have all the ingredients – i.e. fruits, etc. – ready in front of you.

Fill the piping bag with the almond cream.

Lay the apricots in the bottom of the mould then pipe a fine layer of cream over them. For the next layer place three biscuit fingers along the middle of the length of the terrine, then cover with the wild strawberries; pipe a fine layer of cream all over them. Continue thus, using the cherries, nectarines, raspberries and blackcurrants, with a thin layer of cream between each. Put the remaining three sponge biscuit fingers between the raspberries and the final layer of blackcurrants. Finally, top the pudding with the second piece of sponge biscuit sheet, brush with the remaining Kirsch syrup, cover with cling film and refrigerate for 24 hours.

Serving

Remove the cling film from the top of the pudding. Dip the blade of a knife into hot water then insert all around the inside of the terrine between the silicone paper and the terrine. Pull both overlaps of silicone paper on each side of the terrine, lift out the pudding and place it on to a board. Pull down the silicone sheet and with a hot serrated knife,

2 nectarines, stoned and quartered
20g (¾oz) caster sugar
25ml (1fl oz) water
a drop of lemon juice

3 apricots, halved and stoned
200ml (7fl oz) Stock Syrup (see page 46)
juice of ¼ lemon

FOR THE APRICOT COULIS:
approx. 700g (1½lb) fresh apricots, stoned and quartered
150g (5oz) caster sugar
juice of 1 lemon

FOR SOAKING THE BISCUIT:
300ml (10fl oz) Stock Syrup (see page 46)
100ml (3½fl oz) Kirsch

cut slices of the pudding and place on plates. Spoon the apricot *coulis* around the slices, and serve to your guests.

CHEF'S NOTES

When making the apricot *coulis*, you may wish to alter the amount of sugar. This will depend on the quality of the fruit you use and also your own personal taste.

Any remaining pudding may be kept for up to 2 days in the refrigerator, and should be kept in the original terrine to retain its nice shape.

Diplomate aux Fruits d'Été et Coulis d'Abricots

Entremet aux Fraises

*The lightest strawberry mousse
lined with sponge biscuit*

Lining the pastry ring
The dessert will be built upside down. Wrap and stretch cling film around the base of the pastry ring. Place the ring (cling film down) on a tray. Slice the garnish strawberries lengthways, 2–3mm (⅛in) thick, and arrange them in two concentric circles against the cling film. Reserve.

Preparing the mousse
Purée the strawberries and force the pulp through a fine sieve into a mixing bowl (there should be about 300g/11oz pulp). Put one-fifth of the strawberry pulp and the sugar into a small saucepan and bring to near boiling point. Add the softened gelatine leaves, which will dissolve almost instantaneously. Remove from the heat, combine with the raw pulp, and leave to cool. (If using powdered gelatine, follow the instructions on the packet.)

Whip the cream to soft peaks, then gently incorporate into the strawberry pulp.

Filling the pastry ring
Pour the creamy mousse into the pastry ring, making sure you do not disturb the strawberries.

Using a pastry brush, moisten the sponge biscuit circle with the stock syrup mixed with the Kirsch or Grand Marnier. Place on top of the mousse. Cover with cling film and leave to set for at least 4–5 hours in the refrigerator.

Serving
Remove the cling film from the top. As the dish is upside down, you now have to unmould it the right way up. Place a cake stand or serving dish over the top of the ring and invert the ring on to it. The sliced strawberries are now on top. Remove the cling film.

Dip the blade of the knife in hot water, and slide this along the inside of the ring to free the mousse. Lift the pastry ring off. Serve the mousse to your guests.

Variations
The strawberries could be replaced by wild strawberries or raspberries. You could also glaze the sponge biscuit with jelly.

For eight people

Preparation time: 1 hour

Chilling time: 5 hours

Special equipment:
1 stainless-steel pastry ring, 18cm (7in) in diameter, and 6cm (2½in) high.

Planning ahead: This dessert can be prepared at least a day in advance.

*1 round of Sponge Biscuit, 18cm (7in)
in diameter and 1cm (½in) thick
(see page 21)
85ml (3fl oz) Stock Syrup
(see page 46)
1 tablespoon Kirsch or Grand Marnier*

FOR THE MOUSSE:
*400g (14oz) strawberries,
washed, drained and hulled
75g (3oz) caster sugar
5 gelatine leaves, soaked in cold
water to soften
(or 10g/¼oz powdered gelatine)
250ml (8fl oz) whipping cream*

FOR THE GARNISH:
*2 large or 4 medium strawberries,
washed and hulled*

 WINE

A glass of Monbazillac or sweet Jurançon will be fine.

Iles Flottantes
Façon Maman Blanc

Floating islands, my mother's way

A dessert from my childhood especially for the children – and all the grown-ups – a real vanilla custard topped with islands of poached meringue masked with caramel. It must be the most celebrated dessert of France, whether served at home, in small brasseries or great restaurants alike.

Preparing and poaching the meringue
Put the milk and split vanilla pods in a large shallow pan and bring to the boil. Reduce the heat to just below simmering point and infuse the vanilla pods for about 5 minutes.

Meanwhile, in an electric mixer on medium speed, beat the egg whites to a light peak, then add the sugar, increase to full speed, and beat until firm.

Scoop out twelve large chunks of meringue and poach six at a time in the simmering milk for 2 minutes. Turn them over and poach for 2 more minutes. Remove with a slotted spoon and leave to drain on a small tray. Poach six more meringues in this way, cool and refrigerate. Strain and reserve the milk (about 800ml/1⅓ pints).

Making the custard
See Vanilla Custard, page 46, for more information.

In a bowl, whisk the egg yolks and sugar together until pale yellow. Stirring constantly, pour over the hot milk from the poaching. Pour back into the saucepan and place over medium heat. Stir continuously with a wooden spoon until the custard begins to thicken and coats the back of the spoon. Strain immediately into a large serving bowl and leave to cool.

Add the poached meringues to the bowl, and refrigerate for at least 4 hours.

Making the caramel
Pour the water into a straight-sided saucepan, then add the sugar in a mound in the centre of the pan. Over medium heat, cook to a rich caramel, then cool the caramel for a few seconds by dipping the bottom of the pan in hot water. Pour a coating of caramel on to the poached meringues and refrigerate.

Serving
Place the bowl on the table, and let everyone help themselves.

CHEF'S NOTES
Make sure the egg whites are free of any trace of yolk, shell or fat. Your mixing bowl must be scrupulously clean. Any egg yolk will impair coagulation and reduce the volume of beaten egg white by as much as half.

For four people

Preparation and cooking time: 50 minutes

Chilling time: 4 hours

Special equipment:
An electric mixer or hand whisk; a 20cm (8in) shallow saucepan; a straight-sided pan.

Planning ahead: The whole dessert can be prepared well in advance (1 day), and the caramel 1 or 2 hours beforehand.

FOR THE MERINGUE:
6 egg whites
250g (9oz) caster sugar

FOR POACHING THE MERINGUE:
1 litre (1¾ pints) milk
2 vanilla pods, split lengthways

FOR THE VANILLA CUSTARD:
10 egg yolks
75g (3oz) caster sugar
the milk used for poaching

FOR THE CARAMEL:
50 ml (2fl oz) water
100g (4oz) caster sugar

 WINE

Champagne!

The egg whites must be beaten continuously. Never stop, especially at the beginning when the foam is more unstable. Do not add the sugar until soft peaks form; if added too early, it will reduce the final volume considerably and lengthen the beating time.

Do not boil the milk, or the egg whites will expand, then deflate miserably. The poached meringues should be cooked through and firm to the touch.

Variations
You could sprinkle some toasted flaked almonds over the meringue before adding the caramel.

The caramel could be replaced by Raspberry *coulis* (see page 222).

Crème de Riz aux Pêches et Coulis de Fraises

Creamed rice with peaches and strawberry coulis

Preparing the strawberry *coulis*
Cut the strawberries in half, add the sugar and lemon juice, then liquidise. Pass through a fine sieve, then reserve in the fridge until required.

Preparing the creamed rice
Prepare the creamed rice, following the method on page 240, and reserve in the four cooking dishes.

Preparing the garnish
Poach the peaches for 1 minute in a pan of water at full boil. Drain and refresh, then skin, halve and stone. Slice the flesh finely.

Serving
Pour a little of the strawberry *coulis* into the centre of each of the four plates.

Dip the blade of a sharp knife in hot water, then slide the blade around the creamed rice to free it from the ramekin dish. Invert the creamed rice on to the centre of the plates on top of the *coulis* and arrange overlapping peach slices decoratively around it.

For four people

Preparation time: 45 minutes

Cooking time: 1¼ hours

Special equipment:
4 ramekin dishes, 10cm (4in) in diameter and 4cm (1½in) high.

Planning ahead: The creamed rice and strawberry *coulis* may be prepared up to a day in advance and refrigerated.

1 quantity Creamed Rice (see page 240)

FOR THE STRAWBERRY COULIS:
*250g (9oz) ripe strawberries,
washed and hulled
75g (3oz) caster sugar
1 tablespoon lemon juice*

FOR THE GARNISH:
4 ripe peaches

 WINE

Try a very nice sweet Jurançon wine, Domaine Cauhape.

La Mousse Brûlée
à l'Abricot

Puréed apricots topped with vanilla and Amaretto mousse, coated with ground almonds and gratinated

For four people

Preparation and cooking time: 1 hour

Special equipment:
4 egg dishes, 10 cm (4in) in diameter.

Planning ahead: This dessert can be prepared 2–3 hours in advance and kept refrigerated.

FOR THE APRICOT *COULIS*:
2 medium ripe apricots
30g (1¼oz) caster sugar
juice of ⅛ lemon
1 tablespoon water

FOR THE MOUSSE BASE:
½ vanilla pod, cut lengthways
(see page 18)
300ml (10fl oz) double cream
4 egg yolks
50g (2oz) caster sugar

TO FINISH THE MOUSSE:
100ml (3½fl oz) double cream
1 tablespoon Amaretto (almond liqueur)

FOR THE *CASSONADE*:
25ml (1fl oz) water
150g (5oz) caster sugar
30g (1¼oz) flaked almonds
1 teaspoon corn oil or any
non-scented oil (see page 17)

Preparing the apricot *coulis*
Halve and chop the apricots. Place the sugar, lemon juice and water in a saucepan over a low heat and bring to simmering point. Add the chopped apricots, cover and cook for 6–8 minutes.

Cool down the apricots and purée in a liquidiser, then sieve the purée back into a saucepan. Over a medium heat, reduce it until it thickens, whisking continuously. Cool down, then spread the *coulis* to about 3mm (⅛in) thickness, in the bottom of each dish.

Preparing the base of the mousse
Scrape out the inside of the vanilla pod and add it all to the cream. Simmer for 5 minutes. In a separate saucepan, whisk the egg yolks and sugar together for 30 seconds and, while whisking, pour the cream into this. Place the saucepan over a medium heat and cook until the cream thickens (see page 46, Vanilla Cream). Do *not* allow to boil or the egg mixture will curdle. Strain the cream into a bowl, cool down and refrigerate for a minimum of 2 hours.

Finishing the mousse
Whip the cream with the Amaretto until it has thickened, and fold into the mousse base. Divide the mousse between the egg dishes, and tap so that it is evenly distributed. Refrigerate when cool.

Preparing the *cassonade*
Place water and sugar in a saucepan and bring to a gentle boil. When the syrup becomes a light brown colour, add the flaked almonds. Cook for a further 30 seconds until light caramel in colour.

Spread a thin film of cooking oil on a stainless-steel tray or marble top and pour the mixture over it. Cool down. The mixture will then solidify; cool for a further 20 minutes, break into pieces, then liquidise until it becomes sandy in texture.

Finishing and serving the dish
Place the egg dishes in a freezer for 1 hour.

Preheat the grill to very hot.

Remove the egg dishes from the freezer and spread a layer of the *cassonade* (about 1mm (¹⁄₁₆in) thick) over the mousse. Place under the hot grill for 30 seconds (according to the power of your grill), and remove when gratinated. Refrigerate the dessert for 15–30 minutes before serving to your guests.

Variations
Apricots can be replaced by fresh cherries cooked for 6–8 minutes – in this case the Amaretto should be replaced by Kirsch.

La Mousse Brûlée à l'Abricot

A purée of raspberry or peaches can replace the apricots; whole diced poached fruits can also be used instead of the *coulis*; or you could simply prepare the mousse without a fruit base.

 WINE

A Vin Santo or an Asti Spumante.

Crème de Riz

Creamed rice

This dessert can be eaten on its own, but it's better if accompanied by seasonal fruit.

Cooking the rice
Blanch the rice in boiling water for 2 minutes, then drain. Bring the milk to the boil with the vanilla pod and sugar. Add the blanched rice and simmer for 30 minutes, then drain. Reserve.

Binding the rice pudding
In a large bowl, whisk the egg yolks and caster sugar together and reserve.

Bring the milk and vanilla pod to the boil. Allow to cool for 2 minutes and then pour on to the egg yolks and sugar and whisk together well. Pass through a sieve and allow to cool.

Pour on to the rice and mix together.

Preheat the oven to 350°F (180°C) Gas 4.

Finishing the pudding
Make the caramel. Place the water and sugar in a saucepan and cook until a dark colour. Divide between the four moulds.

Divide the rice pudding mixture between each mould, place in a *bain-marie* containing warm water and cook in the preheated oven for 25 minutes.

Allow to cool then reserve in the refrigerator.

Sorbet au Framboises

Raspberry sorbet

Place the washed, hulled raspberries in a stainless steel bowl, and pour over the stock syrup.

Purée the raspberries and syrup in a food processor then force the pulp through a fine sieve. Taste and correct with a tiny drop of lemon juice or caster sugar, depending on the ripeness of the fruit.

Churn for 15–20 minutes according to the cooling power of your machine.

Using 2 dessertspoons dipped in hot water, place the sorbet into the frosted glass bowls or glasses and serve to your guests.

Variations
You can replace the raspberries with strawberries or wild strawberries.

Beignets d'Ananas au Coulis de Fruits de la Passion

Pineapple fritters with a passion fruit sauce

Preparing the *coulis*

Halve the passion fruit, remove the seeds and pulp with a spoon and reserve in a bowl. Halve the orange and squeeze and strain all the juice into the passion fruit pulp. Add the sugar and the water. Liquidise the fruit pulp mixture for 20 seconds and then bring to the boil in a small saucepan for about 2 minutes, skimming the froth from the surface. Over a bowl strain the mixture through a fine sieve, pressing with a ladle to extract all the juice. Cool the juice, cover with cling film and store in the fridge.

Preparing the pineapple

With a serrated knife, cut off the top and bottom of the pineapple, then peel. Divide into eight circular slices and remove the hard, woody central core. Cut each slice into four pieces, place on a small tray, and sprinkle with the sugar. Leave to marinate for 10 minutes.

Preparing the batter

Separate the eggs into two different bowls. Add a third of the lager to the bowl of egg yolks, and whisk. Add the flour, sugar and salt, and whisk until smooth, gradually adding the remaining lager. Whisk the egg whites until they form soft peaks, then add the lemon juice and carry on whipping until you obtain firm peaks. Mix a third of the egg whites into the batter, whisk briefly and then fold in the remaining whites.

Cooking the dish

Over a moderately hot ring heat the oil to about 320°F (160°C). (*Do not* overheat the fat or it will seal and brown the fritters too quickly.) Test the temperature by frying a little of the batter mixture: it should sizzle immediately.

Dip two pieces of pineapple at a time into the batter making sure they are completely covered. Deep-fry on each side for 30 seconds until golden coloured. Repeat for the other slices. Place them on absorbent paper and reserve.

Serving

Turn the grill to high. Place the fritters on a tray, dust with icing sugar and caramelise under the hot grill for about 2 minutes. Either place fritters into a dish and serve the passion fruit *coulis* separately in a sauce boat, or divide the *coulis* between six plates and place fritters in a mound in the middle.

Variations

The pineapple can be replaced by other fruits such as peaches, apples, mangoes or apricots.

241

For four to six people

Preparation and cooking time: 45 minutes

Planning ahead: The sauce can be prepared 3 days in advance and kept in a sealed container in the fridge.

1 small ripe pineapple weighing about 600g (1lb 6oz)
1 tablespoon caster sugar
1 litre (1¾ pints) good vegetable oil for frying
icing sugar to glaze

FOR THE FRITTER BATTER:
3 eggs
200ml (7fl oz) lager
75g (3oz) plain flour, sieved
1 teaspoon caster sugar
a pinch of salt
½ teaspoon lemon juice

FOR THE PASSION FRUIT *COULIS*:
(makes 300ml/10fl oz):
12 passion fruit
1 large orange
65g (2½oz) caster sugar
3 tablespoons water

WINE

Why not try a small glass of chilled rum?

Sablé aux Poires au Caramel et Citron

*Poached pears sandwiched in shortbread pastry,
served with a lime caramel sauce*

For four people

Preparation time: 25 minutes

Cooking time: 40 minutes

Special equipment:
An 8cm (3¼in) round pastry cutter.

Planning ahead: The shortbread pastry should be made in advance and refrigerated (see page 21). The pastry and the pears can be prepared in advance.

*1 quantity Sweet Shortbread Pastry dough
(see page 21)
icing sugar for sprinkling*

FOR THE PEARS:
*2 pears, preferably William
400ml (14fl oz) water
150g (5oz) caster sugar
juice of ½ lemon
½ vanilla pod,
split in half and scraped,
or 2 drops vanilla essence (see page 18)*

FOR THE LIME CARAMEL SAUCE:
*50ml (2fl oz) water
100g (4oz) caster sugar
200ml (7fl oz) double cream
50g (2oz) unsalted butter
juice of ½ lime*

Very early September is the ideal time to do this dish. William pears are at their very best then, and it is worthwhile to seek out this variety.

Preheat the oven to 350°F (180°C) Gas 4.

Preparing and cooking the pastry
Lightly flour your work surface and roll out the pastry dough to 3mm (⅛in) thickness. Using the pastry cutter, cut out eight rounds. Place these on a non-stick pastry tray, and cook for 15 minutes in the preheated oven. Remove from the oven and leave to cool.

Preparing and cooking the pears
Peel the pears, cut them in half lengthways and remove the cores.

Cut out a round of greaseproof paper the same size as a small saucepan and make a hole in the middle. In the small saucepan, bring to the boil the water, sugar, lemon juice and vanilla. Add the pears and lower the heat to barely simmering. Place the round of greaseproof paper on to the pears – this will prevent discoloration and help to cook the pears thoroughly.

After 15–20 minutes, remove from the heat and let the pears cool down in the syrup.

Making the lime caramel sauce
Combine the water and sugar in a saucepan and bring to a gentle boil. Brush the sides of the pan with a little water from time to time during cooking, to prevent the sugar from crystallising and burning.

When the sugar becomes dark caramel in colour, add half the cream and stir with a wooden spoon. Remove from the heat and add the remaining cream. Stir until the texture is smooth, then add the butter and lime juice and mix again.

Finishing and serving the dish
Drain the pears from the syrup and slice them finely. Place one pastry round in the middle of each plate (three rounds per plate), and top with slices of pear. Place the second shortbread round over the pear slices, and top with more pear slices. Put the third pastry round on top and sprinkle a little icing sugar on it. Pour the warm caramel sauce around the pastry on each plate, and serve to your guests.

CHEF'S NOTES
Be careful not to boil the pears; they should be cooked gently or they will break up and the texture will be spoiled. The cooking time may alter in accordance with the ripeness of the pears; they could take up to 30 minutes to cook.

Sablé aux Poires au Caramel et Citron

If you wish to give an attractive shiny texture to the pastry, lightly brush with egg yolk and a pinch of salt before baking.

Variations
The lime caramel sauce could be replaced by chocolate sauce (see page 45). Also the pears could be substituted by raspberries or strawberries, etc. In this latter case, use a raspberry *coulis* (see page 222).

 WINE

An original suggestion would be an orange Muscat from Australia. Search for the name Brown Brothers.

243

Semoule Soufflée aux Pommes

Apples baked in a semolina soufflé

My mother used to make this dish when I was a child which made me love her ten times over. It's delicious!

Preparing the dish
Melt 10g (¼oz) of the butter and spread a film of it inside the dish, then sprinkle with 20g (¾oz) of the caster sugar. Clean the edge of the dish. Reserve.

Preheat the oven to 350°F (180°C) Gas 4.

Pre-baking the apples
Wash the apples and pat dry. Melt the remaining butter and brush over the apples, then coat with the remaining caster sugar. Place on a buttered pastry tray and bake in the oven for approximately 25–30 minutes, according to ripeness. Remove from the oven and reserve.

Preparing the semolina soufflé
Bring the milk to the boil together with the vanilla essence (or pod), then lower the heat and add 60g (2¼oz) of the caster sugar, the semolina and sultanas. Simmer for about 3 minutes until the mixture thickens, whisking all the time to prevent any lumps forming or burning the bottom. Cool for 2–3 minutes, and pick out the vanilla pod if used.

In a bowl, whisk the egg whites until soft peaks form, and then slowly add the remaining caster sugar. Continue whisking until stiff peaks have been achieved.

Mix the egg yolks into the semolina mixture. Briskly whisk in one-third of the egg white, then fold the remainder in gently with a spatula.

Baking the soufflé
Pour the semolina soufflé mixture into the prepared baking dish and imbed the apples in it. Dab a knob of butter on each apple, sprinkle sugar over the dish, and bake in the preheated oven for 25 minutes.

Serving
Remove the dish from the oven, place it on your table, and let your guests help themselves.

CHEF'S NOTES
It is essential that the apples are pre-baked as this will partly cook them. The apples must be perfectly ripe and I personally find the James Greaves variety to be particularly delicious. Do not peel the apples as the skin will hold their shape, and they will have a nice texture.

Of course, if this dish is for the kids, golden syrup will be welcomed!

For four people

Preparation time: 25 minutes

Cooking time: 25 minutes

Special equipment:
A large earthenware or Pyrex oval dish 34 × 24 × 7cm (13½ × 9½ × 2¾in), or a rectangular heatproof dish, 28 × 23 × 7cm (11 × 9 × 2¾in).

Planning ahead: The apples must be pre-baked. The semolina can be prepared half an hour in advance and kept warm in a *bain-marie* (sprinkle with sugar so no crust is formed). Then all you have to do is whip the meringue and incorporate it into the semolina.

*4 large ripe eating apples
(James Greaves, Junagold or Golden Delicious are recommended)
25g (1oz) butter
60g (2¼oz) caster sugar*

FOR THE SEMOLINA SOUFFLÉ:
*500ml (18fl oz) milk
2 drops vanilla essence,
or ½ vanilla pod cut in half and scraped
(see page 18)
100g (4oz) caster sugar
70g (2¾oz) semolina
70g (2¾oz) sultanas
(as pale as you can find them)
4 eggs, separated*

TO FINISH THE DISH:
*20g (¾oz) unsalted butter
caster sugar for sprinkling*

➥ WINE ↩

A fresh young Quarts de Chaume will be delightful, and if the children are at the table, a bottle of sweet farm cider will be perfect.

Semoule Soufflée aux Pommes

Tarte Tatin, Façon Cecile

Upside-down caramelised apple tart

For eight people

Preparation time: 25 minutes

Cooking time: 50 minutes

Special equipment:
1 *tarte tatin* mould or round cake tin, 24cm (9½in) in diameter and 5cm (2in) deep.

Planning ahead: The tart can be made half a day in advance and kept at room temperature. It can be reheated for 15 minutes in an oven preheated to 350°F (180°C) Gas 4.

150g (5oz) best quality puff pastry
300ml (10fl oz) double cream
or lots of clotted cream (optional),
to serve

FOR THE FILLING:
1.8kg (4lb) Granny Smith apples
(approx. 12 apples)
60g (2¼oz) unsalted butter, diced
2 pinches of powdered cinnamon
135g (4¾oz) caster sugar

FOR THE CARAMEL:
75g (3oz) caster sugar
30g (1¼oz) unsalted butter

This dessert was part of a most memorable autumn meal put together by a dear friend, who kindly gave me her recipe. It is sumptuous, decadent and so good . . . and I hope that Cecile will forgive me for having slightly changed the recipe.

Rolling out the pastry
Roll the puff pastry out on a lightly floured surface to about 2–3mm (up to ⅛in) in thickness. Place on a tray lightly dusted with flour and refrigerate for 30 minutes.

Cut out a circle 26cm (10½in) in diameter (slightly larger than the dish) and refrigerate until required.

Preheat the oven to 375°F (190°C) Gas 5.

Preparing the apples
Peel all the apples. Cut eight of them in half vertically, and scoop out the cores. Cut the remaining four apples into quarters and remove the cores. Reserve, covered.

Cooking the caramel
Put the caster sugar in the *tarte tatin* mould and place over a medium heat until the sugar turns a dark caramel colour. Turn off the heat and stir in the butter. Cool down for a few minutes.

Building the tart
Place the 16 halves of apple upright around the mould, rounded side to scooped-out side, and arrange the quarters in the middle. Press the apple halves tightly together so that there are no gaps. (The apple halves will rise above the rim of the mould, by approximately 3cm/1¼in.)

Dot the apples with the diced butter. Mix the cinnamon with the caster sugar and sprinkle over the apples.

Cooking the tart
Bake the tart in the preheated oven for 25 minutes.

Remove it from the oven and place the puff pastry circle on top of the apples, tucking the edge of the pastry inside the mould. Cook for a further 30 minutes.

Remove the tart from the oven and allow to cool down for 30 minutes.

Serving
Turn the tart out on to a flat serving dish, pastry side down, and serve it with lots of fresh double cream or, even better, clotted cream – blissfully delicious!

CHEF'S NOTES
It is important to use Granny Smith apples as they are very firm, have a high degree of acidity and a delicious taste; they will hold together beautifully.

Tarte Tatin, Façon Cecile

When building the tart, the apples have to be packed tightly together so that there are no gaps; this ensures that the tart will hold together well.

The round of pastry must be placed *loosely* over the apples: do not try to stick the pastry to the mould. The steam produced by the apples, and not allowed to escape, would give a soggy texture to the pastry.

Variations
This tart can be made with just-ripe William pears or ripe but firm bananas. If you use the latter, the total cooking time should be altered to 20 minutes, and the pastry should be placed on the tart at the start of cooking.

 WINE

I have discovered a pleasant Vin Santo Muscato (Italy) with a beautiful caramel taste.

Tartes Fines aux Pommes
Apple tarts

For four people

Preparation time: 30 minutes

Cooking time: 20–25 minutes

Planning ahead: The apple tarts can be prepared a few hours in advance, ready for baking.

400g (14oz) bought puff pastry (made with butter if possible)
1 egg, beaten

FOR THE TOPPING:
6 Granny Smith apples
100g (4oz) unsalted butter
1 teaspoon lemon juice
3 tablespoons caster sugar
1 tablespoon Calvados (optional)

This is one of the best apple tarts I know. The delicious texture and taste of the soft caramelised apple with the thin crust of the puff pastry make this simple dessert a very special one.

Preparing the pastry
Allow the pastry to come to room temperature.

On a lightly floured work surface, roll the pastry out until it is 1mm ($\frac{1}{16}$in) thick maximum. Place the pastry on a floured tray and refrigerate for 10 minutes, then remove from the refrigerator.

With an upturned 13cm (5in) plate, cut out four rounds; place these on to a dampened 30 × 40cm (12 × 16in) baking sheet, and reserve in the refrigerator.

Press all the pastry trimmings together and roll out until 30cm (12in) long and 5mm (¼in) thick. Place this in the freezer for 10 minutes so that the pastry firms up and will be easy to cut.

Remove the pastry from the freezer and cut into four bands of 30cm (12in) long. Remove the pastry rounds from the fridge, moisten the edges with egg, and stick the bands of pastry around each. Reserve.

Preheat the oven to 450°F (230°C) Gas 8.

Preparing the topping
Peel, quarter and core the apples. Cut into segments of about 5mm (¼in) thick. Place them in two concentric circles, overlapping, inside the banded rim of the pastry rounds.

Melt the butter, add the lemon juice, 2 tablespoons of the sugar and the Calvados (if using), then brush all over the apples. You won't use all of this mixture.

Cooking the apple tarts
Bake the tarts in the hot oven for 20–25 minutes.

Remove from the oven, brush with the remaining butter mixture, and sprinkle with the remaining tablespoon of caster sugar. Carefully, slide on to plates and serve to your guests.

CHEF'S NOTES
I personally find Granny Smith apples to be the best type of apple for this dish.

The thickness of the pastry is vital to the success of this dish. If it is too thick, the bottom of the tarts will be totally uncooked and soggy. The little band placed on the edge of the pastry circle will hold all the juices in.

Variations
The apples can be replaced by ripe William or Comice pears, or with segments of quince poached in stock syrup (see page 46) for 20 minutes. Omit the Calvados in all cases.

⇌ *WINE* ⇌

A Quarts de Chaume or a sweet Vouvray, both from the Loire Valley, will be good, or a glass of farm cider.

Sorbet aux Pommes Vertes

Apple sorbet

Place the whole apples in the freezer for at least 12 hours. Remove them and place in the microwave on the 'defrost' setting for 15 minutes. Chop the unpeeled apples into quarters, remove the core and stalk, then chop the quarters into small pieces.

Liquidise the chopped apples, apple jelly and caster sugar then strain through a sieve into the bowl of the *sorbetière*, pressing with a ladle to extract as much juice as possible.

Churn for 10–15 minutes, according to the cooling power of your machine.

Using 2 dessertspoons dipped in hot water, place the sorbet into frosted glass bowls or glasses and serve to your guests immediately.

CHEF'S NOTES

Apple jelly can be found in most supermarkets, usually in the preserves and jams department. If you cannot find it, use apricot jelly.

It is important to freeze the apples for a minimum of 12 hours, to prevent oxidisation.

This sorbet is not cooked so as to retain all the freshness and taste of the apples. It is 'cooked' by freezing.

For six to eight people

Freezing time: 12 hours

Preparation time: 40 minutes

Special equipment:
A *sorbetière* (see page 32).

Planning ahead: The sorbet can be prepared in advance. Before serving, chill the glass bowls or glasses in the freezer for 30 minutes.

1.4kg (3lb) Granny Smith apples
170g (6oz) apple jelly
150g (5oz) caster sugar

Assiette de Fruits au Caramel

Autumn fruits in caramel

This dessert holds the colours and flavours of autumn.

Preparing the creamed rice
Prepare the creamed rice, following the method on page 240, and reserve in the four cooking dishes.

Preparing the fruits
Peel the quince, pear and apple and cut each of them into eight segments. Remove cores, pips and stalks. Cut the plums in half and remove the stones.

Cooking the fruits
Poach the quince segments in the stock syrup for 15 minutes, covered with a round of paper with a hole cut in the middle. Drain.

Melt half the butter and 65g (2½oz) of the sugar in a saucepan for 30 seconds over a medium heat, then add the quince segments. Caramelise them lightly for 5–7 minutes. Reserve.

Caramelise the apple and pear segments in much the same way in a further, similar quantity of butter and sugar for 5–7 minutes. Add half of the water, and reserve.

Place the plum halves in a saucepan with the remaining water and sugar and cook gently for 15 minutes. (Add more water if necessary.) Reserve on a plate.

Serving
Dip the blade of a sharp knife in hot water, then slide the blade around the creamed rice to free it from the dish. Invert the creamed rice on to the centre of four individual plates. Arrange the fruit attractively around; spoon the caramel fruit juices around as well.

Variations
Other autumn fruits could be added such as blackberries and blackcurrants.

For four people

Preparation and cooking time: 1½ hours

Special equipment:
4 moulds, 10cm (4in) in diameter, and 4cm (1½in) high.

Planning ahead: The rice pudding and fruit can be prepared half a day in advance.

1 quantity Creamed Rice (see page 240)

FOR THE FRUITS:
1 quince
1 pear (preferably William)
1 apple (preferably Granny Smith)
2 red plums
200ml (7fl oz) Stock Syrup
(see page 46)
40g (1½oz) unsalted butter
150g (5oz) caster sugar
120ml (4fl oz) water

⇒ *WINE* ⇐

If you can find a Vin de Paille (straw wine) from my home country of the Jura, you will experience one of the most delicate sweet wines.

Assiette de Fruits au Caramel

Tarte au Chocolat

Chocolate tart

For eight people

Preparation time: 20 minutes

Cooking time: 15 minutes

Special equipment:
1 pastry ring, 28 × 3cm (11 × 1¼in),
and 1 baking sheet.

Planning ahead: The tart can be
prepared half a day in advance.

*150g (5oz) best cooking chocolate
(see page 16)
50g (2oz) unsalted butter, in pieces
50ml (2fl oz) whipping cream
7 egg whites
60g (2½oz) caster sugar
5 egg yolks
50g (2oz) plain flour
30g (1¼oz) unsweetened cocoa powder
extra butter and flour
for the pastry ring*

FOR THE WALNUTS:
*100g (4oz) walnuts, roughly chopped
icing sugar*

FOR COATING THE TART:
*150g (5oz) plain chocolate
50ml (2fl oz) milk*

⇒ WINE ⇐

Why not try a glass of old Malmsey
Madeira? It may be surprising, but both
flavours will complement each other
very well. Equally, the Muscat wine,
Essensia from California, would go
well. But I recommend the first.

Or, you could try a glass of the
orange wine on page 299, made by
yourself!

Preheat the grill to its hottest.
Preheat the oven to 350°F (180°C) Gas 4.

Preparing the walnuts
Place the chopped walnuts on a baking tray, sprinkle lightly with icing
sugar, and grill for 1 minute. Reserve.

Preparing the pastry ring
Place the ring on the baking sheet. Butter the inside of the ring and
the baking sheet base, and sprinkle with flour. Shake off the excess flour.

Preparing the chocolate mixture
Melt the chocolate in a warm *bain-marie*. When the chocolate has melted,
stir in the butter pieces with a spatula until they are totally incorporated
and mixture is of a smooth texture. Stir in the cream and remove from
the heat.

In a mixing bowl, whisk the egg whites until they reach soft peaks,
adding the caster sugar gradually, then stir in the egg yolks. Sprinkle
in the flour and cocoa powder. Fold in the chocolate and butter mixture
and mix slowly with a spatula.

Cooking the tart
Pour half of the chocolate mixture into the pastry ring, sprinkle the
walnuts in the middle, and then add the remaining chocolate mixture.
Bake in the preheated oven for 12–15 minutes.

Remove from the oven and leave to cool for at least 10 minutes.
Turn the tart out carefully on to a cooling rack and rest for at least
1 hour.

Finishing the tart and serving
Place the rack on a tray. Melt the chocolate in a *bain-marie* and thin
down with the milk. Spread the chocolate over the tart with a spatula
and leave to cool for about 10 minutes.

With two spatulas, lift the tart and place it on a large round plate.
Serve to your guests.

CHEF'S NOTES
Make sure the *bain-marie* does not boil, otherwise the chocolate will
cook and become granular.

Variations
To simplify the tart, you could omit the chocolate coating and instead
sprinkle with cocoa powder or icing sugar.

Sliced poached pears can be placed into the mixture instead of walnuts.

Coffee Cream sauce (see page 46) can be served as an accompaniment
to the tart.

Tarte au Chocolat

Soupe de Fruits Exotiques au Poivre Vert

Exotic fruit salad spiced with green peppercorns

For four to six people

Preparation time: 40 minutes

Planning ahead: The soup must be prepared at least 12 hours in advance to allow the flavours to infuse.

1 pawpaw
1 baby pineapple or ¼ large pineapple
1 small firm mango
8 lychees
½ very ripe star fruit
2 kiwi fruit
12 Chinese gooseberries (physalis)
1 banana
2 ripe guavas

FOR THE FRUIT SYRUP:
juice of 5 oranges
100ml (3½fl oz) water
4 passion fruit (cut fruit in half, and remove pulp, juice and seeds with a teaspoon)
juice of ¼ lime
60g (2¼oz) caster sugar
1 tablespoon green peppercorns, rinsed for 10 minutes under running water

The shops are full of strange-looking exotic fruits, a lot of them belonging to the early days of *nouvelle cuisine*. Some are simply horrible, others are indifferent, but some are delicious. Although in winter most native fruits such as raspberries are out of season, exotic fruits from the Caribbean and elsewhere are plentifully available. This fruit salad will bring a bit of colour to a drab winter's night.

Preparing the fruit
Peel the pawpaw, cut it in half and remove the seeds. Cut into large cubes and reserve.

Cut the rind off the pineapple and cut the fruit in half lengthways. Remove the core and cut the flesh into slices of 5mm (¼in) thickness. Reserve. Keep the rind and core too.

Peel the mango, place on its flat side and, with a knife, slice against the stone to remove the first half. Turn the mango over and do the same again. Cut the flesh in large dice. Keep the stone, and mix with the trimmings and core of the pineapple.

Peel and stone the lychees. Reserve the fruit.

Wash the star fruit and cut into slices of 5mm (¼in) thickness.

Remove the Chinese gooseberries from their paper leaf surrounds, then wash well. Cut in half.

Peel the banana and cut it into thin slices.

Peel the guavas and cut in half. Remove the seeds.

Preparing the fruit syrup
Place the orange juice, water, passion fruit, lime juice and caster sugar in a saucepan and add the reserved fruit trimmings (rind and core of pineapple and the mango stone). Mix and bring to the boil, then skim and simmer for 5 minutes. Strain the syrup into a large bowl and add the rinsed and drained peppercorns.

Marinating the *soupe*
Cool the syrup until it is tepid then add all the fruit. Cover with cling film, refrigerate and marinate for 12 hours.

Serving
Simply place in a large bowl, and serve to your guests.

CHEF'S NOTES
Star fruit can be quite delicious but only if they are very ripe. If an all over yellow colour, this can be taken as a good indication of ripeness.

The green peppercorns are refreshed under running cold water to get rid of some of their fire.

The fruits are placed into the tepid syrup so that all the flavours can

WINE

This dessert is lively with spicy flavours, so a dessert wine such as Sauternes, Monbazillac will be good.

infuse. During the marinating time, the flavours will further improve.

Variations
Various fruits can be added or substituted such as Chinese melon and orange segments.

Truffière de Chocolat

Chocolate mousse

A very good, impressive and simple dinner-party dessert for chocolate lovers!

Lining the biscuit base
Mix the cold stock syrup and the rum together and, with a pastry brush, dampen the biscuit round with this. Place the biscuit on to the cardboard cake base in the middle of a tray, and fit the pastry ring over it. Reserve.

Preparing the chocolate mousse
Break the chocolate into pieces and melt in a bowl placed over a *bain-marie*. Do not let the water temperature rise above 140°F (60°C). Stir and make sure that all of the chocolate has melted. Cool slightly.

Separately in a large bowl, whip the cream. Briskly mix one-quarter of the whipped cream into the cooled chocolate, then pour the mixture into the bulk of the whipped cream. Fold in gently with a spatula until just homogenised.

Pour the mixture into the ring on top of the biscuit. Smooth the top with a palette knife and refrigerate for at least 6 hours.

Serving
Sprinkle the surface of the mousse with cocoa powder. Place a warm damp cloth around the ring for a few seconds and lift the ring off.

With two palette knives, lift and place the mousse on its cardboard base on to a serving dish. Serve to your guests.

Serve the coffee cream sauce separately, if used.

CHEF'S NOTES
Use the best cooking chocolate you can find (see page 14).

Always put the chocolate in a bowl and place over water not exceeding a temperature of 140°F (60°C); ideally the chocolate should melt at a temperature of 104–113°F (40–45°C). If the water is too hot, the starch within the chocolate will start burning and will become granular.

Do not whip the cream too stiffly as it must remain quite loose. If the cream is too stiff it will be impossible to incorporate it with the chocolate mousse; it will be far too firm and could become grainy.

Variations
Some fine slices of pineapple poached in syrup, or cherries soaked in brandy, can be placed on the biscuit base first.

For eight people

Preparation time: 30 minutes

Special equipment:
1 pastry ring, 18 × 6cm (7 × 2½in) or 25 × 4cm (10 × 1½in);
1 cardboard cake base the same size.

Planning ahead: This dessert must be prepared 12 hours in advance. It will benefit if it is prepared a day in advance.

*50ml (2fl oz) Stock Syrup
(see page 46)
50ml (2fl oz) dark rum
1 round of Chocolate Sponge Biscuit,
the same diameter as the pastry ring
(see page 22)*

FOR THE CHOCOLATE MOUSSE:
*350g (12oz) bitter chocolate
500ml (18fl oz) whipping cream
25g (1oz) unsweetened cocoa powder*

TO SERVE (OPTIONAL):
*500ml (18fl oz) Coffee Cream sauce
(see page 46)*

⇔ *WINE* ⇔

An orange Muscat from Australia or California will accompany the taste of chocolate very well, or a glass of Madeira.

Mousse au Chocolat Amer

Bitter chocolate mousse

For four people

Preparation time: 20 minutes

Planning ahead: This dessert must be prepared at least 3 hours in advance and refrigerated.

*120g (4½oz) best-quality
cooking chocolate (see page 16)
5 egg whites
40g (1½oz) caster sugar
2 egg yolks*

Most French children are made to remain at the table all through the meal and, of course, they are expected to behave. This, as I remember, was quite an ordeal, especially when the 'grown-ups' talked about unexciting topics such as politics, religion, education, etc., and ignored us totally. This sweet made it all worthwhile — the price of patience!

Break the chocolate into small pieces and place them in a large bowl. Melt in a *bain-marie* of warm water, stirring from time to time.

Beat the egg whites until they form soft peaks, then add the caster sugar and continue to whisk until firmer peaks are formed.

Stir the egg yolks into the warm melted chocolate.

Briskly whisk one-third of the egg white into the chocolate mixture, then fold in the remaining egg white delicately.

Spoon the chocolate mousse into a large serving bowl or four individual dishes, and refrigerate for at least 3 hours. Serve to your guests.

CHEF'S NOTES
The water in the *bain-marie* must not boil. If it is too hot, the chocolate would cook and become granular.

The egg whites must be firm enough but not too stiff, as it would be difficult to incorporate them into the chocolate mousse. The meringue mixture should form soft peaks and be perfectly homogeneous.

The addition of one-third of egg white to the chocolate is to lighten the base; this makes it easier to incorporate the remaining egg white.

Variation
A dash of Grand Marnier would give a lovely flavour.

 WINE

As for Truffière de Chocolat (see page 255).

Mousse au Chocolat Amer

Soufflé au Chocolat

Chocolate soufflé

For four people

Preparation time: 10 minutes

Cooking time: 15 minutes

Special equipment:
4 soufflé ramekins,
10cm (4in) × 7cm (2¾in)

Planning ahead: Please read the piece on soufflé-making, page 23, before commencing this dish. The cocoa paste can be prepared well in advance.

*50g (2oz) cocoa powder
(use the best unsweetened variety
you can find)
100ml (3½fl oz) cold water
8 egg whites
60g (2¼oz) caster sugar*

FOR THE RAMEKINS:
*1 teaspoon unsalted butter
1 tablespoon caster sugar mixed with
1 tablespoon cocoa powder*

Preparing the cocoa paste
In a saucepan, combine the cocoa and cold water over a medium heat. Bring to the boil and whisk continuously until the mixture is well blended. Remove from the heat after boiling for 10 seconds.

Preheat the oven to 375°F (190°C) Gas 5.

Preparing the ramekins
Melt the butter and, with a pastry brush, butter the inside of the ramekins. Sprinkle the mixed sugar and cocoa powder into each ramekin until coated. Put aside.

Making the soufflé mixture
Place the cocoa paste into a mixing bowl.

In a separate bowl, with an electric mixer, whisk the egg whites until soft peaks are formed. Add the sugar and continue whisking at high speed until the peaks become firmer (1 minute approximately).

Add a quarter of the egg white to the cocoa paste, and whisk briskly until thoroughly blended. Very delicately, using a spatula, fold in the remaining egg white (do not over-mix, so that the soufflé remains light).

Cooking and serving the soufflé
Fill each prepared ramekin with the chocolate soufflé mixture and, using a palette knife, smooth the surface. Run your thumb around the rim of the ramekin pushing away the soufflé mixture, so that it does not stick on the edge, and will rise evenly.

Cook the soufflés in the preheated oven for 14–16 minutes.

Serve immediately to your guests.

CHEF'S NOTES
You will be left with 8 egg yolks. These could be used for a Vanilla Custard or Pastry Cream (see pages 46 or 47).

 WINE

Any champagne would be a good accompaniment, or a good Californian wine made from Muscat grapes.

Soufflé aux Fruits de la Passion and Soufflé au Chocolat

Nougat Glacé
au Grand Marnier et Amandes
Iced Grand Marnier and almond nougat

Preheat the oven to 400°F (200°C) Gas 6.

Preparing the almonds and cream
Place the almonds on to a roasting tray and sprinkle the icing sugar over them. Turn them over, so they are completely coated with icing sugar. Caramelise the almonds in the preheated oven for about 4–5 minutes, then leave to cool down.

Crush the almonds, not too finely. Reserve.

Whip the double cream, not too stiff, and add the Grand Marnier. Refrigerate.

Making the meringue
In a saucepan mix the honey, lemon juice, orange zest and caster sugar. Bring to the boil slowly.

Place the egg whites into a mixing bowl and whip until light peaks are reached. Have whisk at medium speed, then add the *boiling* liquid to the egg whites, making sure it is poured in between the bowl and the whisk.

Increase the whisk to full speed and whisk for 3–4 minutes until the meringue is cold.

Filling the terrine
When the meringue is cold, fold the whipped cream into it, using a spatula, along with the crushed almonds. Fill the terrine with the mixture, then tap the terrine bottom on the table so that the mixture is evenly distributed. Cover with cling film, then place in the freezer for at least 6 hours.

Making the apricot *coulis*
Wash the apricots, remove the stones and chop roughly. Place the water, sugar, lemon juice and apricots in a covered saucepan. Bring to the boil, reduce the heat, and simmer for 5–8 minutes. Leave to cool, then purée. Force through a fine sieve and taste. Add the Kirsch or Amaretto, if using, when cold.

Serving
Dip the terrine into a hot water bath for 4 seconds, then turn upside down and release the iced nougat. Serve either on a serving dish with the *coulis* separately, or prepare eight plates, carve slices with a hot knife, and surround each slice with apricot *coulis*.

CHEF'S NOTES
When adding the hot liquid to the egg white meringue, do not let it hit the whisk – this could prove dangerous. The boiling sugar will cook the meringue which, as it cools, will become firm and smooth.

For eight people

Preparation and cooking time: 1¼ hours

Freezing time: 6 hours

Special equipment:
1 terrine, 24cm (9in) long, 8cm (3¼in) wide and 9cm (3½in) deep.

Planning ahead: The dessert can be prepared 2–3 days in advance.

100g (4oz) flaked almonds
70g (2¾oz) icing sugar
300ml (10fl oz) double cream
50ml (2fl oz) Grand Marnier

FOR THE MERINGUE:
100g (4oz) honey
juice of ¼ lemon
finely grated zest of 1 orange
50g (2oz) caster sugar
5 egg whites

FOR THE APRICOT *COULIS*:
400g (14oz) fresh apricots
150ml (5fl oz) water
100g (4oz) caster sugar
juice of ¼ lemon
1 tablespoon Kirsch or Amaretto (optional)

WINE

This sweet would welcome a full, sweet dessert wine such as a Sauternes, Quarts de Chaume, or Muscat de Beaumes de Venise.

You may need a little less or more sugar or lemon, so *taste* and correct accordingly.

Variations
The apricot *coulis* can be replaced by a raspberry *coulis* (see page 222).
    This iced nougat dish can also be flavoured with lemon or mandarin zests.

Bouchées d'Orange

Orange buns

These delicious buns can be served either with Spiced Amber Pots (see page 262) as a dessert, or on their own as *petits fours* (cooked in small 4cm/1½in tartlet moulds). They are deliciously crisp on the outside and crumbly inside, and are also wonderful served warm, with afternoon tea.

Preheat the oven to 425°F (220°C) Gas 7.
    Whisk together the egg, melted butter and caster sugar, and add the orange zest and ground almonds. Sprinkle on the flour and fold into the mixture.
    Grease the bun tins with a little butter, and dust with flour. Divide the mixture between the bun tins, and bake in the preheated oven for 8 minutes.
    Remove from the oven and place on a cooling rack for 10 minutes. Serve to your guests.

For four people

Preparation and cooking time: 10 minutes

Special equipment:
8 bun tins, 5–6cm (2–2½in) in diameter, and 1cm (½in) high.

1 egg
40g (1½oz) unsalted butter, melted
50g (2oz) caster sugar
finely grated zest of 1 orange
25g (1oz) ground almonds
25g (1oz) self-raising flour, sifted
butter and flour for the moulds

For four people

Preparation and cooking time: 20 minutes

Planning ahead: The jelly must be made at least 2 hours in advance to allow it to set.

FOR THE JELLY:
2 gelatine leaves (or 1 dessertspoon powdered gelatine)
150ml (5fl oz) fresh orange juice, strained (half from blood oranges if possible)
300ml (10fl oz) Muscatel de Valencia (a sweet wine)
4 tiny sprigs of rosemary, crushed peel of 1 large orange
a generous grating of nutmeg

FOR THE TOPPING:
100ml (3½fl oz) whipping cream
10g (¼oz) icing sugar
a dash of almond essence or almond liqueur

⇒ *WINE* ⇐

A glass of the same wine used in the jelly would be welcome.

DESSERTS

Vin de Muscatel en Gelée

Spiced amber pots

This recipe is a small tribute to a lady who competed in the *Masterchef* programme. I found this dessert, one of the dishes she prepared, absolutely delicious and fresh. I thank Miss Riddell for allowing me to include her recipe in my book, and I hope you will enjoy it too.

Preparing the jelly
Soften the gelatine leaves in cold water. Reserve. (If using powdered gelatine, follow the instructions on the packet.)

Bring the orange juice to the boil, add the softened gelatine leaves, and simmer for 2–3 minutes. Add the wine, rosemary sprigs, orange peel and grated nutmeg to the orange mixture and simmer for 10–15 seconds. Turn off the heat and strain through a fine muslin cloth.

Cool down and pour into four glasses. Refrigerate for a minimum of 2 hours until the jelly sets.

Making the topping and serving
Whip the cream, add the icing sugar and the almond essence or liqueur, then place in a piping bag and pipe over the jelly. Serve to your guests.

CHEF'S NOTES
This dish does not need any sugar due to the presence of the sweet wine. Muscatel wine can be replaced by Beaumes de Venise, sweet Jurançon or any dessert wine.

Bouchées d'Orange (see page 261) would be delicious served with this dessert.

Crème Caramel à la Mandarine

Mandarin crème caramel

As this recipe does not contain any egg whites and is bound only with egg yolks, you will get a perfect melting texture. Despite its simplicity, this dish remains one of my favourite desserts. If you do this dessert for the children, omit the mandarin zest.

Preheat the oven to 350°F (180°C) Gas 4.

Cooking the caramel
Place the water and caster sugar in a saucepan and cook until you obtain a dark caramel. Pour the caramel into the four ramekins, allow to cool down, then reserve.

Preparing the cream
If you are using the vanilla pod, cut it in half lengthways, scrape out the insides and put in the milk. Chop the two halves of the pod and add to the milk as well, together with the finely grated zest. Simmer the milk for about 5 minutes.

In a separate bowl, whisk together the egg yolks and caster sugar. Pour the milk in gradually while whisking the egg yolk and sugar mixture. Strain into another bowl and divide the cream between the four ramekins.

Cooking the cream
Place the ramekins in a wide, low-sided pan or small roasting tray. Fill the pan or tray with enough hot water to come two-thirds up the sides of the ramekins. Bring to simmering point on top of the stove, then place in the oven. Cover the ramekins loosely with aluminium foil to prevent a skin from forming, and cook for 35 minutes.

Remove the ramekins, allow to cool down, then refrigerate.

Serving the dish
Run the blade of a knife around the sides of the ramekins and turn them out on to dessert plates. Serve to your guests.

Variation
The *crème caramel* will be absolutely delicious even if the mandarin zest is not used. You can also transform this dessert into a *crème brûlée*. Once cold, sprinkle brown sugar over the surface and place under the grill for 1 minute.

For four people

Preparation time: 10 minutes

Cooking time: 40 minutes

Special equipment:
4 ramekins, 7.5cm (3in) in diameter, 4cm (1½in) in height.

Planning ahead: This dish can be prepared a day in advance.

FOR THE CARAMEL:
2 tablespoons water
80g (3¼oz) caster sugar

FOR THE CREAM:
½ vanilla pod,
or 1 drop vanilla essence
400ml (14fl oz) milk
very finely grated zest
of 2 mandarin oranges
6 egg yolks
80g (3¼oz) caster sugar

 WINE

Vin Santo is a wine which will be a fantastic experience. Its scent and flavour will be delightful with this dessert.

For five people

Preparation time: 10 minutes

Cooking time: 15 minutes

Special equipment:
5 non-stick tartlet moulds, 10cm (4in) in diameter.

Planning ahead: This dish can be prepared an hour in advance but of course it is best served warm, about 10 minutes after it is taken out of the oven.

1 firm ripe kiwi fruit
25g (1oz) caster sugar
1 teaspoon lemon juice
10g (¼oz) unsalted butter
1 small orange, peeled and segmented
icing sugar for sprinkling

FOR THE FILLING:
2 eggs, separated
40g (1½oz) caster sugar
50g (2oz) plain flour
175ml (6fl oz) whipping cream
a pinch of salt
finely grated zest of ¼ lemon
1 drop vanilla essence
½ tablespoon Cointreau (optional)

WINE

I would recommend an orange Muscat from Australia.

Tartelettes aux Kiwis et Orange

Small kiwi and orange tartlets

The kiwi fruit has suffered a great deal under the abuse of *Nouvelle Cuisine*. Once there was not a dish without a slice of this colourful fruit, and subsequently the kiwi fruit lost some of its originality and interest. I find it to have a delicate and clear flavour which, served warm, is full and deliciously refreshing.

Preparing the kiwi fruit
Peel and cut the kiwi fruit into 5mm (¼in) slices, then sprinkle with ¼ teaspoon of the sugar and the lemon juice. Reserve on a plate.

Preparing the tartlet moulds
Butter the inside of the tartlet moulds and sprinkle with a little of the remaining sugar.

Preparing the filling
In a large mixing bowl whisk together the egg yolks and caster sugar until the mixture is well blended. Add the flour and continue whisking until the texture is smooth; while whisking, gradually add the cream and salt, then the finely grated lemon zest, vanilla and Cointreau (if using).

Whisk the egg whites until soft peaks are formed. Pour one-third of the egg white into the egg yolk mixture and whisk. Gently fold the remaining egg white into the mixture.

Preheat the oven to 350°F (180°C) Gas 4.

Filling the moulds and cooking the tartlets
Divide one-third of the filling mixture between the tartlet moulds, place two kiwi slices and three or four segments of orange on the top, then pour the remaining mixture over the fruit. Sprinkle generously with the remaining caster sugar and bake in the preheated oven for 15 minutes.

Remove from the oven and cool down until just warm. Remove the tartlets from the moulds, sprinkle with icing sugar, and serve to your guests.

CHEF'S NOTES
The tartlets can be accompanied by a lemon-flavoured Vanilla Cream (see page 46) or a simple purée of kiwi fruit, served warm.

Variations
The kiwi fruit and orange segments can be replaced by caramelised segments of apple or pear (see page 250), and would be equally delicious.

Gâteau au Citron

Lemon cake

This cake is a perfect accompaniment to morning coffee or afternoon tea.

Preheat the oven to 350°F (180°C) Gas 4.

Preparing the cake mixture
Combine the lemon zest, eggs, caster sugar and salt in a mixer bowl, then whisk at top speed for 5–7 minutes, until the mixture has thickened. Add the lemon juice towards the end.

Place the bowl on a work surface and fold in the cream. Sieve the flour and baking powder over the mixture and fold in delicately with a spatula. At this stage, add the melted butter, little by little, folding and lifting the mixture gently.

Preparing the cake tin
Grease the inside of the cake tin with butter, then dust with flour – about 10g (¼oz) of each. Turn the tin over and knock it against the table, to remove excess flour.

Baking the cake
Pour the cake mixture into the prepared tin, ensuring that the mixture reaches up to 2cm (¾in) from the top. Place on the middle rack in the preheated oven and cook for 55 minutes.

The cake will be cooked when the top is slightly convex. To be certain, slide a needle into the middle of the cake, and wait 2 seconds; remove the needle, which should be very clean and hot. Remove the cake from the oven, and turn on to a cooling rack for at least an hour until cold.

Increase the oven temperature to 400°F (200°C) Gas 6.

Glazing the cake
Thoroughly mix the lemon juice and the icing sugar until you obtain a homogeneous, loose mixture. Warm the orange marmalade in a small casserole.

Place the cake on a pastry sheet and, using a pastry brush, glaze the top and sides with the marmalade. Cool down for 5 minutes. Lightly heat the lemon and icing sugar for 1 minute until just warm, then brush over the cake. Place the cake in the oven for 30 seconds.

Remove the cake from the oven and allow to rest for a further hour so that the glaze can solidify. When completely cold, serve to your guests.

CHEF'S NOTES
The orange marmalade is first brushed all over the cake so that the icing can fix itself on to it.

For ten people

Preparation and cooking time: 1 hour, 10 minutes

Resting time: 1 hour

Special equipment:
1 cake tin, 30 × 10 × 8cm (12 × 4 × 3¼in).

Planning ahead: The cake can be made 1 day in advance.

finely grated zest of 2½ lemons
5 whole eggs
350g (12oz) caster sugar
a pinch of salt
juice of 1 lemon
150ml (5fl oz) double cream
275g (10oz) plain flour
10g (¼oz) baking powder
100g (4oz) unsalted butter, melted
butter and flour for lining the tin

FOR GLAZING THE CAKE:
juice of ½ lemon
100g (4oz) icing sugar
2 tablespoons orange marmalade

Papillote de Banane au Coulis de Fruits de la Passion

Bananas cooked in a parcel with vanilla and passion fruit coulis

For four people

Preparation and cooking time: 30 minutes

Planning ahead: The dish can be prepared half a day in advance and cooked at the last moment.

4 bananas
1 teaspoon lemon juice
1 tablespoon caster sugar
1 vanilla pod, cut in half lengthways,
then in half widthways
1 egg white

FOR THE PASSION FRUIT *COULIS*:
12 passion fruit
¼ fresh mango
juice of 1 large orange
70g (2¾oz) caster sugar
juice of ¼ lemon
2 tablespoons water

Preheat the oven to 400°F (200°C) Gas 6.

Preparing the passion fruit *coulis*
Cut the passion fruit in half, and spoon the pulp out into a bowl. Peel and stone the mango and chop the flesh. Add to the passion fruit pulp. Pour the fresh orange juice into the bowl. Add the caster sugar, lemon juice and water. Mix and then push through a sieve into another bowl. Reserve.

Preparing the bananas
Peel the bananas and cut into halves widthways. Remove any black threads and place the flesh in a bowl. Add the lemon juice and sprinkle with caster sugar. Reserve.

Preparing and cooking the *papillotes*
Cut four circles, 30cm (12in) in diameter, out of greaseproof paper or aluminium foil. Lay the four rounds of paper or foil on a table. Spoon equal amounts of the *coulis* into the middle of each. Place two banana halves into the centre and top with a strip of vanilla pod.

Using a pastry brush, brush the outer edges of the paper or foil with egg white. Draw up one side of the paper or foil to form a half moon. Brush the outside edges with egg white, and pinch together to seal the *papillotes*.

Transfer the *papillotes* to a baking tray and cook in the preheated oven for 7 minutes.

Serving
Transfer the *papillotes* to four warmed plates, unwrap foil or paper, and serve immediately to your guests.

 WINE

A fruit cocktail or an exotic fruit punch is the answer, or a glass of white rum.

Papillote de Banane au Coulis de Fruits de la Passion

For ten people

Preparation time: 30 minutes

Freezing time: 6 hours, approximately, depending on your freezer.

Special equipment:
A terrine or mould, $28 \times 8 \times 7$cm ($11 \times 3\frac{1}{4} \times 2\frac{3}{4}$in);
silicone (or greaseproof) paper to line the mould.

120g (4½oz) chestnuts in their own syrup (marrons glacés)
165ml (5½fl oz) syrup from the chestnuts (or make a syrup using 100g/4oz caster sugar and 65ml/ 2½fl oz water)
200g (7oz) each of sweetened and unsweetened chestnut purée (available in cans)
3 tablespoons dark rum
7 egg yolks
200ml (7fl oz) whipping cream

Le Parfait aux Marrons Glacés

Iced chestnut parfait

This is an ideal dessert for Christmas lunch or dinner.

Preparing the *marrons glacés* and chestnut purée
Drain the *marrons glacés* and keep the syrup. (If not available, make the syrup as left.) Break the *marrons glacés* into pieces, place them in a bowl together with 1 tablespoon of the rum, and leave to marinate.

Liquidise the two chestnut purées together with the remaining rum. Reserve in a bowl.

Making the *sabayon*
Place the egg yolks in the bowl of an electric mixer and mix at high speed for 6–7 minutes until the yolks have tripled in volume.

Separately, boil the chestnut syrup to 248°F (120°C). If you do not have a sugar thermometer, fill a bowl with cold water, take a drop of the boiling syrup with a spoon and pour it in the cold water. If the syrup is ready, a soft sugar ball will form within the water.

At this stage, lower the speed of the mixer and trickle the syrup on to the egg yolks, making sure you pour it between the sides of the bowl and the beaters. Leave to cool down.

Finishing the dish
Whip the cream. Using a spatula, mix together the chestnut purée and *marrons glacés*, add the whipped cream, and mix lightly. Fold in the *sabayon*.

Line the terrine mould with silicone paper, pour the *parfait* mixture into the mould, and smooth the top with a palette knife. Place in the freezer for a minimum of 6 hours.

Serving
Place a flat serving plate in the freezer.

Dip the terrine in hot water (to loosen the sides of the *parfait*), then gently ease the *parfait* out of the mould on to the chilled serving plate. Peel off the silicone paper. With a serrated-edged knife, slice the *parfait* into ten portions at the table. Serve to your guests.

CHEF'S NOTES
There is an emulsifier in the egg yolks. The volume of the egg yolks will expand due to the air incorporated by the whisking; the hot syrup poured over will partly cook the egg yolks, and make the *sabayon* stable. This operation must be done with great care. If the syrup trickles against the side of the bowl, it could solidify; and if it is poured over the beaters, it could fly out and be very dangerous.

It is important that the *parfait* is placed on to a chilled serving plate straight from the freezer.

Le Parfait aux Marrons Glacés

Variation
The *parfait* can be served with a Chocolate or Coffee sauce (see pages 45 and 47), as above, and flakes of chocolate shaved from a large bar.

 WINE

For this dessert I would recommend a champagne, *demi-sec*.

La Galette des Rois

Twelfth night cake

For eight people

Preparation time: 40 minutes

Cooking time: 30 minutes

Resting time: 2½ hours

Special equipment:
A non-stick pastry baking sheet 30cm (12in) square;
2 greaseproof paper sheets of the same size.

2 × 200g (7oz) square pieces of best bought puff pastry (made with butter)
100g (4oz) flour (for dusting)
1 egg, beaten

FOR THE FRANGIPANE CREAM:
100g (4oz) unsalted butter, softened
100g (4oz) icing sugar
100g (4oz) ground almonds
4 eggs
finely grated zest of 2 lemons
2 teaspoons almond essence

 WINE

This sweet is traditionally served in the afternoon, a couple of hours after the midday meal. Sometimes it is accompanied by champagne, or more humbly with coffee or tea; it is simply a matter of mood.

It is interesting that the French Republic starts its year celebrating . . . kings! It is also typical of the French to choose any historic, religious or political event, and turn it into a cake or dish! This Twelfth Night cake commemorates the kings who went to honour the birth of Jesus. The tradition is to place a small china king and queen in the middle of the cake, the crowns made of silver (the queen) and gold (the king). Ceremoniously, the slices are carved and the lucky ones having the queen or king are instantly consecrated for a day and are allowed to use the power of their own status. It is fun for everyone from children to grown-ups, but, a simple piece of advice – no matter how good the cake is, do not bite it too hard!

Preheat the oven to 400°F (200°C) Gas 6.

Rolling out the puff pastry
Lightly dust the table with some of the flour to prevent the puff pastry from sticking.

Place one piece of puff pastry in front of you and sprinkle it with a little more of the flour. Roll into a circle about 30cm (12in) in diameter and 2mm (¹/₁₆) thick. Dust a tray with yet more flour, place the circle of pastry on it and refrigerate for about 30 minutes, so that the pastry will lose its elasticity; this will also prevent retraction during cooking.

Repeat the same process for the second piece of pastry.

Preparing the frangipane cream
While the pastry is resting prepare the frangipane cream. Place the softened butter in a bowl and add the icing sugar. Whisk it in very well. Add the ground almonds and whisk into the mixture thoroughly. Add the eggs one by one along with the lemon zest and almond essence, whisking the mixture well after each egg has been added. Reserve.

Building the *galette des rois*
Line the pastry baking sheet with greaseproof paper and reserve. Using a plate 28cm (11in) diameter, cut out two circles in each of the puff pastry rounds. Place one of the pastry circles on the lined pastry baking sheet and brush all around the edge of the circle with egg wash. Pour the frangipane cream into the middle of the circle and spread it over about 1cm (½in) thick to form a concentric circle about 2cm (¾in) away from the edge of the pastry.

Place the second pastry circle on top of the frangipane cream and, using your fingertips, press all around the edge of the circle to seal the pastry together. With a small knife, press down with the blade to scallop and make a fluted edge to the pastry; this also strengthens the join between the two circles of pastry. Glaze the top of the pastry with egg wash and, using a small knife again, lightly score it to create an attractive design.

Cooking the *galette des rois*
Place in the preheated oven for 15 minutes, then reduce the temperature to 350°F (180°C) Gas 4, and cook for another 15 minutes. Remove from the oven, allow to cool down for 15 minutes, and serve to your guests.

CHEF'S NOTES
Be careful not to put egg wash on the sides of the puff pastry. The egg wash will stick to the layers and will prevent the puff pastry from rising. Be careful, too, not to cut *through* the puff pastry when you score it.

At the end of the cooking you could, if you wished, glaze the top of the *galette des rois* to get a better shine. When you take the *galette des rois* from the oven, dust the top with icing sugar and place under the grill for 30 seconds until the icing sugar has melted.

Sorbet au Chocolat

Chocolate sorbet

Place all the ingredients together into a saucepan and bring to the boil, whisking continuously. When all the ingredients have blended together, strain through a fine sieve directly into the bowl of the sorbet machine. Leave to cool down.

Churn for 15–20 minutes according to the cooling power of your machine.

Using 2 dessertspoons dipped in hot water, place the sorbet into the frosted glass bowls or glasses and serve to your guests.

CHEF'S NOTES
When bringing all the ingredients to the boil, it is important to whisk the mixture continuously to prevent the chocolate from burning on the bottom of the saucepan.

Although the sorbet can be kept frozen, it is always best consumed when it is freshly made.

Variations
This sorbet would be delicious served with Tuiles or Bouchées d'Orange (see pages 278 and 261).

For six to eight people

Preparation and cooking time:
30 minutes

Special equipment:
A *sorbetière* (see page 32).

Planning ahead: The sorbet can be prepared well in advance. Before serving, chill the glass bowls or dishes in the freezer for 30 minutes. (See the note on chocolate on page 14.)

500ml (18fl oz) water
50ml (2fl oz) liquid glucose
100g (4oz) caster sugar
75g (3 oz) unsweetened cocoa powder
50g (2oz) cooking chocolate, grated

Bûche de Noël au Chocolat

Chocolate Christmas log

Preheat the oven to 425°F (220°C) Gas 7.

Making the sponge biscuit
Follow the directions on page 21.

Making the chocolate mousse
Melt the chocolate gently in a *bain-marie* to 104°F (40°C). Remove from the heat. Whip the cream until it forms soft peaks. Pour a third of the whipped cream into the hot chocolate and mix very well. Pour the remaining cream into the chocolate and fold in until well blended.

Building the *bûche*
Mix the stock syrup and Cointreau together, then, using a pastry brush, soak the sponge with it. Spread 120g (4½oz) of the chocolate mousse over the soaked sponge, then roll the sponge up into a tight tube of 30cm (12in) long. Wrap this tube in a damp cloth tightly, and refrigerate for 15 minutes.

Unwrap the *bûche* and place it on a dish, 35cm (14in) long, and pipe the remaining chocolate mousse all over the *bûche*. Using a fork, fluff up the mousse to give the impression of a log. Refrigerate for 30 minutes.

Serving
Slice the *bûche* into eight pieces using a hot knife, place a slice on each plate and serve with Vanilla Cream or Custard (see page 47).

For eight people

Preparation time: 45 minutes

Cooking time: 6–8 minutes

*1 quantity Sponge Biscuit
(see page 21)*

FOR THE CHOCOLATE MOUSSE:
*120g (4½oz) extra bitter chocolate
175ml (6fl oz) whipping cream*

FOR SOAKING THE SPONGE BISCUIT:
*50ml (2fl oz) Stock Syrup
(see page 46)
25ml (1fl oz) Cointreau*

 WINE

It is a Christmas cake; champagne is the perfect festive wine.

Sorbet à la Banane

Banana sorbet

The banana usually is a fruit which has a very rich texture and can sometimes be unpleasant. Banana sorbet is one of the most delicious sorbets I know; it still contains the banana's richness but creates a lively freshness on the palate when the sorbet is served.

Peel the bananas and cut them in half lengthways. Using a teaspoon, scrape out and discard all the black seeds from the middle. Liquidise the banana, lemon juice and sugar together.

In a saucepan, bring the milk to the boil, cool it then pour it over the banana pulp and liquidise for a further minute; strain through a fine sieve into the bowl of the *sorbetière*.

Churn for 25–30 minutes according to the cooling power of your machine.

Using 2 dessertspoons dipped in hot water, place the sorbet into the frosted glass bowls or glasses and serve to your guests.

CHEF'S NOTES

In order to obtain the best possible taste, the bananas must be ripe but not stained.

The sorbet can be kept for up to 1 week in the freezer.

Variations

This sorbet would be delicious served with Coconut Tuiles (see page 276).

For four to six people

Preparation time: 20 minutes

Special equipment:
A *sorbetière* (see page 32).

Planning ahead: The sorbet can be prepared well in advance. Before serving, chill the glass bowls or glasses in the freezer for 30 minutes.

5 ripe bananas (but they must be firm), or 450g (1lb) banana pulp
juice of 2 lemons
60g (2¼oz) caster sugar
200ml (7fl oz) milk

Sorbet aux Fruits de la Passion

Passion fruit sorbet

Cut the passion fruit in half with a serrated knife and scrape out all the pulp, seeds and pink skin with a teaspoon.

Mix the fruit pulp and seeds with the cold stock syrup. Purée in a food processor fitted with a plastic blade for about 2 minutes, then force the pulp and juices through a conical sieve, pressing with a small ladle to extract as much juice as possible.

Churn for 20–25 minutes, according to the cooling power of your machine.

Using 2 tablespoons dipped in hot water, shape the sorbet into ovals and place three on each chilled plate or in a glass. Serve to your guests.

CHEF'S NOTES

Do not use a liquidiser when puréeing the pulp, as the blades will grind the little black pips, discolouring the pulp. Use the plastic blade of your food processor, which will detach the pulp from around the pips.

If you wish, you can replace the stock syrup with caster sugar, but reduce the quantity by half.

Variations
Add 100g/4oz mango pulp.

Keep some of the passion fruit shells and fill them with the sorbet, or serve in tulip-shaped tuiles (see page 276).

For four people

Preparation time: 45–60 minutes

Special equipment:
A *sorbetière* (see page 32).

Planning ahead: The syrup must be and the sorbet can be prepared well in advance. Chill the plates or glasses in the freezer for 30 minutes before serving.

17 passion fruit (for 400g/14oz pulp)
200ml (7fl oz) Stock Syrup (see page 46)

CHAPTER NINE

Petits Fours

Petits fours are definitely not for everyday cooking, but at a dinner party it is a delightful touch when the coffee reaches the table. Here are a number of very simple *petits fours* which are easily made at home.

Tuiles Coco

Coconut tuiles

Makes 12 pieces

Preparation and cooking time: 15 minutes

Resting time: 1 hour

Special equipment:
A non-stick tray.

50g (2oz) desiccated coconut
2 egg whites
60g (2¼oz) icing sugar
40g (1½oz) unsalted butter, melted

Preheat the oven to 325°F (160°C) Gas 3.

In a bowl mix the coconut, egg whites and sugar until homogeneous, using a wooden spatula. Then add the melted butter and mix again.

Using all the mixture, put 12 spoonfuls on the non-stick tray. Refrigerate for 1 hour.

To flatten the mixture to discs about 5cm (2in) in diameter and about 1mm (¹⁄₁₆ in) thick (or as thin as possible), use the base of a small, flat-bottomed bowl. Dip this in very hot water before using each time, so that the mixture does not stick.

Cook in the preheated oven for 3 minutes. Remove from the oven, let them rest for 2 minutes, then lift the tuiles with a spatula. Whilst still hot, place them over a rolling pin to give them a curved shape. Leave to cool.

Store in an airtight rigid container until ready to serve to your guests.

Tuiles aux Amandes

Almond tuiles

Makes 16 pieces

Preparation and cooking time: 10 minutes

Resting time: 1 hour

Special equipment:
A non-stick tray.

1 egg
1 egg white
125g (4½ oz) icing sugar
30g (1¼oz) plain flour
1 teaspoon double cream
30g (1¼oz) unsalted butter, melted
125g (4½oz) flaked almonds

Preheat the oven to 325°F (160°C) Gas 3.

In a bowl whisk the egg and the egg white together with a wooden spatula. Add the icing sugar, flour, cream, then the melted butter in that order, and mix until smooth. Add the almonds with a spatula, working carefully.

Using all the mixture, put 16 spoonfuls on to the non-stick tray. Refrigerate for 1 hour.

Flatten each of the discs as above, then cook in the preheated oven for 8 minutes, until the discs are golden brown around the edges. Remove from the oven, let rest, then shape, cool and store as above.

Petits fours

Tuiles à l'Orange

Orange tuiles

Makes 16 pieces

Preparation and cooking time: 13 minutes

Resting time: 1 hour

Special equipment:
A non-stick tray.

100g (4oz) icing sugar
30g (1¼oz) unsalted butter, melted
25g (1oz) plain flour
50ml (2fl oz) orange juice
50g (2oz) flaked almonds
finely grated zest of ½ orange

Preheat the oven to 350°F (180°C) Gas 4.

In a bowl mix all the ingredients together with a wooden spatula. Do not mix them too much, or the almonds will be crushed and not remain whole.

Using all the mixture, put 16 spoonfuls on the non-stick tray. Refrigerate for 1 hour.

Flatten each of the discs as above, then cook in the preheated oven for 5 minutes until golden brown. Remove from the oven, let rest, then shape, cool and store as above.

Biscuit Financier

Makes 30 pieces

Preparation and cooking time: 30 minutes

Special equipment:
30 *petits fours* tins, 4cm (1½in) square, and 1 cm (½in) deep.

50g (2oz) unsalted butter
80g (3¼oz) icing sugar
30g (1¼oz) ground almonds
40g (1½oz) plain flour
1 teaspoon self-raising flour
75g (3oz) egg whites

Preheat the oven to 425°F (220°C) Gas 7.

Brown the butter over a low heat, pass through a very fine sieve to remove the solid particles, and reserve (see page 30).

Combine the icing sugar, ground almonds and flours in a mixing bowl. Pour in the egg whites and mix with a spatula until smooth. Gradually mix in the warm butter.

Fill the generously buttered tins three-quarters full and cook in the preheated oven for 5 minutes.

Remove from the moulds while they are still hot. Reserve until required.

Tartelettes de Framboises

Raspberry tartlets

Makes 15 tartlets

Preparation and cooking time: 30 minutes

Special equipment:
30 tartlet moulds, 4cm (1½in) in diameter, and 1cm (½in) deep;
a fluted pastry cutter 5cm (2in) in diameter;
a sugar thermometer.

Planning ahead: The cooked pastry cases can be made 1 day in advance and kept in a sealed container.

125g (4½oz) Sweet Shortcrust Pastry (see page 20)
60g (2¼oz) raspberries
icing sugar

FOR THE RASPBERRY *GELÉE*:
150g (5oz) good quality seedless raspberry jam
juice of ¼ lemon
50g (2oz) Raspberry Coulis (see page 222)

Preheat the oven to 350°F (180°C) Gas 4.

Preparing and cooking the tartlet cases
Roll the pastry out on a floured board to 1.5mm (¹⁄₁₆in) thick. Using the pastry cutter, cut out 15 rounds. Place each round in a tartlet mould and top it with another mould, so that the pastry keeps its shape when baking. Cook for 3 minutes in the preheated oven. Remove the cooked tartlet cases carefully, cool down and reserve.

Making the raspberry *gelée*
Boil together the jam, lemon juice and raspberry *coulis* then allow to cool to 104°F (40°C), stirring occasionally.

Coating the raspberries
Dip all the raspberries in the *gelée* at the same time, ensuring that they are totally covered. Pour gently on to a tray so that you can separate the raspberries from the warm *gelée*.

Building the tartlets
Place the raspberries one by one into the baked tartlet cases. You should allow 2–3 raspberries per tartlet. Sprinkle with icing sugar and serve to your guests.

CHEF'S NOTES
The tartlet moulds do not need to be greased as the pastry is quite rich.

Variation
For lemon tartlets, pipe some good quality lemon curd into the tartlet cases.

Truffes au Whisky

Whisky truffles

Makes 50 pieces

Preparation and cooking time: 1 hour

Special equipment:
A piping bag with a 1–2mm ($^1/_{16}$ in) nozzle;
a baking tray lined with silicone paper;
a sugar thermometer.

140g (4¾oz) extra bitter chocolate, flaked
90ml (3¼fl oz) whipping cream
50ml (2fl oz) old Scotch whisky
250g (9oz) unsweetened cocoa powder
500g (18oz) best plain cooking chocolate for the
truffle coating

Place the chocolate flakes in a bowl. Bring the whipping cream to the boil and pour it on to the chocolate flakes. Whisk together and allow to cool down to room temperature.

Place the mixture into the bowl of an electric mixer and add the whisky. Whisk until the mixture has doubled in volume and is smooth in texture. Then place the mixture in the piping bag and pipe it into balls of 2cm (¾in) in diameter on to the lined tray. Allow to cool down in the fridge.

Place the cocoa powder in a deep tray.

Break the cooking chocolate for the coating into pieces, and place in a bowl in a *bain-marie* of warm water until melted. Stir from time to time. Turn off the heat and leave to cool for a while. It must still be liquid though.

Using a fork, dip the truffles in the chocolate. Immediately place them in the cocoa powder and roll them to coat. Place the truffles in a sieve and shake off the excess cocoa powder. Reserve in a dry and cool place.

CHEF'S NOTES

Truffles can be kept in a dry and cool place for 1 week.

When melting the chocolate in a *bain-marie*, ensure that the water does not boil or the chocolate would become granular. The ideal temperature is between 104° and 122°F (40° and 50°C).

If the chocolate is too hot when dipping the truffles, it will be too fluid and not coat the truffles properly. It would also melt the fragile inside. It should be cooled down to about 90°F (32°C).

Variations
Candied orange zest, chopped walnuts, diced *marrons glacés*, etc. could be added to the inside of the truffle.

Madeleines

Makes 35–40 pieces

Preparation and cooking time: 30 minutes

Special equipment:
Petits fours madeleine pan or tins (with shell-shaped indentations).

2 eggs
75g (3oz) caster sugar
10g (¼oz) brown sugar
a small pinch of salt
15g (½oz) honey
90g (3½oz) plain flour
½ teaspoon baking powder
90g (3½oz) unsalted butter, melted
butter and flour for the moulds

Preheat the oven to 400°F (200°C) Gas 6.
Beat together the eggs, sugars, salt and honey until smooth in consistency.
Fold in the flour and baking powder, then add the melted butter. Mix until well blended.
Butter and flour the tin or tins. Half fill with the mixture and cook for 5 minutes in the preheated oven.
Take out of the oven and remove from the tin immediately. Cool on wire racks. Do not allow to cool in the tin.
Reserve in a dry place until needed.

Caramels à l'Ancienne

Fudge

Makes 150 pieces

Preparation and cooking time: 30 minutes

Special equipment:
A deep tray, 20 × 30cm (8 × 12in), lined with silicone paper;
a sugar thermometer.

310g (11¼oz) caster sugar
100g (4oz) liquid glucose
310ml (11¼fl oz) double cream
100g (4oz) unsalted butter
110g (4oz) hazelnut praline paste or gianduja

In a pan, heat the sugar, glucose and cream until the temperature reaches 250°F (123°C), stirring from time to time. Remove from the heat.
In a separate pan melt the butter and *gianduja* together. Add to the glucose mixture in the first pan, and put back on the heat. Heat until the temperature again reaches 250°F (123°C), stirring rather more frequently than before.
Remove from the heat, and pour while still hot into the lined tray. Leave to cool.
When the mixture is cold, it will crystallise and firm up. Cut the fudge into 2cm (¾in) squares.

CHEF'S NOTES
Please read the chocolate notes on page 14.

The hazelnut praline paste can be replaced by any chocolate such as white chocolate melted with half a vanilla pod.

Gianduja is a praline, almond-flavoured chocolate. It can be found in good food stores.

Rochers aux Amandes

Almond rocks

Makes 50 pieces

Preparation and cooking time: 30 minutes

Special equipment:
A baking tray lined with silicone paper.

70g (2¾oz) extra bitter chocolate, broken into pieces
30g (1¼oz) cocoa butter
300g (11oz) nibbed almonds, toasted

Melt the chocolate and cocoa butter together in a bowl in a *bain-marie* of simmering (not boiling) water. Add the cold toasted nibbed almonds, and remove from the heat. Keep on stirring until the mixture is cool enough to be made into little rock-like shapes. (It thickens as it cools.)

Place the rock-like shapes on the lined tray, and set in the fridge for 15 minutes.

CHEF'S NOTES
See chocolate notes on page 14.

If you can't find cocoa butter, unsalted butter can be used instead.

Variations
Other nuts can be used; other varieties of chocolate can be used as well.

Pralines au Kirsch

Caramelised almonds with Kirsch

Makes 200g (7oz)

Preparation and cooking time: 15 minutes

Planning ahead: The pralines can be made a few days
in advance and kept in an airtight container.

150g (5oz) whole shelled almonds, skinned
or unskinned
150g (5oz) icing sugar
100ml (3½fl oz) Kirsch
20g (¾oz) unsalted butter

A delicious garnish for ice cream, or an accompaniment to coffee.

Combine the almonds, icing sugar and Kirsch in a heavy-bottomed saucepan. Cook over a strong heat until the Kirsch has evaporated and the sugar has a sandy texture.

Reduce the heat and cook for a further 5 minutes, stirring continuously, until lightly caramelised. Draw off the heat and stir in the butter. Cool on a lightly oiled tray and store in an airtight container, separating the caramelised almonds.

Varations
Mix hazelnuts with the almonds, or use hazelnuts alone.
Use water instead of Kirsch.

CHAPTER TEN

Breads

Bread has been a symbol of both spiritual and physical nourishment from biblical times to today. In France bread has always played an important part in daily life, and there is no good meal without good bread, from one in a 3-star restaurant right down to the family day-to-day meal. In my childhood I remember that my father alone carved the slices from the huge crusty loaf. This I could understand; it was surely a way to show us that he was the provider. But then his ritual would extend to tracing a cross on the bread with the point of a knife. Knowing that my father was a total atheist, this puzzled me. When asked the explanation, it became clear and simple: that was the only and best way he knew to show his respect for bread. I must say that it was beautiful bread, made by the village baker, following traditional recipes.

Today it is a different story. Industrialisation and machinery have taken over; and have dismissed the craft of bread-making, hence the poor quality on the shelves − more often than not a very anaemic loaf with dead white crumbs, the whole thing wrapped in plastic and, needless to say, tasteless. These last few years, though, have seen a revival of interest in bread. An interest in healthy eating has generated many organic flours which come from grains grown free of pesticides and soil additives. The direct result is a higher quality of flour, producing better bread.

Bread-making demands time − a minimum of half a day − but it can be the most fulfilling, soothing, enjoyable and rewarding activity.

The Basic Ingredients for Bread-Making

There is an incredible variety of different flours you can use (plain, wholegrain, rye, etc), and ingredients that can be added to bread. Once you have mastered the basic techniques, you can explore many other varieties of flours and ingredients such as carrots, herbs, walnuts, dried currants, almonds, ham, smoked bacon and spices, etc.

Bread is made from four basic ingedients − flour, water, yeast and salt.

FLOUR

People often ask me the difference between English and French flours. For a start, the flours just *are* different because they come from different wheats, or different mixtures of wheats. Then they are treated differently in the milling process or at the bakery. The bread-making properties of a flour are much improved by prolonged storage − the flour able to produce more loaf volume and a finer, softer crumb after 12 months' storage. In the last twenty years or so, it has become common practice to simulate this natural ageing process by the use of oxidising agents and improvers, particularly in Great Britain.

In France, legislation controlling flour milling is very strict, and millers can use only a very short list of biological, *natural* improvers:

Bean flour (a natural compound, used as a bleaching agent)

Malt extract (to give taste)

Amylase

Gluten powder (to strengthen the flour if necessary)

Ascorbic acid (or Vitamin C)

Soya extract (which helps conservation)

In Britain, the legislation on flour milling is much more lenient. Some of the accepted chemical 'improvers', bleaching and oxidising agents are:

Potassium bromate

Azodicarbonamide

Emulsifiers (E 471, E 472)

Benzoyl peroxide and Chlorine dioxide (bleaching agents)

The use of many of these improvers gives the dough an excess of strength which, in my opinion, results in a loaf that has developed too quickly, giving very often a white and insipid crumb.

With the aid of M. Dadé, who has his own bakery in London and has helped me to write this chapter, we have tried many British flours. We have selected two brands which are more likely to give you good results, Allinson and Asda, both of which are organically grown, and unbleached. They can be found in many outlets.

When it comes to pâtisserie, use quite a strong flour for all pastries made with yeast, such as croissants, bread and brioche; for everything else, use a medium-strength flour.

Delicious home-made bread

WATER

In order to regulate the temperature of the dough which should not go over 24°C, the temperature of the water is adjusted according to the temperature of the room and the flour, and according to the speed of the hook. If the speed of the hook is very fast, the friction produced will create heat; if the dough reaches around 30–32°C it would affect the strength of the gluten. Equally the dough would prove too fast and the taste and texture of the bread would be affected. Below is a formula which illustrates the way to find this temperature. (These calculations work only with Celsius.)

We use a base figure of 52°C. (This has been calculated using a Kenwood machine, speeds 1 and 2.) Assuming that the flour is 20°C (or 23°C) and that the room temperature is 24°C (or 22°C), the formula is:

Flour:	20°C	+	or	23°C	+
Room temperature:	24°C		or	22°C	
=	44°C		=	45°C	
Base temperature:	52°C	–		52°C	–
	44°C			45°C	
The water must therefore be adjusted to:	8°C	or		7°C	

The temperature of the water will determine the kneading and proving time. If the water is too warm, it will activate the proving time and the bread will be less tasty and heavier in texture. More simply, have the temperature of the room at approximately 21°C, and place all the ingredients at this room temperature for several hours in advance of the bread-making.

YEAST

In these recipes, we have used moist fresh yeast which is available from your delicatessen or local bakery (though in the latter your request might prove less popular!). Dry yeast can also be used, but the flavour of the bread will be affected.

Yeast is made from sugars, mineral and nutrient compounds, and oxygen, and it is manufactured. Reproduction of yeast cells takes place in laboratory conditions.

The main function of yeast is to produce carbon dioxide which causes the dough to grow in volume and give the bread its light texture.

SALT

Salt is obviously used to give flavour to the bread. It must never be mixed with the yeast, as this would cancel the latter's effect.

Special Equipment for Bread-Making

You will need very little that is not already in your kitchen, but the most important piece of equipment is an electric mixer fitted with a dough hook. You also need a thermometer, a spatula, a sieve, a razor blade or scissors, bowls, and cloths to cover the dough while it is proving.

The Process of Bread-Making

The first important thing is to weigh all your ingredients very carefully, keeping them entirely separate. The yeast and salt, for instance, must not come in contact with each other.

MIXING THE DOUGH

According to the type of mixer you have, read the instructions on bread-making in your manual. This will give you the speed to set your mixer on; for a Kenwood this should be slow, speed no. 1, medium, speed no. 2.

The mixing will aerate the dough, and further its development of gluten which will determine the texture and the lightness of the bread. The first mixing should be done at the lower speed – no. 1 – then the speed should be increased to medium speed – no. 2 – when you add the yeast. Do not use the high speed, and do not *over* mix or the temperature of the dough will be too high. Check with a thermometer that the dough temperature does not go over 24°–25°C.

PROVING OR FERMENTING THE DOUGH

This should be done in a draught-free environment, and the dough should be covered with a cloth to prevent a dry skin forming.

Generally speaking, the dough will be ready when it has doubled in size.

SHAPING THE DOUGH

Work each piece of dough separately on a lightly floured surface. With the palm of your hand, push the sides towards the centre of the loaf or roll. Rotate the dough, pushing in the same way until it is smooth and even.

The breads and rolls can be made into oblong or round shapes according to your personal taste.

BAKING THE DOUGH

Preheat the oven well in advance of putting the bread dough in. Boil 300ml (10fl oz) water and place it in a deep-sided tray in the bottom of the oven. The steam rising will help to give the bread colour and texture. If the crust were to cook too quickly, it would prevent the dough from rising. The steam also helps the carbon dioxide trapped in the dough to expand more fully; it helps the caramelisation of the sugars contained in the bread which are responsible for the pleasing brown crust.

The baking tray should be placed towards the top of the oven, where the heat is reflected and is strongest.

COOLING AND STORING THE BREAD

Remove the bread from the oven when it is ready and leave to cool on a rack for a minimum of 1 hour.

If you cannot use all the bread immediately, it can be frozen while still slightly warm. To serve, place directly from the freezer into an oven preheated to 415°F (210°C) Gas 6½ for 4–8 minutes.

All the following bread recipes make three loaves or 20–25 rolls.

Fermented Dough Starter

100g (4oz) white unbleached flour
4 tablespoons water, 22°C

5g (⅛oz) moist baker's yeast

Using a fermented dough starter is the traditional way to make good, light, tasty bread. Fermented dough is composed of flour, water and a small quantity of yeast which is left to ferment, then added to the other ingredients of the bread recipe. The living yeast cells will reproduce during the fermentation and, when mixed into the basic ingredients of the bread, will activate the other yeast cells in the fresh dough, giving a light acidity which is important to the taste of the bread. Fermentation will also develop the strength of the dough.

One can, of course, make bread *without* this dough starter, but it will be less tasty and of a heavier texture.

Knead the flour and water in the bowl of the electric mixer at a low speed, no. 1, for 3–5 minutes. Crumble in the yeast, and knead at medium speed, no. 2, for 10 minutes. Remove the bowl from the mixer, and cover with a cloth. Prove the dough for 3 hours at room temperature.

Break or knock back the dough by lifting it. This removes the fermentation gases from the dough. Replace in the bowl, cover with the cloth, and prove for another 3 hours for a second fermentation.

This fermented dough can be prepared 1–2 days in advance, and kept in the fridge. If you do this, omit the second fermentation as the dough will go on fermenting slowly in the fridge.

When making bread with the fermented dough, the dough must be removed from the fridge at least 2 hours in advance, so it can prove.

Granary Bread

*500g (18oz) granary flour (Allinson),
at room temperature, sieved
300ml (10fl oz) water, 8°C*

*12g (just under ½oz) moist baker's yeast
15g (½oz) salt
165g (5½oz) Fermented Dough Starter (see page 287)*

Mix the flour and water slowly in the bowl of the electric mixer for 3 minutes at speed no. 1. Crumble in the yeast. Knead on medium speed – no. 2 – for a further 10 minutes. Add the salt and the fermented dough starter, and knead again at the same speed for another 5 minutes.

Take the dough out of the bowl and shape it into a big ball on a lightly floured surface, cover with a cloth and leave to prove at room temperature for 1 hour.

Knock it back and prove it for a further hour.

Divide the risen dough into three equal pieces for loaves or 20 pieces for rolls, and shape them. Place a cloth on a tray and lift the dough pieces on to it, separating with folds of the cloth. Cover with another cloth and prove for another hour. Preheat the oven to 500°F (250°C) Gas 9.

When the dough is ready, place the water in the oven. Lightly flour the baking tray and very delicately lift the pieces of risen dough on to it, leaving as much space as possible between them. Make sharp incisions into the loaves or rolls and bake the loaves for about 25–30 minutes, the rolls for about 8–10 minutes. Cool down for a minimum of an hour on a cooling rack.

CHEF'S NOTES

Granary bread can be moulded in a tin. Simply grease with vegetable oil.

The dough must be knocked back twice in order to give it strength; granary flour has a smaller amount of gluten.

Perfect for a simple meal

Pain de Campagne

White bread

500g (18oz) plain unbleached flour (Allinson), at room temperature, and sieved
350ml (12fl oz) water, 7°–8°C

12g (slightly under ½oz) moist baker's yeast
15g (½oz) salt
165g (5½oz) Fermented Dough Starter (see page 287)

Place the flour in the bowl of the electric mixer. Pour the water in, and start mixing at speed no. 1 for 3 minutes. Then crumble the yeast in and knead at speed no. 2 for a further 8 minutes. Add the salt and fermented dough starter and mix on the same speed for a further 5 minutes.

Take the dough out of the bowl and shape it into a big ball on a lightly floured surface. Cover with a cloth and leave to prove at room temperature, approximately 1 hour.

Divide the risen dough into three equal pieces for loaves – or 20 for rolls – and shape them according to personal taste (oblongs, rounds, etc).

Place a cloth on a tray and lift the dough pieces on to it, separating each with a fold in the cloth. Cover again with another cloth and prove the dough for about another 1–1½ hours, depending on room temperature; the dough will be ready when it has doubled in volume, and if, when you press the surface with your finger, it springs back. The dough is now ready for baking. With a fine sieve, dust the loaves with a little extra flour.

Meanwhile, preheat the oven to 500°F (250°C) Gas 9 or as high as your oven will go and put a tray of boiling water at the bottom of the oven.

Lightly flour a baking tray and very delicately lift the pieces of risen dough on to the tray, leaving as much space as possible between them. Then make some very sharp incisions into the loaves – four or five widthwise or one long one lengthways right in the middle of the bread or rolls.

Slice the tray into the preheated oven immediately after making the cuts, and bake the loaves for about 25–30 minutes, the rolls for about 8–10 minutes. Remove when the bread or rolls have beautiful golden crusts, and leave to cool for a minimum of 1 hour.

CHEF'S NOTES

Hold the blade of the razor against the surface at about a 30° angle. It is essential that the cuts are not too deep – they should be about 2–3mm ($\frac{1}{16}$–⅛in) – and not too vertical. If the angle is not sharp enough the fold will close up during the cooking, and if too deep the loaf is very likely to open up during baking. Each cut should be a minimum of 3cm (1¼in) apart.

Variation

Once you have shaped the bread, before proving, you can brush the surface with water (or spray with water). Place a generous amount of sesame seeds on a cloth and roll the dough on it gently so that the surface is coated with the seeds.

Le Benoiton

Bread with currants and hazelnuts

500g (18oz) farmhouse brown flour
(Asda), at room temperature, sieved
350ml (12fl oz) water, 8°C
12g (just under ½oz) moist baker's yeast

15g (½oz) salt
165g (5½oz) Fermented Dough Starter (see page 287)
80g (3¼oz) each of currants and
cold toasted hazelnuts

This bread goes well with game and cheese, or it can be eaten any time you are hungry.

In the bowl of the electric mixer, place the flour and water. Knead at speed no. 1 for 3 minutes. Crumble in the yeast and knead at speed no. 2 for 10 minutes, before adding the salt and the fermented dough. Knead again for 5 minutes at the same speed, then add the currants and hazelnuts until well mixed in.

Take the dough out of the bowl and shape it into a big ball on a lightly floured surface. Cover with a cloth and leave to prove at room temperature for approximately 20 minutes. Knock back, divide the dough into three pieces for loaves or 20 for rolls, and shape according to personal taste. Place on a cloth on a tray, separating with the cloth folds, cover with another cloth, and prove at room temperature for another hour.

When the dough is ready, lightly flour a baking tray and very delicately lift the pieces of risen dough on to it, leaving as much space as possible between them. Cover and prove at room temperature for about another 1¼–1½ hours.

Preheat the oven to 425°F (220°C) Gas 7, and place a tray of water in it.

Do not cut these loaves or sprinkle them with flour. Bake the loaves for 25–30 minutes, and the rolls for 8–10 minutes. You can give the crust a lovely shine by brushing the top of the loaf with soft butter just as it is coming out of the oven. Cool on a rack for a minimum of 1 hour.

Pains aux Olives

Olive Bread

500g (18oz) farmhouse brown flour
(Asda), at room temperature, sieved
350ml (12fl oz) water, 8°C
12g (just under ½oz) moist baker's yeast
15g (½oz) salt

165g (5½oz) Fermented Dough Starter (see page 287)
160g (5¼oz) pitted olives in olive
oil, black or green, drained
½ teaspoon powdered rosemary

This bread will go particularly well with any Provençal dish and also with goat cheese.

Mix, knead, prove, shape and bake exactly as for Le Benoiton.

CHAPTER ELEVEN

Liqueurs and Aperitif Wines

A small tribute to my grandmother.

I first made acquaintance with liqueurs rather early on in life, at about the age of seven. No, I was not a budding alcoholic; it was simply that my grandfather had a huge cellar with an enormous press where he would distil his fruits. I became an enchanted and frequent visitor to this Aladdin's cave. Needless to say, tasting this forbidden fruit was an exhilarating experience. My grandfather would distil the hard stuff from such as mirabelle plums to produce a minimum of 65° proof alcohol! My grandmother was an alchemist, concentrating on gentler liqueurs with many different tastes and colours. The mysterious bottles, the product of both their labours, would stand on the old oak dresser, ready to be savoured. Traditionally the men would drink the very hard alcohols after their meals, and the women would gather in another corner of the room to sip these divine concoctions.

These liqueurs and aperitif wines are traditionally made in France with 90° proof alcohol which you can get in any chemist. In Britain this is impossible and against the law. I have had to replace this by the most neutral alcohol available with the highest alcohol content, which is tequila.

I'm still fascinated at the amazing sense of creativity and adventure that these recipes hold. My grandmother was quite a lady. The recipes here are examples of her fascinating skills.

Liqueurs

The principles involved in the making of these liqueurs are very simple. The basic requirement is time – time for the fruit or flavouring to macerate in the alcohol, hence giving it taste and colour, and for the liqueur to mature. This is done in a clean, covered and sealed bowl or jar; Kilner jars look good. Light and warmth are damaging, though, so the maturation must take place in a dark, cool and dry place. The time involved ranges from 2 days to 3 months.

When ready, the alcohol is filtered by pouring it through a doubled layer of muslin into a clean container. This filtering is very important, as is the *double* layer of muslin. Thereafter, in most cases, the flavoured alcohol is mixed with a simple sugar and water syrup, then poured through a funnel into clean bottles. Seal these with screw tops or corks. The liqueurs will now be ready to drink.

Liqueur de Lait Grand-mère Blanc

Grandmother's milk liqueur

Makes about 1.2 litres (2 pints)

300ml (10fl oz) milk
500g (18oz) caster sugar
500ml (18fl oz) tequila
2 vanilla pods, halved
1 lemon, cut into 8

Mix all the ingredients together in a bowl. Cover with cling film or lid and leave to macerate at room temperature for a fortnight. Then filter the liquid into a container, bottle and seal. It can then be enjoyed straightaway.

CHEF'S NOTES

During maceration all the solid matters in the milk will separate; so filter *very carefully* to separate the solids from the liquid.

What better way to end a dinner party?

Liqueur d'Estragon

Tarragon liqueur

Makes about 900ml (1½ pints)

60g (2¼oz) fresh tarragon leaves
500ml (18fl oz) tequila

FOR THE SYRUP:
400ml (14fl oz) water
400g (14oz) caster sugar

Macerate the tarragon leaves in the alcohol for 3 months in a covered and sealed jar. Filter the liquid into a container.
Make a syrup with the water and sugar. Allow to cool down. Add the filtered, tarragon-scented alcohol to the syrup, then bottle and seal. The liqueur is ready to be served.

Liqueur de Cassis

Blackcurrant liqueur

Makes about 1.4 litres (2½ pints)

500g (18oz) ripe blackcurrants, washed and drained
1 litre (1¾ pints) tequila

300g (11oz) caster sugar
1 clove
a few blackcurrant leaves (optional)

Crush the blackcurrants with a fork, and place them in a jar with the remaining ingredients. Seal the jar and macerate for 2 months. Filter into a container, and then store in a sealed bottle. The liqueur is now ready to be enjoyed.

Liqueur d'Angélique

Angelica liqueur

Makes about 1.3 litres (2¼ pints)

*150g (5oz) fresh angelica stalks,
washed and finely chopped*
1 litre (1¾ pints) tequila

1 tiny piece of cinnamon
2 cloves

FOR THE SYRUP:
250ml (8fl oz) water
400g (14oz) caster sugar

Place the angelica, tequila, and spices into a large jar, cover and seal, and macerate for 2 months. Filter the liquid into a container.
Make a syrup with the water and caster sugar, and allow to cool down. Mix with the angelica alcohol, then pour into a bottle and seal. It is now ready to be enjoyed.

Liqueur de Genièvre

Juniper berry liqueur

Makes about 800ml (1¼ pints)

75g (3oz) fresh juniper berries
500ml (18fl oz) tequila
½ lemon, cut into 4
10 anise seeds

1 vanilla pod, halved
5g (⅛oz) piece of cinnamon

FOR THE SYRUP:
100ml (3½fl oz) water
200g (7oz) caster sugar

Place the juniper berries, tequila and lemon in a jar, cover and seal, and macerate for 3 days. Filter into another jar.
Make a syrup with the water and sugar. Allow to cool, then mix with the alcohol in the second jar.
Wrap the anise seeds, vanilla and cinnamon in a piece of muslin. Tie with a string and add to the alcohol in the jar. Macerate for a month, then filter, bottle and seal. It is now ready for use.

Liqueur de Café

Coffee liqueur

Makes about 900ml (1½ pints)

6 bitter almonds
50g (2oz) coffee beans, crushed
500ml (18fl oz) tequila

FOR THE SYRUP:
100ml (3½fl oz) water
300g (11oz) caster sugar

Preheat the oven to 400°F (200°C) Gas 6.
Brown the almonds in the preheated oven for 5–6 minutes, then allow to cool down. Crush them, and add to the coffee beans and tequila in a jar; cover and seal. Macerate for a fortnight. Filter into a container.
Make a syrup with the water and sugar, and allow to cool, then mix with the filtered alcohol. Place in a bottle and seal. It is now ready for use.

Liqueur de Coings

Quince liqueur

Makes about 1.3 litres (2¼ pints)

6 quinces
1 litre (1¾ pints) tequila

FOR THE SYRUP:
100ml (3½fl oz) water
320g (11½oz) caster sugar

For this recipe you will only need the peel of the quinces. (Use the flesh in the purée on page 30.) Wash the fruit and pat dry, then cut off the peel. Place the peel in a jar with the tequila. Cover, seal and macerate in a dry dark place for 6 weeks. Filter into a container.
Make a syrup with the water and sugar, cool, then mix with the alcohol. Pour into a bottle and seal. It is ready for use.

Liqueur de Noyaux d'Abricots

Apricot kernel liqueur

Makes about 1.2 litres (2 pints)

FOR THE SYRUP:
100ml (3½fl oz) water
250g (9oz) caster sugar

10 apricot stones
1 litre (1¾ pints) tequila
½ vanilla pod

Break the stones of the apricots to release the kernels. Crush both the kernels and the woody stones of the apricots. Place them in a jar with the tequila and vanilla pod, cover and seal, and macerate for 6 weeks. Filter into a container.

Make a syrup with the caster sugar and water, and allow to cool down before mixing with the alcohol. Pour into a bottle. It is ready to be tasted.

Liqueur de Fleurs d'Oranges

Orange-flower liqueur

Makes 1.4 litres (2½ pints)

FOR THE SYRUP:
100ml (3½fl oz) water
500g (18oz) caster sugar

50g (2oz) dried orange flowers
dried zest of 6 oranges (see page 297)
dried zest of 1 lemon
1 litre (1¾ pints) tequila

Place the orange flowers and zests in a jar and cover with the tequila. Cover and seal the jar and macerate for 6 weeks. Filter into a container.

Make a syrup with the water and sugar. Allow to cool down and mix with the alcohol. Pour into a bottle and seal. It is ready for use.

Liqueur d'Anis

Anise liqueur

Makes about 1.5 litres (a good 2½ pints)

1 litre (1¾ pints) tequila

FOR THE SYRUP:
100ml (3½fl oz) water
600g (1lb 6oz) caster sugar

40g (1½oz) anise seeds, crushed
10g (¼oz) coriander seeds, crushed
a tiny piece of cinnamon, crushed
a tiny piece of whole mace

Place the spices in a jar, mix with the alcohol, and cover and seal. Macerate for a month. Filter into a container.

Make a syrup with the water and sugar, and allow to cool down. Mix both liquids together. Pour into a bottle and seal. It can be tasted straightaway.

Liqueur de Curaçao

Curaçao liqueur

Makes about 1.2 litres (2 pints)

dried zests of 6 oranges
1 litre (1¾ pints) tequila

FOR THE SYRUP:
100ml (3½fl oz) water
250g (9oz) caster sugar

FOR THE CARAMEL:
50g (2oz) caster sugar

Place the dried zests and tequila into a jar, cover and seal, and macerate for 2 months. Filter into a container.
  Make a syrup with the water and sugar, then cool down before mixing with the alcohol.
  In a small pan heat and caramelise the sugar until it is quite dark. Add 100ml (3½fl oz) of the alcohol syrup to the caramel, and simmer for 2 minutes. Allow to cool down, and mix with the bulk of the liqueur. Pour into a bottle and seal. It is now ready for use.

CHEF'S NOTES
Remove zests or rind from citrus fruit with a potato peeler. Place in a tray and leave in a warm place (close to the oven, for instance) for about 40 hours to dry it.

Cerises au Kirsch

Cherries in Kirsch

Preparation time: 30 minutes

Maceration time: 2 months minimum

Special equipment:
a 2 litre (3½ pint) jar with a rubber-sealed lid.

2kg (4½lb) Morello cherries
150g (5oz) white sugar cubes
1 vanilla pod
750ml (1¼ pints) Kirsch

These Morello cherries, macerated in Kirsch, will be heavenly at the end of a dinner party. If you cannot find Morello cherries, use the best cherries you can get. They should be slightly unripe, firm and unbruised.

Morello cherries must be perfectly ripe. Wash them briefly then dry them. Cut the stalks so they are only 2cm (¾in) long.
  Place the cherries in the jar, and add the sugar cubes, vanilla pod and Kirsch. Seal the jar tightly with the lid and place in a dark place for a minimum of 2 months.

CHEF'S NOTES
The maceration process is essential to enable the alcohol to permeate the flesh of the cherries.

This liqueur will keep for a minimum of a year.

Variation
You can replace cherries with raspberries which would also be delicious; follow the recipe exactly, but replace the Kirsch with a raspberry alcohol.

Liqueur de Framboises

Raspberry liqueur

Makes about 1.3 litres (2¼ pints)

450g (1lb) raspberries
1 litre (1¾ pints) tequila

FOR THE SYRUP:
50ml (2fl oz) water
350g (12oz) caster sugar

Crush the raspberries and mix with the tequila in a jar. Cover, seal and macerate for 2 months. Filter into a container.

Make a syrup with the water and sugar, and allow to cool before mixing with the alcohol. Pour into a bottle and seal. It is ready to be tasted.

Les Aperitifs

Aperitif wines

Here are just a few aperitif wines that my mother and my grandmother would make − with a mother and grandmother like them, how could I *not* become a chef! Ladies would also enjoy these lighter fruit- and wine-based aperitifs.

Vin de Pêche

Peach wine

Makes about 1 litre (1¾ pints)

120 fresh peach tree leaves
500ml (18fl oz) red wine
500ml (18fl oz) dry white wine
100ml (3½fl oz) tequila

FOR THE SYRUP:
100ml (3½fl oz) water
200g (7oz) caster sugar

Mix the peach leaves, wines and tequila together in a jar. Cover, seal and macerate for 8 days. Filter into a container.

Make a syrup with the sugar and water and allow to cool down. Mix both liquids together, then pour into a bottle and seal. It is ready for tasting.

Vin de Pamplemousse

Grapefruit wine

Makes about 1.2 litres (2 pints)

peel and pith of 1 grapefruit
1 litre (1¾ pints) dry white wine
1 heaped teaspoon ground chicory

FOR THE SYRUP:
100ml (3½fl oz) water
200g (7oz) caster sugar

Chop the grapefruit peel and pith roughly, into about 15−16 pieces, then place in a jar with the wine and chicory. Cover and seal and macerate for 48 hours. Filter into a container.

Make a syrup with the water and sugar, and allow to cool down before mixing with the alcohol. Pour into a bottle and seal. It is ready for use.

CHEF'S NOTES
The flesh of the grapefruit can be used for another recipe (see page 82).

Oranges can replace the grapefruit in this recipe.

LIQUEURS AND APERITIF WINES

Guignolet

Cherry leaf wine

Makes about 1.2 litres (2 pints)

FOR THE SYRUP:
100ml (3½fl oz) water
350g (12oz) caster sugar

100 cherry tree leaves
1 litre (1¾ pints) red wine
200ml (7fl oz) tequila

Mix the cherry leaves, wine and tequila together in a jar. Cover, seal and macerate for 3 days. Filter into a container.

Make a syrup with the water and sugar and allow to cool before mixing with the alcohol. Pour into a bottle and seal. It is now ready for use.

Sangria

Makes about 1.3 litres (2¼ pints)

FOR THE SYRUP:
100ml (3½fl oz) water
100g (4oz) caster sugar

2–3 oranges, sliced
1 lemon, sliced
1 litre (1¾ pints) red wine
200ml (7fl oz) tequila

Mix the citrus fruit slices, wine and tequila in a jar. Cover, seal, and macerate for 2 days. Filter into a container.

Make a syrup with the water and sugar, and allow to cool down before mixing with the alcohol. Pour into a bottle and seal. It is ready for tasting.

CHAPTER TWELVE

Jams and Preserves

Confitures

Jams

Jam-making is associated with wonderful childhood memories of bringing baskets of home-grown or wild fruits to my mother. She would then use her traditional skills and perform the small miracle of jam-making. Large black saucepans would simmer the divine juices while suspended jelly bags would drip the essences of the fruits; the aroma of jam would waft through the entire house. The jars would then be filled with the colourful jams and jellies, stored away, ready to be enjoyed throughout the year – to adorn the breakfast table, to fill pancakes or one of her delicious cakes . . .

I find jams made in the traditional way have too high a concentration of sugar which totally obliterates the wonderful freshness and basic characteristics of the fruits. They are also mashed and discoloured through the over-long cooking process.

In the traditional recipes, one is told to boil the fruits until they reach a temperature of 221°–224°F (105°–107°C); Besides diminishing the yield by 30 per cent, this increases the concentration of sugar up to around 80 per cent (jams sold in shops often have a sugar content ranging from 70–80 per cent). This long cooking also damages the pectin and thus the fragile pectin/sugar balance, and the jam could clot together to produce a granular jam.

So, last year, I began in earnest to question the traditional ways of making jam. Stunning results came of various trials, producing the most well-textured, colourful and refreshing jams.

The Process of Jam-Making

It is really simple to make jam but, like all other forms of cooking, it is an inexact science: so many factors can influence the final result – ripeness, size, water content and acidity of the fruit, the length of cooking, etc. I am sure you have experienced jams which never set or the ones which set like concrete! For maximum success, let us understand how to achieve the best results.

Special equipment You don't need much, but these few pieces are essential. A large cast-iron casserole (Le Creuset, for example); a fine conical sieve; a sugar thermometer.

Fruits These must be extremely fresh, just ripe, and dry. Over-ripe fruit will squash easily, and will have less pectin and acid content. If the fruit is under-ripe, it will not hold enough sugar, will have too much acid, and the pectin will not be as soluble; this will make the jam more difficult to set. The fruit must be dry; if it is picked wet, it will have too high a water content, and will dilute acid and pectin.

All fruits must be cut to an even size so that they need the same cooking time. If they have traces of dirt on them, wash them carefully and briefly in cold water, then drain well in a colander.

Sugar Preserving sugar is not essential, granulated or caster will do just as well.

According to which fruit you use, more or less sugar will be added. Sugar of course acts as a sweetener. Its density helps the fruit to keep its shape and texture and it also acts as a preservative, killing off the microbes. It helps the setting of the jam by increasing its thickness.

Lemon juice Although there is acid in the fruit, citric acid needs to be added in different quantities according to the type of fruit you are using. It will also help the binding of the jam and will counterbalance the sweetness of the sugar.

First let us look at the ingredients involved in a traditional recipe, which was made with 1kg (2¼lb) each of strawberries and sugar, and the juice of 1 lemon. My observations were: *colour*, dark red; *texture*, thick and highly set; *taste*, too sweet; *fruits*, mushy.

Because of the high concentration of sugar (70–80 per cent) the jam will have a long shelf life (it could, in fact, live forever), but I feel that it would not honour my guests to place such a jam on their breakfast tray.

The following recipes from Le Manoir are truly part of the magic of the breakfast tray. The approach is different, based on the idea of diminishing the lengthy boiling of the fruits, the amount of sugar and the high temperature.

Tasty and wholesome home-made jams

The jams produced are very colourful, with a pleasant sweetness and good texture; the sugar content will also be as low as 55 per cent and once the jars have been sterilised the jams can be kept for use all year round.

Cooking the fruit We simply boil the fruit and sugar to 212°F (100°C), a temperature which can be achieved within 5–8 minutes. To check this you will need a sugar thermometer. We then make up for this short boiling with the addition of dried pectin. Pectin is a substance naturally present in most fruit (although in varying quantities) that causes pulp to set. None of the liquid pectins that I have tried in Britain are very efficient, and I would recommend dried pectin. This can be bought from a chemist or grocer. However, as all pectin extracts have different concentrations it is wise to test the one you buy before trying these recipes.

Checking for setting point The jam should be enabled to set well by boiling to 212°F (100°C), and the addition of the dried pectin. But to test in the traditional way, place a tablespoon of the hot jam on a cold saucer, and place in the fridge for a few minutes. If setting point has been achieved, the jam should wrinkle when pushed with a finger. If not ready, cook for a few minutes more or add a small amount of pectin.

Filling the jars The jam is then poured into the jars and left to cool. Pour in through a special jam funnel, or a plastic one with a 5–7.5cm (2–3in) opening. I prefer to use jars with a screw-top lid, and the jars and lids should be very clean and dry before filling.

Fill them to 1mm ($\frac{1}{16}$in) from the top, and leave to cool.

Sterilising the jams The jams will need to be sterilised to ensure they keep well because there is so little sugar (a natural preservative) in them. Simply place the filled jars, sealed tightly with their lids, into a large pan of cold water. This must cover the jars completely to ensure the sterilisation process takes place. It is a good idea to put a double layer of paper or cloth, or a wire grid, on the bottom of the pan so that the jars do not come in contact with the heat coming through the bottom of the pan. You could also separate the jars by using paper or cloths.

Bring the water to the boil gently, then simmer for 20–25 minutes from boiling point. The jars *must* be placed in cold water; if it were boiling the glass would break.

Remove the jars from the water (there are special tongs for this) and leave to cool down. Dry and label.

Storing jams and preserves A dark cool place is best, especially for preserves, to prevent discoloration and deterioration. However, a few jars in the kitchen will look very attractive. Once the jars are opened, it is best to keep them in the refrigerator.

Confiture de Framboises et Groseilles

Raspberry and redcurrant jam

500g (18oz) raspberries, prepared
500g (18oz) redcurrants, prepared
500g (18oz) caster sugar

100g (4oz) caster sugar plus 20 g (¾oz) dried pectin
juice of 1 lemon

Place the sugar in a cast-iron saucepan and warm over a medium heat, stirring all the time with a wooden spoon. Add the prepared raspberries and redcurrants, stir to mix the fruit and sugar, cover and boil rapidly for 5 minutes. Remove the lid and cook the fruit until the temperature reaches 212°F (100°C).

Force the pulp through a conical sieve into another saucepan, pressing with a ladle to extract as much jam as possible. Bring the jam to the boil, and sprinkle in the mixed sugar and dried pectin. Stir with a whisk, add the lemon juice and boil for a further minute.

Check to see if the jam has reached setting point.

Pour the jam into the prepared jars, and leave to cool down. Secure tightly with lids.

Sterilise the jam jars, cool down, label and store.

Framboise Pépin

Raspberry jam with pips

1kg (2¼lb) raspberries, perfectly ripe
450g (1lb) sugar

100g (4oz) caster sugar plus 30g (1¼oz) dried pectin
juice of 1 lemon

Place the sugar in a cast-iron saucepan and warm over a medium heat, stirring with a wooden spoon. Add the whole raspberries and mix. Cover with a lid and boil rapidly for 5 minutes. Remove the lid and cook for a further 5 minutes, until the temperature reaches 212°F (100°C). Skim off any impurities, then sprinkle in the mixed sugar and dried pectin together with the lemon juice. Stir with a whisk, and boil for a further minute.

Check that the jam has reached setting point.

Pour the jam into the prepared jars, cool down, then seal tightly with the lids.

Sterilise the jam jars, cool down, label and store.

Confiture de Fraises

Strawberry jam

1kg (2¼lb) just ripe strawberries, prepared
300g (11oz) caster sugar

100g (4oz) caster sugar plus 50g (2oz) dried pectin
juice of 1 lemon

The best strawberries to use are the small ones; if you use large strawberries, cut them into four.

Place the sugar into a large cast-iron saucepan and warm over a medium heat, stirring all the time. Add the strawberries and stir. Cover with a lid and boil rapidly for 5 minutes; remove the lid and cook the fruit until the temperature is 212°F (100°C), skimming off any impurities. Sprinkle in the mixed sugar and pectin, add the lemon juice and stir with a whisk. Cook on for a further minute.

Check that the jam has reached setting point.

Pour the jam into the prepared jars, cool down, then seal tightly with the lids.

Sterilise the jam jars, cool down, label, and store.

Confiture de Mûres

Blackberry jam

1kg (2¼lb) blackberries, prepared
350g (12oz) caster sugar

100g (4oz) caster sugar plus 50g (2oz) dried pectin
juice of 1 lemon

Place the sugar in a cast-iron saucepan and warm over a medium heat, stirring with a wooden spoon. Add the blackberries and stir, cover with a lid and boil rapidly for 5 minutes; remove the lid and cook the fruit until the temperature reaches 212°F (100°C). Skim off impurities from time to time.

Force the pulp through a conical sieve into another saucepan, pressing with a ladle to extract as much jam as possible.

Bring the jam to the boil and sprinkle in the mixed sugar and dried pectin. Stir with a whisk, add the lemon juice and boil for a further minute.

Check that the jam has reached setting point.

Pour the jam into the prepared jars, leave to cool down and seal tightly with lids.

Sterilise the jam jars, cool down, label, and store.

Confiture d'Abricots

Apricot jam

1kg (2¼lb) apricots, stoned
450g (1lb) caster sugar
100ml (3½fl oz) water

100g (4oz) caster sugar plus 40g (1½oz) dried pectin
juice of 2 lemons

Place the sugar and water in a large cast-iron saucepan, and bring to the boil over a medium heat, until the sugar and water become a syrup.

Add the whole apricots, cover with a lid and cook over medium heat for 10 minutes. Remove the lid and boil gently until the temperature reaches 212°F (100°C). Skim off any impurities, then sprinkle in the mixed sugar and pectin together with the lemon juice and stir with a wooden spoon. Cook on for a further minute.

Check that the jam has reached setting point.

Pour the jam into the prepared jars, leave to cool down then close tightly with the lids.

Sterilise the jam jars, cool down, label and store.

CHEF'S NOTES
According to the size of the apricots you are using, halve or quarter them.

Confiture de Cerises

Morello cherry jam

1kg (2¼lb) Morello cherries, stoned
450g (1lb) caster sugar

100g (4oz) caster sugar plus 40g (1½oz) dried pectin

Place the sugar in a large cast-iron saucepan and warm over a medium heat, stirring with a wooden spoon. Add the cherries and stir, cover with a lid and boil rapidly for 5 minutes; remove the lid and boil for a further 5 minutes until the temperature reaches 212°F (100°C).

Skim off any impurities, then sprinkle in the mixed sugar and pectin; whisk and boil for a further minute. Check that the jam has reached setting point.

Pour the jam into the prepared jars and leave to cool down. Seal tightly with the lids.

Sterilise the jam jars, cool down, label and store.

CHEF'S NOTES

Morello cherries are the best for this jam. Of course you can substitute them with black or other cherries, but the jam will be much sweeter and will have less character.

Confiture de Cassis

Blackcurrant jam

1kg (2¼lb) blackcurrants, prepared
500g (18oz) caster sugar

juice of 1 lemon

Place the sugar in a large cast-iron saucepan and warm over a medium heat, stirring with a wooden spoon. Add the blackcurrants, stir, cover with a lid and boil rapidly for 5 minutes; remove the lid and boil for a further 5 minutes until the temperature reaches 212°F (100°C), skimming from time to time. Add the lemon juice and stir.

Check that the jam has reached setting point.

Force the pulp through a conical sieve into a bowl, pressing with a ladle to extract as much jam as possible.

Pour the jam into the prepared jars, cool down and seal tightly with the lids.

Sterilise the jam jars, cool down, label and store.

CHEF'S NOTES

Blackcurrants hold enough pectin of their own to give the right texture to the jam. It is therefore not necessary to add any pectin.

Make a Confiture de Groseilles, a redcurrant jam, in exactly the same way, but using 400g (14oz) caster sugar.

Marmelade aux Trois Fruits

Three-fruit marmalade

4 lemons, washed and halved
2 sweet oranges, washed and halved
2 grapefruit, washed

*(Altogether, the lemons, oranges and grapefruit should
weigh a total of approximately 1.4kg (3lb))*
3.4 litres (6 pints) water
2.75kg (6lb) sugar

The French are not expert at making marmalade. I have tried many recipes but failed to achieve the result I wanted, in texture, sweetness or bitterness. Then I had the pleasure of staying with two old and dear friends, Francis Coulson and Brian Sack, at their hotel, Sharrow Bay in the Lake District. Besides enjoying their well-known hospitality and very good food, I had the best breakfast ever! The gem of this breakfast happened to be this delicious marmalade, which we now serve to our guests at Le Manoir.

Cut the lemons and oranges in half and, using your hands, squeeze out the juice and pips. Reserve. Chop the lemon and orange rinds and pith into fine *julienne* strips 2–3mm (⅛in) thick. Reserve.

With a sharp knife remove the grapefruit peel then place the peel on the work surface and remove some of the pith. Reserve both the peel and the pith. Chop the grapefruit peel into *julienne* strips 3mm (⅛in) thick. Chop the grapefruit flesh roughly.

Place the lemon and orange pips and the grapefruit pith in a muslin cloth and tie. Reserve.

In a large cast-iron saucepan, place the *julienne* strips of lemon, orange and grapefruit, the lemon and orange juice, chopped grapefruit flesh, and the muslin bag containing the pips and pith. Add the water, bring to the boil, then skim and simmer gently for 1¼–1½ hours until the *julienne* strips of peel are soft and the contents of the saucepan have reduced by half.

Remove the muslin bag, cool it down on a plate, then squeeze it over the saucepan allowing all the juices to run out. Add the sugar, and continue to simmer, stirring from time to time until it is totally dissolved, then boil rapidly for 15–20 minutes.

Check the marmalade for a set (see page 304). When setting point has been reached, remove the saucepan from the heat, and skim off any impurities with a slotted spoon. Leave the marmalade to cool down for 30 minutes, stirring to distribute the peel.

Pour the marmalade into clean jars, leave to cool down then seal tightly with lids. Label the jars and store in a dark place.

CHEF'S NOTES
No sterilisation is required for this recipe as marmalade has a high concentration of sugar and will keep very well.

Fruits au Sirop

Bottled fruit

These should be made when fruit is plentiful and in perfect condition. There is often a glut of fruit in the summer and the advantage of this is that they can be bought quite cheaply. It is better to keep these bottled fruits in a dry, dark place to be enjoyed during the winter days. But you can also reserve a few to be displayed in your kitchen or dining room.

The principles involved are much the same as those of jam-making. The jars and lids should be meticulously cleaned before filling, as should be the rubber seals: plunge these in boiling water for a few minutes then leave to cool in the water. The recipes have been prepared for 2 litre (3½ pint) jars.

The fruit should be prepared as outlined in the recipes, then packed into the jars and covered with syrup. The jar is then sealed and placed in a large pan of cold water to cover, as for jam, and sterilised (see page 304). The pan could have a false base as for jam, and you could use paper or cloth to separate the jars. Then the water is brought to the boil slowly, before being simmered for 30 minutes from boiling point (see page 304). The jars are removed from the water, allowed to cool, then dried and stored in a dry, dark place.

Stock Syrup for Preserves

Bring 1 litre (1¾ pints) water and 600g (1lb 6oz) caster sugar to the boil together, then skim off any impurities and simmer until the sugar has dissolved. Reserve. Make this well in advance of preserving.

Fruits au Sirop

Conserve aux Nectarines ou Pêches

Bottled nectarines or peaches

1.25kg (2¾lb) fruit
350ml (12fl oz) stock syrup (see page 309)

juice of 1 lemon
1 vanilla pod

Blanch the fruit briefly, then skin. Halve and stone the fruit, and stir in the lemon juice. The net weight should be about 1.1kg (2½lb).

Pack the fruit into the jar, add the vanilla pod, and cover with the cold stock syrup. Seal and sterilise as above.

Conserve aux Poires William

Bottled pears

1.25kg (2¾lb) pears
350ml (12fl oz) stock syrup (see page 309)

juice of 1 lemon
1 vanilla pod

Peel the pears, halve them and remove the stalks and cores. Wash briefly and stir in the lemon juice.

Pack the fruit into the prepared jars. Add the vanilla pod and cover with stock syrup. Seal and sterilise as above.

CHEF'S NOTES
Pears are first stirred in lemon juice to prevent oxidisation and discoloration. The best pears to use are William or Beurre Hardi.

Conserve aux Pruneaux

Bottled red plums

1.25kg (2¾lb) plums
350ml (12fl oz) stock syrup (see page 309)

1 vanilla pod

Wash the plums, halve them and remove the stones.

Pack the plums into the prepared jars, add the vanilla pod and cover with the stock syrup. Seal and sterilise as above.

CHEF'S NOTES
There is enough acidity in the plums so no lemon juice is needed.

Variations
Many other fruits can be prepared by the same method − raspberries, cherries, etc. If using cherries, leave them whole.

Index

Figures in italics refer to picture captions

INDEX

INDEX

INDEX